# Discipleship in the New Testament

# Discipleship in the New Testament

---

### Edited and with an Introduction
### by
### FERNANDO F. SEGOVIA

**FORTRESS PRESS**          **PHILADELPHIA**

### Library of Congress Cataloging in Publication Data

Main entry under title:

Discipleship in the New Testament.

   Papers from a symposium hosted by the Theology Dept., Marquette University, April 15–17, 1982.
   Bibliography: p.
   1. Christian life—Biblical teaching—Congresses.
2. Bible. N.T.—Criticism, interpretation, etc.—
Congresses.   I. Segovia, Fernando F.   II. Marquette
University.   Theology Dept.
BS2545.C48D57   1985      225.6      85–47730
ISBN 0–8006–1873–4

1275D85   Printed in the United States of America   1–1873

# Contents

## CONTENTS

# Contributors

RICHARD A. EDWARDS
Associate Professor of Theology,
Marquette University

JOHN H. ELLIOTT
Professor of Theology and Religious Studies, University of San Francisco

LUKE T. JOHNSON
Associate Professor of Religious Studies, Indiana University

WERNER H. KELBER
Isla Carroll and Percy E. Turner Professor of Biblical Studies, Rice University

WILLIAM S. KURZ, S.J.
Associate Professor of Theology, Marquette University

ELISABETH SCHÜSSLER FIORENZA
Talbot Professor of New Testament, Episcopal Divinity School

FERNANDO F. SEGOVIA
Associate Professor of New Testament and Early Christian Literature, Vanderbilt Divinity School

CHARLES H. TALBERT
Professor of Religion, Wake Forest University

ROBERT A. WILD, S.J.
Associate Professor of Theology, Loyola University of Chicago

# Preface

In the spring semester of 1982, the Theology Department at Marquette University hosted a three-day symposium (April 15–17) on the theme of "Call and Discipleship: New Testament Perspectives." In the course of the symposium, ten papers were given in all, including the Pere Marquette Theology Lecture for 1983, "The Theology and Setting of Discipleship in the Gospel of Mark," by the Rev. John R. Donahue, S.J. The present volume includes nine of these presentations. Since Fr. Donahue's Pere Marquette address has already been published by Marquette University Press and will also be included in a forthcoming publication by Fortress Press of Fr. Donahue's previously published Markan studies, it was not included in this present volume. To be sure, however, that presentation was a major part of the symposium, and I shall make reference to its various contributions to the topic under consideration in the course of my introductory remarks to this volume.

There is no question that the completion of a project such as this one presupposes and entails the contributions of many an individual. I should like to thank, first of all, Marquette University and, more specifically, Dr. Edward D. Simmons, Vice President for Academic Affairs, for the generous grant from the Humanities Excellence Fund that made this symposium possible. A special word of thanks should be extended as well to the Rev. Philip J. Rossi, S.J., Acting Chairman of the Theology Department, who vigorously supported the project from its very inception and through its earliest stages, and to the Rev. William J. Kelly, S.J., who saw it through to its successful completion and who supported my work both as coordinator for the symposium and as editor for this volume in every possible way. A very special word of thanks is also due to Ms. Carol Maher and Dr. June Edwards for their kind patience and professional excellence in the typing of the manuscript. Finally, I should like to express my deep gratitude to all those who took part in the symposium and who, in a very concrete and specific way, made that gathering a thorough success as well as a most enjoyable occasion. Among those present at the symposium was John A. Hollar of Fortress Press, whose help and support in the planning, preparation, and publication of this volume have been constant, invaluable, and deeply appreciated; to him and to Fortress Press a final and most gracious word of thanks.

This volume is dedicated to my former colleagues and students in the Theology Department at Marquette University.

FERNANDO F. SEGOVIA
Marquette University

# Abbreviations

| | |
|---|---|
| AB | Anchor Bible |
| AnBib | Analecta Biblica |
| ASNU | Acta seminarii neotestamentici upsaliensis |
| *ATR* | *Anglican Theological Review* |
| BAGD | Walter Bauer, William F. Arndt, F. Wilbur Gingrich, and Frederick Danker, eds., *A Greek-English Lexicon of the New Testament and Other Early Christian Literature* |
| BDF | Friedrich Blass, Albert Debrunner, and Robert W. Funk, eds., *A Greek Grammar of the New Testament and Other Early Christian Literature* |
| BETL | Bibliotheca ephemeridum theologicarum lovaniensium |
| *BH* | *Buried History* |
| BHT | Beiträge zur historischen Theologie |
| *Bib* | *Biblica* |
| *BibLeb* | *Bibel und Leben* |
| *BR* | *Biblical Research* |
| *BTB* | *Biblical Theology Bulletin* |
| BZNW | Beihefte zur Zeitschrift für die neutestamentliche Wissenschaft |
| CBC | Collegeville Bible Commentary |
| *CBQ* | *Catholic Biblical Quarterly* |
| CBQMS | Catholic Biblical Quarterly Monograph Series |
| *Computer-Konkordanz* | H. Bachmann, W. A. Slaby, et al., eds., *Computer-Konkordanz zum Novum Testamentum Graece von Nestle-Aland, 26. Auflage und zum Greek New Testament, 3rd Edition* |
| EBib | Études bibliques |
| EdF | Erträge der Forschung |
| EKKNT | Evangelisch-katholischer Kommentar zum Neuen Testament |

| | |
|---|---|
| *EstBib* | *Estudios bíblicos* |
| ETL | *Ephemerides theologicae lovanienses* |
| *ExpTim* | *Expository Times* |
| FRLANT | Forschungen zur Religion und Literatur des Alten und Neuen Testaments |
| FzB | Forschung zur Bibel |
| GBS | Guides to Biblical Scholarship Series |
| *HeyJ* | *Heythrop Journal* |
| HNT | Handbuch zum Neuen Testament |
| HNTC | Harper's New Testament Commentaries |
| HSCL | Harvard Studies in Comparative Literature |
| HTKNT | Herders Theologischer Kommentar zum Neuen Testament |
| *HTR* | *Harvard Theological Review* |
| Iamblichus | |
|   *VP* | *Vita Pythagorica* |
| ICC | International Critical Commentary |
| *IDBSup* | Keith Crim, ed., Supplementary Volume to the *Interpreter's Dictionary of the Bible* |
| *Int* | *Interpretation* |
| IRT | Issues in Religion and Theology |
| *JAAR* | *Journal of the American Academy of Religion* |
| *JAC* | *Jahrbuch für Antike und Christentum* |
| *JBL* | *Journal of Biblical Literature* |
| *JR* | *Journal of Religion* |
| *JRelS* | *Journal of Religious Studies* |
| JSNTSup | Journal for the Study of the New Testament— Supplement Series |
| LCL | Loeb Classical Library |
| LD | Lectio divina |
| LSJ | Henry George Liddell, Robert Scott, and Henry Stuart Jones, eds., *A Greek-English Lexicon* |
| LXX | Septuagint |
| MeyerK | H. A. W. Meyer, Kritisch-exegetischer Kommentar über das Neue Testament |
| Moulton-Geden | W. F. Moulton, A. S. Geden, and H. K. Moulton, eds., *A Concordance to the Greek Testament* |
| NAB | New American Bible |
| NCB | New Century Bible |
| NICNT | New International Commentary on the New Testament |
| *NovT* | *Novum Testamentum* |

| | |
|---|---|
| NovTSup | Novum Testamentum, Supplements |
| NTAbh | Neutestamentliche Abhandlungen |
| NTD | Das Neue Testament Deutsch |
| NTM | New Testament Message |
| *NTS* | *New Testament Studies* |
| OBT | Overtures to Biblical Theology |
| Philo | |
| *Abr.* | *De Abrahamo* [*On Abraham*] |
| *Cher.* | *De cherubim* [*On the Cherubim*] |
| *Decal.* | *De decalogo* [*On the Decalogue*] |
| *Det.* | *Quod deterius potiori insidiari soleat* [*The Worse Attacks the Better*] |
| *Fug.* | *De fuga et inventione* [*On Flight and Finding*] |
| *Her.* | *Quis rerum divinarum heres sit* [*Who Is the Heir*] |
| *Leg. All.* | *Legum allegoriae* [*Allegorical Interpretation*] |
| *Leg. Gai.* | *De legatione ad Gaium* [*On the Embassy to Gaius*] |
| *Mig.* | *De migratione Abrahami* [*On the Migration of Abraham*] |
| *Moses* | *De vita Mosis* [*On the Life of Moses*] |
| *Mut.* | *De mutatione nominum* [*On the Change of Names*] |
| *Op.* | *De opificio mundi* [*On the Creation of the World*] |
| *Plant.* | *De plantatione* [*On Noah's Work as a Planter*] |
| *Praem.* | *De praemiis et poenis* [*On Rewards and Punishments*] |
| *Q. Gen.* | *Quaestiones in Genesin* [*Questions on Genesis*] |
| *Sacr.* | *De sacrificiis Abelis et Caini* [*On the Sacrifices of Abel and Cain*] |
| *Sobr.* | *De sobrietate* |
| *Spec. Leg.* | *De Specialibus legibus* [*On the Special Laws*] |
| *Virt.* | *De virtutibus* [*On the Virtues*] |
| Plutarch | |
| *Am. Mult.* | *De amicorum multitudine* [*On Having Many Friends*] |
| *Frat. Am.* | *De fraterno amore* [*On Brotherly Love*] |
| Porphyry | |
| *VP* | *Vita Pythagorae* |
| *PRS* | *Perspectives in Religious Studies* |
| PTMS | Pittsburgh Theological Monograph Series |
| *RAC* | *Reallexikon für Antike und Christentum* |
| RechBib | Recherches bibliques |
| *RechSR* | *Recherches de science religieuse* |
| *RevExp* | *Review and Expositor* |
| *RGG* | *Religion in Geschichte und Gegenwart,* 3d ed. |
| *RSR* | *Religious Studies Review* |
| RSV | Revised Standard Version of the Bible |

## ABBREVIATIONS

| | |
|---|---|
| SANT | Studien zum Alten und Neuen Testament |
| SB | Sources bibliques |
| SBLASP | Society of Biblical Literature Abstracts and Seminar Papers |
| SBLDS | Society of Biblical Literature Dissertation Series |
| SBLMS | Society of Biblical Literature Monograph Series |
| SBLSBS | Society of Biblical Literature Sources for Biblical Study |
| SBLTT | Society of Biblical Literature Texts and Translations |
| SBS | Stuttgarter Bibelstudien |
| SBT | Studies in Biblical Theology |
| SD | Studies and Documents |
| *SE* | *Studia Evangelica* |
| *SJT* | *Scottish Journal of Theology* |
| SNTSMS | Society for New Testament Studies Monograph Series |
| *SP* | *Studia Philonica* |
| SUNT | Studien zur Umwelt des Neuen Testaments |
| *TBT* | *The Bible Today* |
| *TDNT* | G. Kittel and G. Friedrich, eds., *Theological Dictionary of the New Testament* |
| TI | Theological Inquiries |
| TorSTh | Toronto Studies in Theology |
| TTS | Trier Theologische Studien |
| TU | Texte und Untersuchungen |
| *TZ* | *Theologische Zeitschrift* |
| *USQR* | *Union Seminary Quarterly Review* |
| *VC* | *Vigiliae Christianae* |
| VTSup | Vetus Testamentum, Supplements |
| WMANT | Wissenschaftliche Monographien zum Alten und Neuen Testament |
| *ZNW* | *Zeitschrift für die neutestamentliche Wissenschaft* |
| *ZTK* | *Zeitschrift für Theologie und Kirche* |

# Introduction: Call and Discipleship— Toward a Re-examination of the Shape and Character of Christian Existence in the New Testament

## FERNANDO F. SEGOVIA

Without a doubt, one of the most fundamental and recurring questions in the history of the Christian tradition has been the definition of Christian discipleship: that is, what exactly does it mean to be a disciple of Jesus Christ, and what precisely does the concept of "following" entail not only in terms of an overall conception or attitude toward life in general but also in terms of concrete day-to-day living and existence? The proposed answers have been considerable, to say the least, and indeed quite often at variance with, if not in direct contradiction to, one another.

The present times have certainly not been immune to such questionings and such disagreements. Indeed, despite the rise of a vigorous and healthy strain of ecumenism in the Christian tradition, it seems at times as if the very process of questioning itself has become more divisive, the enunciated positions more exclusive, and the resulting disagreements more unyielding, not only among the different Christian churches but also, quite frequently, within those very same groups. Furthermore, more often than not, it is an appeal to the witness and authority of the New Testament that lies at the very center of the searching and thus at the very core of the disputes as well.

Thus, when the proposal for a major New Testament symposium was first conceived and advanced, the choice and designation of "Call and Discipleship" as its major focus was in many respects immediate and instinctive. The times did seem ripe for another look at the theme and concept of discipleship at the very beginnings of the Christian tradition. At the very least, the kind of sustained and systematic analysis that such a project would bring to bear on this question would serve to clarify the issues and problems

1

involved in any appeal or recourse to the New Testament as the grounds for any proposed definition of discipleship.

Furthermore, the times also seemed quite ripe within the field of New Testament studies for a thorough, scholarly re-examination of the shape and character of discipleship in the New Testament texts. At the very least, such a project would naturally call forth and utilize the more recent exegetical developments, directions, and perspectives to be found in the discipline, thus raising and posing new questions to the texts as well as refining or refocusing the more traditional questions and concerns.

In order to facilitate such a re-examination, the symposium—and thus the theme of discipleship itself—was deliberately defined in very broad terms; a number of thoroughly established scholars in their respective fields within the discipline were extended invitations; and complete freedom was given to each participant, not only with respect to the exegetical approach and methodology to be employed but also with respect to the specific topic or title to be developed. In effect, only a common interest in discipleship would initially unite the participants and ultimately bring them together.

## TERMINOLOGY

First of all, the term "discipleship" quite clearly admits of a narrow as well as a broader definition. In the former sense, it is to be understood technically and exclusively in terms of the "teacher"/"disciple" relationship with all its accompanying and derivative terminology (for example, "following" or "on the way"). Such a restricted usage would have limited the symposium of necessity to a re-examination of the evidence in the Gospels and Acts as well as in the pre-Gospel tradition. In the latter sense, discipleship would be understood more generally in terms of Christian existence—that is, the self-understanding of the early Christian believers as believers: what such a way of life requires, implies, and entails. Such a wider usage would then apply across the entire spectrum of the New Testament writings.

It was with the latter sense in mind that the symposium was conceived, defined, and organized so that the proposed re-examination could encompass and address itself not only to the very specific relationship of "teacher" and "disciple" with its different conceptions and elaborations in the gospel tradition but also to the more general patterns and modes of Christian existence and self-understanding in the rest of the New Testament. At the same time, it was deemed important to preserve and convey the distinction in as unobtrusive a manner as possible, and thus a decision was made to arrange the symposium studies in this volume accordingly: the first four studies deal directly or indirectly with the given relationship, while the following five studies reflect the wider understanding and application of the term.

## LITERATURE AND STANDARD APPROACHES

Second, the proposed re-examination was meant to be distinctive in aim and scope from any previous major treatment of this topic. Thus, it would forgo any examination of the circumstances surrounding the historical Jesus and his first followers. It would also forgo any major or explicit consideration of the background, whether Hellenistic or Jewish, for the concept and practice of discipleship in the ancient Mediterranean world, unless, of course, such a background was deemed necessary for the interpretation and understanding of any particular text in question. It would devote itself solely and exclusively to an analysis of specific and concrete conceptions of discipleship in various New Testament texts and in the various communities presupposed by and reflected in such texts. Furthermore, it would do so, as pointed out in the previous section, in as wide a manner as possible, not being exclusively tied down to specific terms or expressions.

Four major treatments of the topic may be found in the literature, all dating from the 1960s. The first of these was Eduard Schweizer's *Lordship and Discipleship*[1] (1960). His approach to discipleship may be described as essentially christological in nature: the confessions of the early church about Jesus and thus the christological titles used of and applied to Jesus convey and reveal the fundamental underlying conceptions about following Jesus. For the most part, therefore, Schweizer is concerned only with those verses or units that witness to and contain such confessions or titles; little attention is given to any writing as a coherent whole or to any author as an independent and creative agent.

Two years later, Anselm Schulz's major monograph on the subject appeared under the title *Nachfolgen und Nachahmen.*[2] The title of the volume reflects quite accurately the approach undertaken by the author, as well as the very structure of the work itself: a thorough examination of the verb "to follow" and related terminology in the Jewish sources and the New Testament, followed by a similar examination of the concept of "imitation" and related terminology in Greek and Jewish sources as well as in the New Testament texts. As in the previous case, a certain lack of specificity and regard for each writing as a whole may be noticed in the author's approach to the various texts, particularly with regard to the Synoptic Gospels material.

Five years later, in 1967, another major study appeared in Germany, Hans Dieter Betz's *Nachfolge und Nachahmung Jesu Christi im Neuen Tes-*

*tament.*[3] The volume is divided into three major sections: the first and briefest deals with the concept of "following" Jesus in the Gospels; the second and by far the longest provides the history and background of the concept of "imitation" in the ancient Mediterranean world; the third and final section turns to and examines the role of "imitation" in the theology of Paul. Although one does find a respect for specificity with regard to the Gospel material, the treatment is rather brief and limited. The main focus of the work is quite clearly the concept of "imitation."

A year later, in 1968, Martin Hengel's *Nachfolge und Charisma*[4] appeared, written, in large part, as a deliberate reaction to these earlier studies. In both the introduction and the conclusion to this work, Hengel argues that the question of discipleship in these earlier studies had focused only briefly and in passing on the historical Jesus and his first followers. The volume is therefore meant to redress that situation and proceeds to do so by approaching the question primarily from a history-of-religions perspective—namely, the roles of charismatic leaders and their followers in the ancient world.

This survey of the pertinent literature confirms quite clearly the very explicit and distinctive tone and character of the present volume and its proposed re-examination of the concept of discipleship—and ultimately, of course, of the symposium from which it originated. Its main emphasis falls, therefore, on the different conceptions of discipleship, again to be understood in the very broad sense of Christian existence and self-understanding, present in various writings and communities of the New Testament. Consequently, its main emphasis also falls on each writing or tradition as a coherent and independent whole with its own unique and characteristic understanding of Christian discipleship.

Finally, it should go without saying that the proposed re-examination was not, is not, and could not be exhaustive in nature and scope; its basic aim in this regard is to encompass and provide a representative view of the various understandings and elaborations of discipleship in the New Testament. As such, it should be looked upon as a beginning step in this direction, not by any means as an already accomplished end.

## METHODOLOGY

An analysis of the specific conception of discipleship present in any writing of the New Testament admits quite clearly of various and rather different exegetical approaches.

Thus, for example, the exegete may choose to do a literary analysis of the way the disciples function as a character in the development of a gospel narrative. On the other hand, the exegete may also choose to do a more traditional redactional study of the term "disciple"—and/or of any other synonymous or related designations—as it is found and used in the gospel or work in question. In a somewhat similar vein, the exegete may turn to a theme, an image, or a metaphor thought to be closely associated with discipleship in the writing under consideration and study it from any number of possible perspectives (e.g., redaction criticism, history of religions, social world, tradition history) to see what further light may be shed on the author's conception of discipleship in that work. In a rather more circumscribed approach, the exegete may also opt instead for a detailed analysis of one or more units central to the exposition of the theme within the work in question—again, from any number of possible perspectives. The possibilities are virtually endless.

Although the actual results of such investigations may at times be quite different, all of these different approaches with their multiple variations are quite valid methodologically and may be said to be, in principle, ultimately complementary in scope and purpose. Indeed, it is quite possible and not altogether infrequent for one and the same exegete to analyze the nature of discipleship in the same writing from more than one of these different exegetical angles. It is, after all, the same reality which is being described from different vantage points.

It was the aim of this proposed re-examination from its very inception to allow the contributors as much latitude as possible in their respective points of departure for and exegetical approaches to the theme of discipleship within the different works in question. It was hoped that such freedom would, in effect, allow these established scholars to select those points of departure which in their opinion would reflect the present state of the question in their respective areas of concentration within the discipline and then employ that particular methodology which would allow them to advance that state of the question in whatever direction was deemed proper and fruitful.

The results of this inquiry go far beyond this initial desideratum and provide not only a solid and fruitful beginning for the proposed re-examination of discipleship but also an excellent overview of the most recent developments and directions within the field of New Testament studies.

## CONTRIBUTIONS

At this point I want to summarize rather briefly the aims and results of each particular study and then proceed to draw certain conclusions concerning these directions and developments, as well as the understanding of Christian discipleship in the New Testament on the basis of these studies.

1. Werner H. Kelber: "Apostolic Tradition and the Form of the Gospel."

Unlike the others, Kelber's study arises out of a dual concern in the discipline and thus deals with discipleship in two different, yet very much interrelated, traditions and areas of research: namely, the oral tradition and the Gospel of Mark.

On the one hand, Kelber believes that the traditional view of the process of gospel formation—an "evolutionary" model in which the written gospel is seen as a basic transcription of oral speech and thus essentially as the preservation of tradition—has paid no attention to the narrative integrity of the canonical Gospels or the world and laws of oral cultures. At the same time, Kelber also believes that Markan scholarship has not yet come to terms with the full narrative impact and consequences of the negative story of the disciples presented in Mark's Gospel. In effect, this study argues that a full realization and appropriation of this negative portrayal leads to a very different view of the process of formation: the Gospel as a refutation of apostolic tradition—a "revolutionary" model.

In approaching the Markan understanding of discipleship, Kelber follows three fundamental literary insights and principles: (a) Markan discipleship can be properly understood only in terms of narrative shape and development; (b) discipleship is a narrative instrument that plays on and solicits responses from the readers; (c) the narrative pattern of discipleship reflects the parabolic dynamic of the Gospel as a whole.

Thus, Kelber argues that, as the narrative develops and unfolds, the disciples, who appear as "insiders" at first, are progressively cast into the role of "outsiders." In fact, by the end of the narrative (Mark 16:8), the disciples are denied any possibility of reunion or reconciliation with the risen Lord and are thus completely banished to the outside. As such, this parabolic ending places the burden of the unexpected outcome upon the readers. For Kelber, this narrative withholding of Easter becomes the key not only to Markan motivation but also to the very form of that Gospel as well. Mark's reserved attitude toward Jesus' sayings, emphasis on Jesus' earthly life with its culmination in death rather than resurrection, and casting of the disciples into the role of complete "outsiders" should be seen, Kelber argues, as an attempt to undermine and correct an oral tradition "fraught with gnosticizing proclivities."

Within this latter tradition, the parabolic sayings of the risen Lord functioned as a means of casting hearers to the outside; Jesus himself was understood and presented as a gnostic redeemer and bringer of esoteric knowledge; Jesus' disciples became the "insiders" or chosen few who received, understood, and guarded such sayings and such knowledge. For Mark, therefore, the mystery of God's kingdom was not to be restricted to the sayings of the risen Lord but encompassed all of Jesus' life and death;

it was not to be limited to the chosen disciples but open to all—the Gospel was meant as a refutation of the oral, apostolic tradition.

2. John R. Donahue: "The Theology and Setting of Discipleship in the Gospel of Mark." Donahue's study calls for and initiates a new direction altogether toward a proper understanding of Markan discipleship within Markan scholarship. Such scholarship has shown in recent times two rather different directions: an explanation of the negative role of the disciples in terms of a polemic against opponents or a positive evaluation, whether from a theological or literary perspective, of this negative role. Although the latter approach is to be preferred, given the fundamentally positive view of discipleship presented in the Gospel, Donahue argues that both lines of interpretation have approached Markan discipleship solely from the point of view of the individual believer and have thus entirely bypassed the essentially communal dimensions of such discipleship.

As a result, Donahue proposes and adopts a social world approach to the question of Markan discipleship: an examination of language associated with household and family. Four key texts serve as primary evidence in this regard: Mark 3:20–35, 10:29–31, 10:42–45, and 13:33–36.

An analysis of these texts yields several essential components of Markan discipleship: (a) being called in the midst of ordinary activity; (b) leaving old sources of identity and becoming members of the new family of Jesus; (c) empowerment for mission and a life doing the things of Jesus; (d) trusting in God even in the face of suffering and death; (e) mutual service and renunciation of all power and prestige. For Donahue, such a conception of discipleship had a specific setting in a house church which attempted to live out its story of Jesus: thoroughly dedicated to missionary activity, radically egalitarian in nature, and characterized above all by a life of mutual service.

3. Richard A. Edwards: "Uncertain Faith: Matthew's Portrait of the Disciples." Edwards's point of departure for this study is quite similar to that of Kelber with respect to Mark: a proper understanding of Matthean discipleship is said to be possible only when the shape and flow of Matthew's narrative as a whole is taken into consideration. Similarly, discipleship is also seen as a narrative instrument which plays on and solicits responses from the reader. Edwards's focus in this study is therefore a dual one: the text and the reader—that is, tracing the portrayal of Jesus' disciples as characters in the narrative as well as observing the cumulative effect of such a portrayal on the reader. Unlike Kelber, however, Edwards deliberately abstains from making any judgments about the historical situation of the reader, the narrator, or the author.

Edwards argues, first of all, that in the case of Jesus' disciples, the narrator provides no basic context or exposition in the beginning chapters from which the reader can judge or interpret their subsequent actions in the narrative. Consequently, the reader is required to fill in the gaps in information by positing a set of hypotheses which will then be confirmed or invalidated by the remainder of the story.

According to Edwards, the reader is encouraged to respond favorably to the disciples when first introduced (Matt. 4:18–20). However, in what follows the narrator is described as keeping the reader quite off balance by means of an alternating pattern of positive and negative portrayals of the disciples. Such a pattern is seen as conditioning the reader to expect neither security nor certainty in the disciples. Even at the end (28:16–20), the pattern continues, and there is no change. Edwards concludes that the reader will thereby come to see discipleship as a situation that is never complete but requires dedication, denial, and a need to comprehend the deeper significance of Jesus' teaching.

4. Charles H. Talbert: "Discipleship in Luke-Acts." Talbert's approach to Lukan discipleship is basically that of redaction criticism, although major arguments are also adduced both from the perspective of genre criticism and the history-of-religions approach: a study of those texts in the whole of Luke-Acts that have to do with disciples of Jesus yields the fundamental, overarching conception of Lukan discipleship as well as its various essential components.

For Luke-Acts, Talbert argues, discipleship means, first and foremost, a complete detachment from old ties and a total attachment to Jesus, repentance and baptism in Jesus' name, and complete submission to the will and purpose of this new authority. Furthermore, this new allegiance involves two interrelated and interacting dimensions: on the one hand, discipleship means being molded by a tradition, being empowered by an experience, and being a participant in a community; at the same time, each of these essential components involves two others: a way to walk and a mission to fulfill. It is only, therefore, through the various interactions of these essential components that one can properly grasp and understand the true dimensions of Lukan discipleship.

Thus, in effect, Luke-Acts shows that Christian discipleship, both in terms of the way to walk and the mission to be fulfilled, is immediately and concretely shaped by the tradition of Jesus; directly and consistently empowered, guided, and protected by divine initiative; radically and thoroughly grounded in and dependent on community. In fact, Talbert concludes, it is a conception of discipleship that defies any attempt at reductionism.

5. Fernando F. Segovia: "'Peace I Leave with You; My Peace I Give to You': Discipleship in the Fourth Gospel." As in the case of Talbert, Segovia's basic approach to Johannine discipleship is also that of redaction or composition criticism. Furthermore, as in the case of both Kelber and Edwards,

he focuses primarily on the characterization of Jesus' disciples in the Gospel narrative and then, like Kelber, proceeds to make certain judgments concerning the historical situation reflected in, presupposed by, and addressed through such a portrayal. Lastly, insofar as such a portrayal is said to point to and reveal the sectarian nature of the community, he also employs, like Donahue, categories from the social world approach.

The Johannine conception of discipleship reveals, according to this study, three fundamental components: (a) the narrative presents a deliberate and sustained contrast between Jesus' disciples and the "world," where the latter term refers primarily to the Jews; (b) exclusive to this contrast lies belief in or acceptance of Jesus' claims regarding his origin, ministry, and goal; (c) such belief is portrayed as necessitating and undergoing a process of gradual understanding and perception, above all with respect to the events comprising Jesus' hour and the necessity for missionary activity.

These essential components are then used to provide different insights into the historical situation of the Johannine community. Thus, for example, the first two are seen as pointing to and addressing a Christian community that was engaged in a bitter and prolonged process of self-definition and self-assertion over against a much larger Jewish "world." Similarly, the third component is used to show further, given the nature and character of this confrontation, that an acceptance of Jesus' death and resurrection as the climax of his mission—as well as a corresponding call to mission regardless of circumstances or consequences—became central and integral elements of this self-definition and self-assertion. Segovia then concludes that the community's relentless antagonism toward the "world" and exclusivistic self-conception as the "children of God" evidenced through such a portrayal of the disciples reveal a highly sectarian group and self-understanding.

6. William S. Kurz, S.J.: "Kenotic Imitation of Paul and of Christ in Philippians 2 and 3." Kurz's point of departure for this study on discipleship in Paul is a call to move away from form and source criticisms toward redactional and compositional studies within Pauline scholarship—that is, toward a study of each letter as it now stands, regardless of its presumed literary history. Thus, in effect, Kurz proposes to study the Pauline conception of discipleship as presented and elaborated in the Letter to the Philippians in terms of the letter's present form and structure. At the same time, however, he also turns to and employs a history-of-religions approach in order to shed further light on what he perceives to be the fundamental motif in the letter's understanding of Christian discipleship—namely, the imitation of personal examples in first-century parenesis.

According to Kurz, therefore, a compositional study of Philippians yields a conception of discipleship which is radically grounded on the imitation of the kenotic examples of both Jesus and Paul: that is, their respective models of surrendering personal prerogatives that would have spared them suffering and of trusting instead in God for vindication and exaltation.

Thus, Kurz continues, just as Jesus gave up equality with God and humbled himself even unto death on a cross, and just as Paul surrendered his Jewish credentials and found himself in prison and facing possible death, so, too, must the believers give up their own self-interests, look to the interests of others, and adopt a unified stand against external persecution from the Jews and internal judaizers who seek to avoid such persecution by compromising with the persecutors. Only then, Kurz concludes, can the disciples expect the kind of eschatological joy in the midst of suffering and conflicts that Paul possesses and promises and hope for the exaltation that Jesus has already been granted.

7. Robert A. Wild, S. J.: "'Be Imitators of God': Discipleship in the Letter to the Ephesians." In this study Wild approaches the question of the conception of discipleship in the Deutero-Pauline literature from the point of view of the Letter to the Ephesians. Furthermore, he chooses as his point of departure one particular statement of the goal or end of Christian discipleship from among many (Eph. 5:1–2) because of a specific theme to be found therein—the imitation of God—which cannot be traced either to the biblical or the Pauline tradition. Wild then proceeds to employ a history-of-religions approach to determine the precise background and context not only for such an unusual articulation of Christian ethical finality but also for the letter as a whole.

Wild locates this background within a long-standing Jewish tradition of biblical interpretation which had recourse to and made use of Platonic perspectives—a tradition thoroughly established in Alexandria by the first century B.C., heavily indebted to the principles and doctrines of Middle Platonism and exemplified, above all, by the exegetical treatises of Philo. Within Middle Platonism and thus within this exegetical tradition as well, the imitation of God was equated with the ethical goal of assimilation to God through virtuous human activity and presented as such as the purpose or end of human existence.

For Wild, therefore, Ephesians stands clearly within a long-standing Platonic tradition mediated through Hellenistic Jewish exegesis and preserves in Eph. 5:1 a specific Middle Platonic statement of the purpose of human existence. Indeed, such an understanding of the goal of Christian discipleship as the imitation of God and, therefore, as assimilation to God through ethical activity is said to underlie other similar statements in the letter on the purpose or end of Christian existence, and thus to be fundamental to the letter as a whole. Wild points out, however, that in Ephesians this ethical demand to imitate God does show two very distinctive characteristics: it is grounded not in the order of creation but of revelation and is thus available as a possibility only to believers; and it is to be carried out not by flight from the world but by and through the ordinary tasks of everyday human activity in this world.

8. Elisabeth Schüssler Fiorenza: "The Followers of the Lamb: Visionary Rhetoric and Social-Political Situation." It is Rev. 14:1–5—the vision of the 144,000 with the Lamb on Mount Zion and the only place outside the Gospels and Acts where the technical terminology for discipleship ("following the Lamb") is employed—and the total lack of scholarly consensus on the identity of this group that provide the concrete point of departure for Schüssler Fiorenza's analysis of discipleship in the Book of Revelation.

In effect, she proposes a literary-critical approach to Revelation in general that would provide a way out of this scholarly impasse by avoiding the two most frequent—and opposing—lines of interpretation: an approach to apocalyptic symbols either as a secret code bearing a one-to-one meaning relationship with specific historical persons or events, or as manifestations of ultimate, transhistorical realities and archetypes.

She argues, therefore, that Revelation should be seen as a poetic-rhetorical construction of an alternative symbolic universe that fits its historical-rhetorical situation. Thus, as poetic construction, first of all, Revelation should be seen as possessing not only a particular meaning but also as opening up rather than limiting meanings. As a rhetorical construction, however, Revelation should also be seen as seeking to persuade and motivate readers to act rightly. Furthermore, as rhetorical construction, Revelation's alternative symbolic universe may also be seen as an active and "fitting" response to a specific rhetorical situation.

Within such a rhetorical perspective, the vision of Rev. 14:1–5 is to be located, first of all, within the overall dramatic movement of the book. As such, it forms part of a series of heavenly/earthly eschatological visions of salvation and provides an antithesis to a different series of visions depicting anti-divine powers. Through such a juxtaposition of antithetical visions, Schüssler Fiorenza argues, the author seeks to persuade the readers to choose the world of God and renounce the world of Rome.

Furthermore, the vision is also said to be surrounded by rhetorical "markers" which seek to channel correctly the readers' understanding of and reaction to the vision: eschatological redemption and salvation are a direct result and consequence of behavior in the past. Through such markers, therefore, the argument continues, the author seeks to encourage, sustain, and strengthen the readers in their decision against Rome in the face of persecution and possible death.

Finally, such a poetic-rhetorical construction is seen as presupposing and addressing a concrete rhetorical situation: persecution and oppression by the Roman Empire; slander and rejection from the Jewish communities;

competing claims of accommodation by rival Christian prophets. Through the construction of Revelation's particular alternative symbolic universe, Schüssler Fiorenza concludes, the author adopts a thoroughly uncompromising stance against the imperial religion of Rome: salvation is possible if and only if the reader and Christian disciple rejects the life and power of Rome in all its aspects—commercial, political, social, and religious—and endures, as Jesus did, all the inevitable consequences of such a rejection.

9. Luke T. Johnson: "Friendship with the World/Friendship with God: A Study of Discipleship in James." Johnson's general point of departure for this study on discipleship in the Letter of James is very similar to that of Kurz: the letter can and should be read as a coherent literary and theological whole, possessing a very definite and discernible structure as well as a very specific theological position or message. Consequently, Johnson's main approach to the teaching of James on discipleship is that of redaction criticism, although, also like Kurz, a history-of-religions approach is also used with respect to two fundamental aspects of that teaching—namely, the treatment of envy as a *topos* in Hellenistic moral philosophy and the understanding of friendship in the Greek philosophical tradition.

The more specific point of departure, then, for this study becomes the warning of James 4:4, the only part of the larger unit comprised by James 3:13—4:10 (said to be a call to conversion from one way of life to another employing a traditional *topos* on envy) for which no parallel can be found in Hellenistic moral philosophy, whether Jewish or Greek. Thus, the redaction-critical study of discipleship in the letter becomes very much focused on this warning and its various components, especially the two central terms, "world" and "friendship."

Such an analysis yields the following results: according to James, first of all, "world" is a measure or standard of reality opposed to that of God; furthermore, for James—and this is confirmed by means of a comparative analysis of friendship in the Greek tradition—"friendship" means a complete sharing in attitudes, values, and perceptions, and implies that one can choose that system of values by which one is to live. Thus, in effect, "friendship with the world" in James 4:4 means quite clearly a profound and willing agreement with a measure of reality which excludes and opposes that of God.

For James, therefore, Johnson concludes, it is impossible for a disciple to be "double-minded," to desire or to attempt to be a friend of the world and a friend of God at the same time, since these measures of reality are diametrically opposed to one another. Those who have received God's word must choose their friends: if they are to be truly God's friends, they must continually renew their conversions and become doers of God's word. As such, they are not called to either ritual or physical separation from the world but rather to full participation in the affairs of the world according to the law of love, which is the law of God's kingdom.

10. John H. Elliott: "Backward and Forward 'In His Steps': Following Jesus from Rome to Raymond and Beyond. The Tradition, Redaction, and Reception of 1 Peter 2:18–25." It is Elliott's main contention in this study that 1 Peter 2:18–25 and, more specifically, 2:21 present not only a conception of discipleship which is very similar to the more technical usage of discipleship terminology in the Gospels but also a more general fusion of concepts and traditions which places the letter very close indeed to the gospel tradition.

The study provides a combination of redaction or composition criticism, social world criticism, and tradition criticism. First of all, Elliott examines the structure, content, and *Tendenz* of the larger unit as a whole, as well as the specific content and function within it of the key verse under consideration. Second, he notes and emphasizes the central importance and significance of such terms as "household servants" and the "household of God" for this unit as well as for the letter as a whole. Finally, he traces the trajectory of the specific fusion of traditions found therein in other early Christian writings.

According to Elliott, first of all, 1 Peter 2:18–25 forms part of a larger section of the letter concerned with the proper conduct of the "household of God" within the structures of society. In this particular unit, then, the proper behavior of "household servants" is addressed: following the general principle at work in the section as a whole, servants are therein exhorted to be subordinate to their masters and to do what is right even in the face of innocent suffering. Furthermore, in 2:21 this exhortation is seen as receiving a very specific grounding: servants have been called to "follow in the steps" of their innocent, suffering Lord. As the obedient, suffering servant of God, therefore, obedient, suffering servants find in Jesus Christ both an exemplar and an enabler.

Second, for Elliott, the status and role ascribed to the "household servants" typify the status and role of the entire "household of God": their precarious social condition matches that of the Christian community as a whole within society and the world; their calling to be obedient and to do what is right despite innocent suffering is the calling of all believers; their bond with the obedient, suffering Lord is likewise the bond of all. Thus, in effect, as the primary ecclesial metaphor of the letter, the "household of God" is said to point to a marginal, sectarian community intent upon affirming and legitimating its identity as the righteous elect of God against an unholy and hostile environment—that is, Judaism and Greco-Roman society.

In conclusion, Elliott argues that the peculiar combination of concepts

13

and traditions to be found in this unit, centering on the specific understanding of "following" Jesus in terms of a solidarity in suffering with the Lord, links 1 Peter with other early Christian writings: *1 Clement*, Polycarp, and the Gospels, especially Mark. The probable Roman provenance of these four writings points further to a common use of local oral tradition, a common social situation, and thus a common socioreligious perspective as well.

## RESULTS

On the basis of the preceding survey and analysis of the studies in this volume (including John Donahue's Pere Marquette Lecture as well), certain conclusions may be drawn, I believe, with respect to different aspects and facets of this scholarly re-examination of the understanding of Christian discipleship in the New Testament.

1. I want to reiterate once again what these results make patently clear: the volume is meant to be a beginning, and thus representative rather than exhaustive in scope. For example, the gospel tradition is very well represented: all four Gospels as well as the pre-gospel oral tradition are thoroughly covered. On the other hand, both the Pauline and the Deutero-Pauline literature are selectively covered by means of individual studies on Philippians and Ephesians, respectively. Similarly, the apocalyptic tradition is represented through a study of Revelation. Finally, the later writings of the New Testament are also selectively covered by means of two studies on the Catholic Letters—namely, James and 1 Peter. The results of the re-examination are thus undeniably limited, but as a beginning, they are also, I believe, quite adequate and quite good.

2. The preceding survey also shows that the individual studies do reflect quite clearly and quite strongly the main and intended thrust of the re-examination: namely, the consideration and analysis of each writing as an independent literary and theological whole, preserving and articulating in each case a unique conception of what Christian discipleship implies and entails.

In this regard, the extensive use of both redaction criticism and narrative analysis encountered in this volume reflects and confirms this goal and this emphasis, especially when one sees the former method being applied to writings such as Philippians and James, which have seldom been examined or analyzed from this perspective. As such, this re-examination is a strong and clear witness to the fact that more than two decades have elapsed since the advent of redaction criticism. Indeed, it is the wide incorporation and profound appropriation of this method—specifically, in terms of its later developments and elaborations, such as composition criticism and narrative analysis—that set this volume apart from the previous treatments of the topic mentioned above, all of which were written during the 1960s and thus in the very early stages of the method.

3. In addition to the pervasive use of redaction criticism in these studies, the preceding survey also shows and reflects the wide variety of methods, often in very fruitful and imaginative combinations, currently in use in the field of New Testament studies (e.g., the history-of-religions approach, genre criticism, tradition criticism), as well as the most recent directions and developments to be found within the discipline as a whole (e.g., literary criticism and the social world approach). Three specific lines of interpretation deserve comment:

a. One finds in these studies, first of all, a very judicious use of that kind of comparative analysis which has traditionally been known as the history-of-religions approach. In this volume, this particular approach is used both as the primary method of interpretation (Wild: the imitation of God within Middle Platonism as the purpose of human existence, in terms of an assimilation to God through virtuous human activity) as well as an ancillary method (Talbert: the portrayal of Jesus' career in terms of the traditional Hellenistic development between beginning and perfection; Kurz: the imitation of personal examples in first-century parenesis; Johnson: envy as a *topos* in Hellenistic moral philosophy and friendship as a sharing in values in the Greek philosophical tradition).

In either case, the comparative analysis is being used to shed further light on the background and context of the particular writing in question in a very strict and circumscribed fashion. Thus, for example, great care is exercised to point out the unique way in which each writing stands, functions, and argues within the proposed background or context. Similarly, great care is taken to avoid the tendency often exhibited in the past by practitioners of the method—aptly characterized by Wild, following Samuel Sandmel,[5] as "parallelomania"—to claim direct and thorough dependence on the part of the writing or author in question.

b. Several of the studies in this volume also reflect a growing awareness of and acquaintance with the aims and methods of contemporary literary criticism and theory. This rather recent orientation in New Testament studies—really no more than a decade in vogue, yet constantly growing in application, sophistication, and prominence—may be observed, above all, in several of the Gospel studies in this volume (Kelber, Edwards, Segovia) but not exclusively so (Schüssler Fiorenza), thus reflecting its wider use in the discipline at large.

With the advent of redaction criticism, the traditional focus of Gospel research underwent a major shift in direction: it was the evangelist as author that had now become the main center of attention. In its earliest stages redaction criticism approached the specific input of the author by examining how the pre-existing traditions, both oral and written, had been edited and arranged in each Gospel.

In time, redaction criticism became what eventually came to be known as composition criticism[6]: the contribution of the author was no longer to be sought solely in terms of his or her disposition toward and handling of the traditional material but rather in terms of the overall conception of each work as well as its inner development, connections, and dynamics. In more recent times, as mentioned above, the main focus of interest has switched once again: the specific character of the Gospel as story has begun to be seriously addressed and examined in terms of contemporary literary theory. As a result, such new topics as the narrator, point of view, plot, characterization, and the implied reader have very much come to the fore in the field of Gospel studies.[7]

In this volume, for example, the studies of Kelber and Edwards on the Markan and Matthean Gospels, respectively, are very much concerned with the question of characterization. Both argue, in effect, that a proper understanding of discipleship in a Gospel narrative is possible only when one takes into consideration the portrayal of the disciples as a character in that narrative (Kelber: completely negative portrayal; Edwards: an alternating pattern of positive and negative portrayals) and the overall effect of such a portrayal on the reader (Kelber: parabolic reversal; Edwards: discipleship as an unfinished and ongoing task). A major difference between them lies, however, in their expressed willingness (Kelber) or unwillingness (Edwards) to make certain historical conclusions on the basis of such a portrayal and its intended effect on the reader.

From a more traditional perspective, and yet very much influenced by these literary developments as well, Segovia's study on John also focuses on the characterization of the disciples in that Gospel (discipleship as entailing a necessary and inevitable progression in perception and understanding) and proceeds to describe how such a portrayal presupposes, reflects, and addresses a concrete historical situation. Finally, Schüssler Fiorenza's study on Revelation clearly shows that recourse to and use of contemporary literary theory is by no means limited to Gospel studies (Revelation as a poetic-rhetorical construction of an alternative symbolic universe which fits a specific rhetorical situation).

c. Along with the rise of literary criticism, New Testament studies have witnessed in the past decade or so a rapidly expanding and deepening interest in the social background, orientation, and dynamics of the earliest Christian groups and communities—what has come to be widely known as the social world approach. Such an interest, moreover, has already taken different forms and directions; however, two overarching lines of investigation may nevertheless be distinguished and differentiated within this approach: historical research into social facts and phenomena, and the interpretation of such facts and phenomena according to models derived from the social sciences.[8]

Three of the studies in this volume very much reflect this new perspective with regard to the New Testament texts and adopt, to a greater or lesser extent, the second line of investigation delineated above. Thus, for example, two of these studies (Donahue, Elliott) use the social world approach as the primary method of interpretation, while the third (Segovia) uses it as an auxiliary and subordinate method. Furthermore, whereas the former rely basically upon the sociology of knowledge in attempting to describe the social world of Mark and 1 Peter, respectively (a self-understanding as the "household of God" in the midst of a hostile world), the latter uses concepts derived from the study of sectarianism within the sociology of religion to describe the self-conception of the Johannine community (a highly sectarian and exclusivistic group).

4. The given emphasis of these studies on each writing under consideration as an independent literary and theological whole, as well as the observed variety of methods and combinations of methods employed in their respective exegetical approaches to these writings, point to and reveal in turn the different aspects and facets of the understanding of Christian discipleship and existence to be found within the New Testament itself. Therefore, I want to underscore the most important and salient findings of this re-examination.

a. First of all, belief in Jesus the Christ emerges as the very ground of discipleship: it is faith that constitutes the basic presupposition and point of departure for all Christian discipleship. However, several of the Gospel studies in this volume (Kelber, Edwards, Segovia) do show that at times the proper character and content of belief itself become a matter of serious concern and discussion.

Nowhere is such a concern more evident than in the Gospel of Mark. For Kelber, the thoroughly negative portrayal of the disciples in the narrative is meant to serve as a direct refutation of the oral, apostolic tradition with its specific understandings of christology (Jesus as a gnostic revealer) and discipleship (the chosen few). Given Edwards's findings, Matthew would present a middle position in this regard—that is, neither complete rejection nor absolute commendation; rather, the alternating pattern of positive and negative portrayals is seen as calling attention to the ever-present need on the part of the disciples to comprehend the deeper significance of Jesus'  sayings. Indeed, even in that Gospel in which faith appears as the sole criterion of discipleship and in which, consequently, the disciples receive a very positive portrayal (John), one does find, according to Segovia, a very sharp and repeated emphasis on the proper understanding and full acceptance of the events comprising Jesus' hour as absolutely essential to proper and correct belief.

b. In the second place, these studies make it quite clear that belief implies and entails a very definite style of life on the part of the believers. Furthermore, the studies also show that such a way of life is, quite often, distinctly patterned on or modeled after the life and ministry of Jesus.

*In the gospel tradition*, as it has already been noted above, this conception of Jesus as model or example for the disciples is conveyed and developed primarily by means of the technical term used with regard to their relationship ("to follow") and its various equivalents (e.g., "to go after"). In this volume, such a conception appears very prominently in the studies on Mark and Luke-Acts, and less so in those on Matthew and John. Moreover, these five studies on the Gospels also show that, with respect to the proposed way and life of discipleship, different gospel traditions draw on and stress different aspects of Jesus' life and ministry.

It is, then, in the works of Kelber, Donahue, and Talbert that one encounters this element of patterning or modeling most prominently. For example, given the proposed parabolic dynamic of the Gospel, Kelber derives by negation the essential attributes of "following" in Mark: inclusiveness, an acceptance of suffering, and a willingness to accept possible death as well. Similarly, by means of a study on household and family language in Mark, Donahue proposes the following characteristics as distinctive of Markan discipleship: being called; leaving behind old ties and embracing the new family of Jesus; being empowered for mission, as well as for a life doing the things of Jesus—namely, mutual service, renunciation of power and prestige, trust in God even in the face of suffering and death. Lastly, Talbert's redaction-critical study yields a rather similar fusion of closely interrelated elements essential to Lukan discipleship: being called; an empowering experience; being molded by the tradition of Jesus; belonging to a new community. All of these elements, moreover, are also said to shape and inform directly two other essential components of discipleship in Luke-Acts: a specific way to walk and a mission to fulfill.

While not as prominent in his study, Edwards does cite nevertheless the strong emphasis in Matthew on the need to make disciples of all nations as well as on the need for constant renewal through dedication and denial on the part of the disciples. Finally, even in the Fourth Gospel, where discipleship is said to rest solely on belief, Segovia does point out a very strong and repeated emphasis to the effect that the disciples are chosen by Jesus and are called to suffer and die as well as to engage in the mission.

*Outside the gospel tradition*, the use of "following" Jesus with respect to the way and life of Christian discipleship is seldom encountered in the New Testament. In fact, it appears but once, in Rev. 14:4 ("following the Lamb"), although a rather similar expression may be found in 1 Peter 2:21 as well ("following in his steps"). Both Schüssler Fiorenza and Elliott use these references as the specific point of departure for their respective studies on the shape and character of Christian existence in Revelation and 1 Peter. In both studies, moreover, the element of patterning mentioned above appears rather prominently once again.

In her literary critical study of Revelation as a poetic-rhetorical construction, Schüssler Fiorenza argues that correct and proper discipleship is described therein as entailing a thorough rejection of Rome in all its various aspects and a corresponding determination to endure all the inevitable consequences of such a rejection—economic loss and deprivation, persecution, and possible death. It should be noted, moreover, that as in the previous case of the Gospels with regard to the proper character and content of faith, such a vision of the Christian life in Revelation has become a matter of serious concern and discussion. It is, in fact, as Schüssler Fiorenza points out, directly being called into question by competing Christian ideologies.

In his examination of household language in 1 Peter, Elliott sees the category and role of the "house slave" as summarizing and representing the position of the entire Christian community in the society at large: innocent and obedient, suffering servants.

Far more frequently encountered in the description of the way of life proper to Christian discipleship outside the Gospels, however, is the concept of *imitation*. In this volume, for example, both Kurz and Wild see this notion of imitation as central to the definition of proper Christian existence in both Philippians and Ephesians, respectively.

Thus, within Philippians, Kurz argues, it is not only the imitation of Jesus but also that of Paul, as well as of other believers and groups of believers, that is used to describe the central thrust of Christian living: a surrendering of all personal prerogatives, including those that would spare suffering and death, and a trusting in God instead for ultimate vindication and exaltation. It should be noted once again that, as in the case of Revelation, such a vision of the Christian life would not be shared by all: it is directly aimed, as Kurz points out, at judaizers within the community. In Ephesians, it is the imitation of God as such, according to Wild, that provides the proper end or purpose of Christian existence: an assimilation to God through virtuous human activity in everyday life.

There are, to be sure, a number of other concepts and expressions which can serve as the primary and essential metaphors for the proper life of the Christian disciple in this world. In this volume, however, only one such other description is encountered: *friendship with God*. Thus, in his redaction-critical study of James, Johnson argues, first of all, that "friendship" for James means a profound agreement in values and attitudes and that, consequently, to be a "friend of God" means continually to renounce friendship with the world, renew one's conversion to God, and become a doer of God's word. Although the idea of Jesus as an exemplar does not appear at all in this study, the implication is made that not all would posit as sharp a dichotomy between the world and God with respect to the way and life of Christian existence (namely, the "double-minded" Christians).

In sum, one may say, first of all, that each of the contributions in this volume presents a different and unique conception of what it means to be a Christian believer, not only in terms of the different metaphors used to describe such a status and role but also, and more important, in terms of the specific, essential characteristics ascribed to discipleship in each tradition, as well as the distinct emphasis placed on certain characteristics vis-à-vis others within the different traditions.

To be sure, certain characteristics do recur in different traditions. In this volume, two immediately come to mind—one solely within the gospel tradition; the other both within and outside the gospel tradition: a commitment to missionary activity (Donahue, Edwards, Talbert, Segovia); a willingness to accept a life of self-denial, persecution, and suffering, including the possibility of death (Kelber, Donahue, Talbert, Segovia, Kurz, Schüssler Fiorenza, Elliott).

Furthermore, as previously mentioned, the proper way and life of discipleship is often patterned after Jesus' own life and ministry; this is true not only, as expected, within the gospel tradition (Kelber, Donahue, Talbert, Edwards, Segovia) but also outside of it as well (Kurz, Schüssler Fiorenza, Elliott). In this regard, Elliott's concluding remarks are very much to the point: Jesus is not only a pattern, a model, an exemplar, but also an enabler. In other words, the proper way and life of discipleship is not only patterned after but also grounded in Jesus' own life and ministry, so that "following" and "imitation" can take place only because Jesus himself has made them possible.

Finally, it should not go unmentioned that in some traditions the proposed delineation of proper Christian discipleship or existence in the world is not without some disagreement or even outright opposition. Very clear in this regard are the studies of Kelber on Mark (versus a gnosticizing apostolic, oral tradition), Kurz on Philippians (versus judaizers), and Schüssler Fiorenza on Revelation (versus a compromise with Rome). To a much lesser extent, certain difficulties are also implied by the studies of Edwards on Matthew (ongoing need for a deeper comprehension of Jesus' sayings and utterances), Segovia on John (belief must encompass the events surrounding Jesus' departure), and Johnson on James (one cannot be of two minds: friendship with God excludes friendship with the world).

Finally, these studies also make it quite clear that, as a result of belief in Jesus Christ and the proper and expected way of life flowing out of and attached to such belief, Christian discipleship or existence in this world implies and entails a very definite position and attitude toward that "world"— that is, toward society as a whole: its fundamental values, means, and goals. Furthermore, this attitude or position is always one of *rejection*, although the specific object, form, and degree of that rejection do vary from tradition to tradition.

In this volume, *rejection* appears in its most extreme form in the studies of Segovia on John (a sustained and progressive contrast between the disciples and the Jews) and Schüssler Fiorenza on Revelation (an uncompromising rejection of Rome and all the various aspects of its life and power). However, whereas the latter looks forward to an imminent destruction of Rome, the former sees the community as having been taken already "out of this world."

A somewhat less extreme position, although quite severe, is shown by the studies of Donahue on Mark (an alternative social structure with alternative values and goals), Kurz on Philippians (a surrendering of all personal prerogatives despite the inevitable persecutions from the Jews), and Elliott on 1 Peter (an alternative social structure called to be submissive in the midst of a hostile environment, both Jewish and Greco-Roman). Only this last position is also described as apocalyptic, although Elliott does see Mark in this light as well.

A much milder stance is revealed by the studies of Wild on Ephesians (assimilation to God in and through ordinary, day-to-day tasks of human activity, but possible only for believers) and Johnson on James (full participation in the affairs of the world, but only as a friend of God).

Thus, as previously mentioned, rejection of the world does vary according to object (Jewish society, Greco-Roman society, or both), form (apocalyptic, introversionist, gnostic), and degree (from limited to total). In this regard, it is interesting to note the correlation that exists between an increasing rejection of the world and the emphasis placed on suffering as an essential component of discipleship (Donahue, Segovia, Kurz, Schüssler Fiorenza, Elliott).

## CONCLUSION

In the preceding remarks I have attempted to point out the specific contribution of this volume and its re-examination of the shape and character of Christian discipleship, broadly conceived, in the New Testament in terms of:

(1) its central and fundamental thrust vis-à-vis previous studies on discipleship—the emphasis on and analysis of each writing in question as an independent literary and theological whole providing a unique and characteristic understanding of Christian discipleship;

(2) its recourse to and use of the newer developments in methodology within the discipline, as well as its rather creative application of the more traditional methodologies, whether by themselves or in combination; and

(3) its distinctive findings concerning the different aspects and facets of the understanding and delineation of Christian discipleship in the various traditions of the New Testament.

I began this introduction by saying that the times did seem ripe within the field of New Testament studies for the undertaking of such a re-examination of the shape and character of Christian discipleship in the New Testament. The results, I noted, more than justify such an undertaking and go far beyond the initial desideratum for such a project. I also remarked, however, that in a much more general sense—the increasingly exclusivistic definitions of what Christian discipleship means, presupposes, and entails in the contemporary scene—the times did seem ripe as well for precisely such an enterprise. Once again, I believe that the given results can be beneficial and instructive with regard to this other facet of the initial desideratum.

Above all else, the results point to diversity. There is diversity, first of all, within individual books of the New Testament. Talbert's concluding remarks in his study on Luke-Acts are very much to the point here: given the number of closely interrelated components of Christian discipleship present in Luke-Acts, no one component can be ignored or bypassed, and no one component can be stressed to the exclusion or detriment of the others. Furthermore, there is diversity as well within the New Testament as a whole: diversity not only with respect to the precise way of life proper to Christian discipleship but also with respect to the proper position or attitude to be taken vis-à-vis the world—that is, the surrounding society and culture.

Any attempt at reductionism or strict exclusivism, therefore—and specifically, any such attempt that would rely on and appeal to the New Testament for its ultimate grounding and justification—would contradict directly the evidence provided by the New Testament as a whole, as well as by individual books within the New Testament. Indeed, what the present results teach and convey, it seems to me, is the great need for patient understanding, open and critical dialogue, and above all, in this day and age, steadfast tolerance both within and among the different churches.

Again, this volume represents but a beginning in the right direction. There is no question that a great deal remains to be done before a complete and thorough grasp of the various conceptions and elaborations of Christian discipleship in the New Testament—and elsewhere as well—becomes a real possibility. Nevertheless, I find the present results most encouraging, and I firmly believe that the cumulative results of such a protracted and systematic re-examination will shed much greater light not only on what Christian discipleship meant, presupposed, and implied for the various traditions and communities in the first century of the Christian church but also, and ultimately, on what Christian discipleship should mean, presuppose, and entail for the various traditions and communities today. And this remains, in fact, the ongoing desideratum.

## NOTES

1. E. Schweizer, *Lordship and Discipleship* (SBT 28; London: SCM Press, 1960). The volume is a translation by the author of his earlier *Erniedrigung und Erhöhung bei Jesus und seinen Nachfolgern* (Zurich: Zwingli Verlag, 1955). The translation is also said to constitute an entirely revised edition of the earlier work: the arrangement of the material is different and more inclusive; more attention is paid to Paul; discussions of disputed exegetical questions have been largely omitted; a treatment of the Hellenistic background has also been omitted.

2. A. Schulz, *Nachfolgen und Nachahmen. Studien über das Verhältnis der neutestamentlichen Jüngerschaft zur urchristlichen Vorbildethik* (SANT 6; Munich: Kösel-Verlag, 1962).

3. H. D. Betz, *Nachfolge und Nachahmung Jesu Christi im Neuen Testament* (BHT 37; Tübingen: Mohr/Siebeck, 1967).

4. M. Hengel, *Nachfolge und Charisma: eine exegetisch-religionsgeschichtliche Studie zu Mt 8,21f. und Jesu Ruf in die Nachfolge* (BZNW 34; Berlin: Walter de Gruyter, 1968). English translation: *The Charismatic Leader and His Followers* (trans. J. Greig; New York: Crossroad; Edinburgh: T. & T. Clark, 1981).

5. S. Sandmel, "Parallelomania," *JBL* 81 (1962) 1–13. According to Sandmel, the word comes from an earlier work written around 1830 whose title and author he does not remember.

6. The term, originally proposed as *Kompositionsgeschichte* by Ernst Haenchen in his *Der Weg Jesu* (Berlin: Alfred Töpelmann, 1966), was adopted and introduced into the American scene by Norman Perrin (see, e.g., *What Is Redaction Criticism?* [GBS; Philadelphia: Fortress Press, 1969]).

7. For a good introduction to and application of this new approach in Gospel studies, see David Rhoads and Donald Michie, *Mark as Story: An Introduction to the Narrative of a Gospel* (Philadelphia: Fortress Press, 1982), and R. Alan Culpepper, *Anatomy of the Fourth Gospel. A Study in Literary Design* (Philadelphia: Fortress Press, 1983).

8. There are several short introductions to the method and its different directions and applications: R. Scroggs, "The Sociological Interpretation of the New Testament: The Present State of Research," *NTS* 26 (1979–80) 164–79; D. Harrington, "Sociological Concepts and the Early Church: A Decade of Research," *TS* 41 (1980) 181–90; T. F. Best, "The Sociological Study of the New Testament: Promise and Peril of a Discipline," *SJT* 36 (1983) 181–94. For longer treatments, see H. C. Kee, *Christian Origins in Sociological Perspective* (Philadelphia: Westminster Press, 1980), and D. J. Tidball, *An Introduction to the Sociology of the New Testament* (Exeter: Paternoster Press, 1983).

# 1

# Apostolic Tradition and the Form of the Gospel

## WERNER H. KELBER

For some time now, the theme of discipleship in Mark has attracted my attention, for nowhere in the canon does a text generate in readers as much alienation from the disciples as in this Gospel.[1] I continue to view it as a puzzle that admits no simple or general answer. The very oddness of the theme ought to have inspired creative explorations, whereas, in fact, it has often given rise to evasive maneuvers. The elaboration of admittedly positive features of the disciples is, of course, very much to the point. But it has not dissuaded me from holding that *the full narrative impact* of the disciples' story is a negative one. The desire to muffle the effects of Markan discipleship still seems less urgent to me than the obligation to explore its fuller ramifications; for the Markan exposition of the theme is more consequential than often assumed. If I take up discipleship in Mark again, therefore, it is out of a conviction that its implications have as yet not been brought to bear upon such issues as the form of the gospel, its connection with what preceded it, and also the role of Easter among competing early Christian traditions.

## EVOLUTIONARY VERSUS REVOLUTIONARY
## GENESIS OF MARK

The assignation of apostolicity to the four Gospels did more than lend legitimacy to what came to be called orthodoxy. It also imposed patterns of continuity upon the early processes of the tradition. Something akin to a straight line was envisioned to lead from Jesus through his oral, apostolic successors to the Gospels. When in the eighteenth and nineteenth centuries historical scholarship probed Christian beginnings, it continued to operate within the framework of linear thinking, partly under the pressure of orthodox assumptions, and partly influenced by modern intellectual disciplines which had themselves adopted linearity as a principal hermeneutical key.

In the twentieth century, both the form critics and their challengers viewed the gospel in direct continuity with tradition. The situation is epitomized by Rudolf Bultmann and Birger Gerhardsson.[2] For Bultmann the gospel results from the upward causation operative in all evolutionary processes. It is assumed that tradition flows predominantly from less to more, and from simple forms to the complex construction of the gospel. Gerhardsson suggested the existence of an authoritative λόγος τοῦ κυρίου ("word of the Lord") programmatically summed up in the speeches of Acts. It formed the basic teaching for the college of the Twelve and also for Paul. Embodying the essentials of Jesus' words and deeds from baptism to ascension, the *logos* constituted the gospel's genetic code inscribed into tradition from its very inception. Thus, both for Bultmann the form critic and Gerhardsson the challenger of form criticism, the gospel appeared to be the natural and expected outcome of the predominantly oral, precanonical tradition.

In view of the fact that form criticism's inability to come to terms with the gospel composition is widely recognized today, it deserves to be pointed out that Bultmann was himself torn between two potentially conflicting viewpoints. There was, on the one hand, his well-known statement that the gospel "offers nothing in principle new, but merely completes what was already begun in the earliest, oral tradition."[3] Yet he also insisted that the "form of gospel is first encountered in Mark; one may say that he has created it."[4] Could Mark, one must ask, become the creator of a new literary form in the Christian tradition by merely bringing oral trends to their destined culmination?

Form criticism's inadequate treatment of orality and its relation to textuality served to enhance the deeply ingrained model of continuity between tradition and gospel. While convinced of the predominance of precanonical, synoptic orality, form critics chose to regard the gospel's written performance as mere transcription of oral speech. On this view, the purpose of the gospel was consistently defined in terms of preservation of tradition. It was a position that accorded well with the classic thesis of the demise of the apostolic generation: when the living chain of apostolic transmitters of tradition was severed, it became imperative that their message be preserved in as authentic a fashion as possible. In view of the massive work undertaken by Eric A. Havelock,[5] Albert B. Lord,[6] and Walter J. Ong, S. J.[7] on orality, it should be obvious that form criticism "paid lip service" to the world of spoken words. Had it seriously sought to explore oral hermeneutics, as well as the processes of transformation of sounded words through textualization, it might well have concluded that preservation is, strictly speaking, not a literary function.

Whether the appeal was to entitlement by apostolic authority, the cumulative force of tradition, the abiding effectiveness of an incipient core message, or to the impulse to stem the tide of forgetfulness—the gospel was invariably viewed as preserver of tradition and guarantor of continuity. It was a view, moreover, that was powerfully strengthened by growing insight into the basic tenacity of linguistic and artistic conventions. No author writes independently from predecessors and without dependency on schemata, and in this sense is inexorably bound up with tradition. The more one recognized the force of linguistic forms and formulas, types and images, genres and styles, the less one trusted the claims to creativity. The gospel, by this logic, was almost always perceived to stand in unbroken or evolutionary continuity with tradition.

Given the deep interiorization of the model of gradualism, the integrity of a gospel and the novelty of its form were consistently underrated. That the gospel could have been written for the purpose of correcting, rather than protecting, tradition, was an idea whose day had not yet come.

The road toward a new appreciation of the composition of a gospel was paved by redaction criticism and literary criticism. Above all, these disciplines demonstrated the narrative integrity of the four canonical Gospels, forcing the conclusion that a distinct authorial intentionality was operative in each of them. The arrangement and revision of traditional materials, the production of novel segments, the artistic interweaving of dramatic features, the employment of christological titles, the whole inner landscape of the narrative with setting, plot, and characters, inside views, ideological point of view, and narrative realism, and in the case of Mark—if one subscribed to Markan priority—the very form of a gospel, all resulted from a linguistic, theological act of creation. In North American biblical scholarship, Norman Perrin took the creative literary production of Mark with utmost seriousness.[8] Much of his Markan scholarship was designed to demonstrate that Mark's Gospel was the result of a "self-conscious . . . editor, redactor, and author."[9] But there is evidence that even Perrin did not fully realize the implications of his work as far as our understanding of the history of the tradition was concerned. He was, under the tutelage of Joachim Jeremias and Bultmann, preoccupied with myth and history and the relation between the historical Jesus versus the kerygmatic gospel, and he never made a sustained effort at revising the gradualist, evolutionary model of tradition and gospel. It was, however, Erhardt Güttgemanns who clearly articulated the impact of redaction criticism upon the model of the history of the synoptic tradition: "If the gospel form is actually a language form first *created* by Mark, then we cannot simultaneously assume an immanent tendency within the tradition history of the material, which leads logically, consistently, causally, and genetically to the gospel form."[10] Güttgemanns's perception of a gospel as "autosemantic language form"[11] carried with it the potential of overturning the time-honored, classic model of continuity with respect to tradition and gospel. Now a gospel could no longer be comprehended solely as product or extension of tradition, and preservation of oral materials proved inadequate as explanation for the writing of Mark. It was not tradition which, empowered by its immanent drives, emanated into a gospel but Mark who had shaped the form of gospel by exercising control over tradition.

Independent of Güttgemanns's theoretically conceived work, Theodore Weeden advanced our understanding of the relation of Mark's Gospel to tradition in his justly famous *Mark—Traditions in Conflict*.[12] Perhaps Weeden's most significant achievement was to introduce into gospel studies the notion of conflicting traditions, and hence to challenge the rectilinear model of the transmission of synoptic traditions. Henceforth, when we speak of the history of the synoptic tradition, we ought to be mindful of *traditions* in the plural. What had long been commonplace in Pauline studies—that is, the recognition of alternate gospels—was about to become reality for the synoptic traditions as well. From this perspective, the synoptic history appeared not as passive transmission of *the* gospel, nor merely as "a process of hermeneutical translation,"[13] but as a struggle between competing and possibly irreconcilable viewpoints. Mark's Gospel, in this view, was an active participant in the conflict between traditions and specifically designed to rebut a distinct view of Christian faith.

The basic argument of Weeden's thesis is well known. In following a principle of Hellenistic, literary hermeneutics, he focused on Mark's characters, especially the disciples, who, he claimed, hold the key to the mystery surrounding the genesis of this Gospel. The evangelist "is assiduously involved in a vendetta against the disciples. He is intent on totally discrediting them."[14] Mark carries out the project dramatically by narrating the disciples' relationship to Jesus as one of progressive deterioration. From the initial stage of imperception of Jesus' miraculous powers, they lapse into misconceiving his messiahship, only to end in rejecting the suffering, dying Messiah. Their failure in discipleship is rooted in a stubborn commitment to a *theios anēr* ("divine man") christology that embraced a messiah in glory and power. What caused Mark to stage this extraordinary scenario was a christological controversy in his own community. It is troubled by suffering and the delay of the Parousia, when certain *theios anēr* apostles arrived and proclaimed a christology of power and presence. It was this heresy that necessitated Mark's Gospel. In projecting the heresy upon the disciples, and by making Jesus the spokesman of his own preferred christology, the evangelist was able to dramatize effectively Jesus' exemplary response to the crisis.

Two obvious objections to Weeden's thesis come to mind immediately. First, the three-stage dramatization of the disciples' failure is a schematization not strictly derived from the plotted narrative. Mark's pattern of discipleship does not follow the tidy progression of unperceptiveness, misconception, and rejection. Second, the *theios anēr* identification of the disciples is questionable. Weeden chose to examine the Markan situation in *theios anēr* terms taken directly from Dieter Georgi's interpretation of 2 Corinthians.[15] What may be obscured by such a procedure is the specificity of Mark. The problem of appropriate, interpretative categories is all the more pressing since Carl R. Holladay has criticized the usefulness of *theios anēr* for New Testament christology.[16] Even if Georgi's application of *theios anēr* is judged successful in the case of 2 Corinthians, its relevance for Mark is not immediately self-evident.

But none of these objections must excuse us from facing up to the depth of the issue raised by Weeden. Whatever the precise narrative pattern of discipleship, did Weeden not correctly see the disciples and their ideological viewpoint discredited by the Markan Jesus? Has he not rightly sensed the total impact of the disciples' story? Yet Weeden's innovative thesis had not yet sufficiently crystallized in his own mind to compel revision of a misleading scholarly convention of designating alternate Christian traditions. Such terms as "opponents," "enemies," or "heresy" are less than helpful in clarifying Mark's motivation for casting the disciples, of all people, in the role of carriers of a competing viewpoint. If, in other words, the alternate tradition was carried by what Weeden calls "certain interlopers,"[17] why would the evangelist see fit to tarnish the disciples with the burden of "heresy"? Could he not, for example, let the false prophets of Mark 13 (vv. 5–6, 21–22) play the role of adversaries? It is a tribute to Weeden's incisive mind that he has, despite deficient nomenclature, pursued the question toward what appears to be a logical conclusion. The "heresy" against which Mark wrote must have appealed to a tradition that claimed to go back to the disciples themselves. In different words, the "heresy" invoked apostolic legitimacy.[18]

Weeden not only broke with the evolutionary model of the genesis of Mark, he also introduced a revolutionary model in a provocative sense: Mark's Gospel arose in refutation of apostolic tradition. Therein lies the real challenge of his work, a challenge rarely understood, let alone taken up by his critics.

## EASTER'S ALLEGED KEY TO MARK, AND THE
## NEGLECT OF NARRATIVE

While the theme of discipleship has received much attention in recent Markan scholarship, its interpretation has remained a serious bone of contention. Three recent studies may serve to illustrate the scope of readings. Klemens Stock[19] interpreted Markan discipleship in a traditional, apostolic sense. Ernest Best[20] viewed it from a pastoral, pedagogical angle. And Günther Schmahl[21] saw it as a function of christology and messianic secret.

In Stock's view, the discipleship theme is designed to underscore close association with Jesus. "Being-with-Jesus" (*Mit-Ihm-Sein*) is the most prominent feature of Markan discipleship. The evangelist consistently assigns to the disciples the role of appointed recipients of Jesus' message and at one particular point initiates them into the mystery of the kingdom of God. Yet being-with-Jesus cannot spare them the pitfalls of apostasy. The theme of their betrayal runs almost parallel to the theme of their being-with-Jesus.[22] But Jesus' tireless efforts to teach the disciples and to challenge their incomprehension confirms the priority of being-with-Jesus. This is so despite the fact that the disciples' flight contradicts their appointed call and brings about a complete break with Jesus. In Stock's view, Mark firmly implicates the disciples in the suspension of relations with Jesus.[23] And yet Jesus' announcement of their fall in 14:28 also contains the seed for a resumption of their being-with-him. In the end, the women's Easter message extends an invitation of reunion with Jesus, which will facilitate the disciples' apostolic mission.

Stock's book raises the question whether discipleship in Mark does in fact admit the pre-eminence of the motif of being-with-Jesus, which subsumes and overrides the failure of the disciples. To some extent an answer will depend on a reading of the ending of Mark's Gospel. But even if we were to share Stock's preference for a happy resolution, it would have to be projected outside the given story. But is such a projection warranted in view of the absence of a narrated resolution? Given the admitted negativity of the disciples, is being-with-Jesus the appropriate designation for the relation between Jesus and the disciples? Granted that the narrator characterizes the disciples both favorably and unfavorably, is there not a point in the story whence the negativity prevails, leading readers to alter their initial, positive impression?

For Ernest Best, Markan discipleship is not primarily polemical and not meant to attack some group within or outside the community. Least of all did the evangelist intend a critique of the historical disciples. Indeed, the weakness of the disciples must not be exaggerated. Their inability, for example, to come to terms with suffering and the cross compares favorably

29

with the ruthless desire of scribes, rulers, and Pharisees to seek Jesus' death. "A failure to understand the death of Jesus is much less serious than an attempt to bring it about."[24] By the same token, Jesus' rebuke of Peter is not "a personal attack on the apostle Peter but on Peter as a sample disciple who in the ultimate analysis represents Mark's community."[25] Mark's principal motive for discipleship is thus pedagogical. "In so far as the disciples appear in a bad light it is because Mark wishes to use them as a foil."[26] Their failure to understand puts Jesus in the role of enunciating the standards of Christian conduct. From him one learns what the disciples failed to learn. From him one learns also that the disciples were to be restored in the postresurrection period, which would be a source of great comfort for Mark's readers. Therefore, "if Mark wishes to show Jesus' power he must show the weakness of his disciples."[27] Rather than attacking the disciples, Mark uses the vehicle of discipleship to teach them the lesson of God's unfailing love in the face of human feeling.

In a general sense, Best's pastoral, pedagogical explication recommends itself to serious consideration. In their incorrigible way of "thinking the things of men," the disciples function indeed as foils for Jesus' proclamation of the kingdom. But Best's interpretation has not absorbed the full implications of Mark's story. In making all too quickly a theological virtue out of dysfunctional discipleship, he tends to blunt the narrative directives and trivialize their impact on readers (or hearers). What strikes him as "perfectly natural"[28] is hardly that at all. Mark's narrative progressively discourages its readers (or hearers) from accepting the leadership of the Twelve. Inasmuch as the Gospel's recipients find themselves disoriented from the disciples, they are also encouraged to reorient themselves, which cannot take full effect until after they have taken in the narrative down to its last word. This carefully plotted distancing of readers (or hearers) from the disciples makes it difficult to seize upon reorientation without absorbing the shock of disorientation. The history of early Christian traditions, moreover, makes it impossible not to be stunned by Markan discipleship, for the well-known Christian preference for apostolic linkage contrasts sharply with Mark's narrative incentive *not* to follow the example set by the disciples.

Günther Schmahl offers the most rigorous assessment of the disciples' negativity. With the possible exception of Peter's confession, he finds the disciples consistently lacking in perception. The explanation, he suggests, lies not in the author's intention to psychologize the disciples but rather in christology. Functionally, failing discipleship resembles Jesus' injunctions to silence. Both themes operate so as to prevent Jesus from becoming fully known during his lifetime. This well-known Markan feature to keep Jesus "under cover" during his earthly career points toward Easter as the time of disclosure. According to this scenario, the disciples play the role of pre-

Easter people, unfinished and shaky in faith. Mark's failing discipleship is, therefore, a function of a christology grounded in Easter and the expected feature of a gospel designed out of Easter faith.

Of the suggested explanations, Schmahl's thesis deserves our most serious reflection. His view, now widely entertained in scholarship, originated, of course, with William Wrede's insight into possible connections between discipleship and secrecy in Mark.[29] For Wrede the disciples' conduct was "quite natural"[30] and entirely compatible with their high estimation in tradition; for while the bulk of the Christian tradition sanctions them in their apostolic, *post*resurrectional role, Mark chose to trace their *pre*resurrectional career. Insofar as vision is bound to be dimmed in the preressurectional status, it is with resurrection that the veil of obscurity is penetrated and clarity of perception restored.

Wrede's position, resumed by Schmahl and others, is highly persuasive and appears close to the mark. But it also runs the risk of misreading Markan discipleship in the interest of a postresurrectional resolution. What comes to mind is Joseph Tyson's objection to correlating the motifs of the disciples' blindness and secrecy: "It is not as if the disciples discerned the nature of Jesus but are prohibited from broadcasting it, but it is that the disciples have a wrong conception about his nature."[31] Tyson has brought the issue into sharp focus: Are the disciples depicted as being excluded from understanding Jesus during his lifetime, only to be enlightened at resurrection, or are they depicted as having misunderstood the earthly Jesus so as to be excluded from representing the risen Lord?

An additional question concerns the Gospel's assumed christological genesis in an orientation toward Easter. Admittedly, the transfiguration projects fulfillment outside the story, gesturing perhaps toward the resurrection, or more plausibly toward the Parousia. But the ending of Mark's Gospel (16:8) seems less designed to assure and more to undercut the disciples' participation in the presence of the risen Lord.[32] Nor is it entirely certain that Easter carries full revelatory weight in Mark. The narrative is somewhat less than perfectly fitted to this conception. When the centurion, in full view of the cross, confesses that Jesus was (ἦν) Son of God (15:39), he appears to locate the cross at the summit of a messianic earthly life. The title "king," moreover, which typifies the Gospel's leading kingdom motif, does not appear until Mark 15, when it is placed over the events of the crucifixion. Those who put Jesus to death endorse the crucified Messiah out of ignorance.[33] There is also Jesus' speaking "openly" (παρρησίᾳ) when first announcing his suffering and rising (8:31–32). This speaking ἐν παρρησίᾳ has been identified as a hallmark of the risen Christ in gnostic Christianity. From this perspective also, Mark's use of παρρησίᾳ marks an "Easter shift," a de-emphasis of the risen Lord in favor of the earthly Jesus moving toward death.[34] The absence of a resurrection appearance story further shifts the focus away from the resurrection toward crucifixion. The point Mark seems to be making is that Jesus' earthly life was perfected in the cross and not directly in resurrection. This does raise the question whether a gospel that projects God's sonship upon Jesus' earthly life, making it culminate in the cross, while not reporting a resurrection appearance, is in fact designed out of Easter faith.

The question needs recasting in different terms. The absence of a resurrection appearance story gives Mark's Gospel a highly distinctive quality. One must ask whether this extraordinary feature is entirely consistent with Wrede's concealing-revealing schematization. If Mark conceals in order to reveal, why does his narrative not reveal the glory of the risen Lord? Why does he withhold from us what Matthew, Luke, and John have found impossible not to report? Why this reluctance to narrate Easter? Is he intent on keeping the risen Lord absent and silent? This line of questioning suggests that Mark's Gospel cannot immediately be assumed to have grown out of Easter faith, at least not until the issue of the unnatural absence of Easter is satisfactorily explained.

The very form of gospel also seems to militate against Mark's genesis in Easter faith. If Easter were the ground of Mark's writing, a most fitting model surely would have been the genre of the revelation dialogue;[35] for it is difficult to find a more authentic product of Easter faith than the genre that presents the risen Lord as revealer of sayings and donor of life. It is not inconsequential that Mark falls woefully short of this Easter genre par excellence. Indeed, the form of Mark's Gospel and the revelation dialogue appear to inhabit opposite conceptual worlds. This observation alone should caution us against uncritically endorsing the notion that Easter gave birth to the form of the orthodox gospel.

Despite their differing readings of discipleship, the studies of Stock, Best, Schmahl, and countless others have a single hermeneutical aspect in common: *a disregard for narrative*. All fail to appreciate discipleship as an integral part of Mark's narrative. The causes for this disregard are deeply rooted in theology and hermeneutics and far from being fully explored.[36] Here we can only touch upon two principal causes.

There is first the issue of story and history. New Testament hermeneutics has found it exceedingly difficult to appreciate the story about Jesus apart from reference to historical actuality. On the assumption that a gospel is not merely related to but also arbitrated by Jesus' historicity, exegesis is often inclined to read the story with assistance derived from the logic of history. Despite growing insight into the linguistic web of narrative connections and strategies, this is a procedure still practiced in New Testament

Gospel studies and subtly in evidence in the work of Best.[37] That a gospel lives by its own internal logic is a principle of special relevance for discipleship, which is one of the most circumspectly plotted features in Mark. It may not be amiss, therefore, to withhold credence from any theory on Markan discipleship that has not seriously attempted to decode the full narrative pattern.

A plea for storied integrity must not necessarily drive us to reduce a gospel to an aesthetic object. This inclination to treat texts as hermetically sealed worlds owes much to what we are able to imagine as children of a venerable print culture. In the perspectives of ancient hermeneutics, however, chirographically produced texts are rarely ever fully closed. They were expected to participate in an ongoing discourse, rewording what preceded them, and subject also to re-imaginings.[38] Each new version awakened hidden potentials and dormant competencies. This hermeneutical openness of ancient texts applies with special force to biblical material. "Scripture is something that is always turning into new versions of itself."[39] Obviously, to consider a gospel's versional status is a far cry from relating it to the alleged historical matrix of its subject matter. Still, it is inadmissible, and hardly even possible, to grasp a gospel's place in the ongoing hermeneutical discourse unless one has first come to terms with its rhetorical and imagistic inner landscape.

A second cause for the neglect of story relates to the hidden assumption that a gospel functions as carrier of ideational content. Best, for example, commences his book on discipleship with Mark 8:27—10:45. Discipleship is here approached conceptually, with a view toward its principal definition, rather than compositionally, in search of progressive narration. Schmahl studies "Twelve" passages, which he divides according to appointment and mission, connection with Jesus' *logoi*, and also their occurrence in the passion narrative. His is an operation that employs formal and analytical criteria irrespective of the flow of narrative. In addition, he analyzes passages that refer to disciples in a nonspecific sense, very briefly reflects on the disciples' misunderstanding, and finally turns to verses that focus on the chosen four or three. Mark's overall concept of the Twelve and of discipleship is then derived from a summary evaluation of those random passages. Stock likewise extrapolates so-called Twelve texts, dividing them into three groups: appointment texts, commissioning texts, and Jerusalem texts. Subsequently, he assesses their interrelationship apart from Mark's story before he determines their position in the story.

What typifies all these approaches is the conviction that a gospel transports concepts and ideas which, in order to be grasped clearly, must be rescued from their narrative entanglement. Here the hermeneutic of story has been stood on its head; for story is not primarily, if at all, designed to serve as carrier of ideas—ideas, that is, that enjoy autonomy apart from the narrative ensemble. Narrativized syntax does not conceptualize, and themes have meaning only insofar as they are narrated. To analyze themes in isolation from narrative amounts, therefore, to a reduction of narrative to meaninglessness.

## TOWARD NARRATIVE DISCIPLESHIP

It is a hallmark of much recent North American work on Mark that it has avoided both historical and ideational fallacies, as when, for example, Norman R. Petersen[40] chose to treat the intrinsic poetics of this Gospel; Robert C. Tannehill[41] studied the narrative patterns of christology and discipleship; Thomas E. Boomershine[42] shed light on the oral, rhetorical nature of the text, that meaning is consistently linked not with referentiality or ideation, but with rhetoric; John R. Donahue[43] explored Mark's parabolic dynamic; the present writer[44] traced the narration of kingdom and discipleship; David Rhoads, together with Donald Michie,[45] composed an introduction to the narrativity of Mark. In these instances, this Gospel's text is seen as resting not on any outside foundation but on the strength of its inner connections. If textual transparency is granted at all, it is not backwards onto Jesus' history but forwards to the implied reader, who is perceived to be the natural extension of the narrative.

When strictly viewed on Markan terms, discipleship emerges in full narrative view, carrying with it stark and virtually forbidding implications. The studies of Petersen and Tannehill, as well as Bommershine's recent reflections on Mark's ending, recommend themselves as entrées into the world of narrative discipleship.

Proceeding on the assumption that narrative is the art of creating time, Petersen singles out two principal plot devices: predictive, anticipatory statements that come to pass as plotted incidents later in the narrative; and predictive utterances that fail to come to pass in the narrative. Both devices "serve to create and reinforce narrative suspense."[46] The former causes short-term suspense, the latter long-term suspense. It is through these devices of prediction and fulfillment that Mark enacts discipleship. On the one hand, he introduces the disciples as privileged sharers of the mystery of the kingdom of God, while from an early point on he casts them into roles which run counter to the expectations raised about them. Since the reader is led to believe that all of Jesus' predictions will come to pass, the full weight of suspense is brought to bear upon the question of when the disciples will finally live up to Jesus' expectations. This long-term suspense

34

created by the disciples' stubborn ignorance "is resolved not in the narrative itself" but according to the predictions of Mark 9:9; 14:28; and 16:7, "in connection with a projected postresurrection meeting between Jesus and his disciples in Galilee."[47]

Petersen's treatment of narrative time progressively closes in on the issue of discipleship, confirming its significance for the plotted story and for a time outside of story. What remains dubious is whether the scheme of prediction and fulfillment accords well with Mark's narration. It seems forcibly theological and curiously tame for a gospel that is known less for a sense of proportionality, and more for rebellion against order imposed from the past.[48] The most serious obstacle to Petersen's thesis is Mark's ending. He has to concede that the women's failure to convey the message of life is "the one potential stumbling block"[49] to his projected postresurrectional resolution. His recent suggestion that "the narrator does not mean what he says in Mark 16:8"[50] proves embarrassing by any standard of criticism, for if Mark's ending does not fit Petersen's scheme, how true is his scheme to Mark?

For Tannehill, Markan discipleship is primarily a story of developing conflict and shifting relations between Jesus and the disciples. When initially the disciples are narrated in a positive light, the author encourages his readers to identify with them. But as their inadequacy begins to surface, and they increasingly "share the blindness of the outsiders,"[51] the readers find themselves under pressure to choose between the disciples' way and that of Jesus. Still, Tannehill cannot bring himself to place the burden of the story's outcome entirely upon the readers. He thinks, although more cautiously than Petersen, that the apocalyptic discourse in Mark 13 "anticipates a continuing role for the disciples beyond the disaster of chapter 14."[52] There is a sense in which the story of the disciples is not over, and a restored relationship appears at least to be a possibility.

Tannehill's perception of the disciples' shift from loyal followers to blind outsiders owes far more to Mark's narrative than Petersen's prediction and fulfillment scheme. What remains unclear is whether Mark 13 does indeed project a role for apostolic succession; for what the discourse *promises* is false messiahs ("christs") and false prophets, strife and persecution, destruction and the coming of the Son of man, and what it *demands* is preaching of the gospel, perseverance, and testimony under pressure. Far from promising the disciples a successful postresurrectional career, Mark 13 is designed to correct their false premises. The one disciple's exultation in view of the magnificent temple stones (13:1) promptly runs into Jesus' prediction of the temple's destruction, while the four disciples' assumed correlation of the temple's demise with the eschaton (13:4) is subject to correction by

Jesus. This corrective function of the discourse, coupled with the disciples' disastrous conduct in Jerusalem, does little to encourage readers to assume that the disciples have ceased to think in human terms.[33]

Boomershine's studies on Mark's ending examine the rhetorical impact of 16:8 on hearers. In his view, the recipients of the Gospel are left with signals "which pull in opposite directions."[54] While the norms associated with the women's flight and silence are strongly negative, the women's response of fear, astonishment, and trembling arouses feelings of compassion among hearers. This combination of negative performance and sympathetic characterization provokes listeners to steadily identify with the women and to reflect on their own response to the dilemma that the women confronted. Speaking to a situation of grave risks for Mark's generation, the ending encourages hearers to consider seriously the future of the Gospel's proclamation. In this way, Mark emphasizes "the same theme as the endings of the other gospels, namely, the apostolic commission to proclaim the gospel."[55]

One must ask whether Boomershine has not unduly softened the negativity of the ending. While it may be true that trembling and astonishment—the motive given for their flight—arouses a glimmer of sympathy for the women, fear—the motive for their silence—definitely does not. Earlier in the story, in Mark 4:41; 9:6; 9:32; and 10:33, the motif of fear contributed to the dysfunctional role of the disciples by underscoring their lack of perception. One cannot be certain, therefore, that the ending that attributes flight and fear to the women encourages progressive identification with them. Their witness of Jesus' death (15:40–41) and burial (15:47) is perceived to be positive, but already their desire to anoint the body (16:1) compares negatively with the anonymous woman's earlier anointment at Bethany (14:3–9). The women's flight, moreover (16:8: ἔφυγον), invites comparison with the disciples' earlier flight (14:50: ἔφυγον πάντες), and the motif of fear, the narrator's parting shot, serves to rank the women with the faithless disciples. Both women and disciples, therefore, receive a similar narrative treatment in Mark. In each case, initial identification with Jesus' followers is reversed by distanciation from them. If it is thus by alienation from the women, and earlier from the disciples, that Mark narrates discipleship, one cannot claim that "all four evangelists end with the theme of the apostolic commission;"[56] for in its classic formulation, apostolic commission suggests discipleship in continuity with the Twelve, whereas Mark enforces discipleship that is discontinuous with the Twelve and also with the women.

What we witness in the studies of Petersen and Tannehill is a methodical exploration of the hermeneutic of story; the intelligibility of discipleship rests on narrative shape and development. Tannehill and Boomershine, moreover, refrain from viewing the story as a system entirely closed in on itself. They both regard discipleship as a narrative instrument that plays on and solicits readers' (or hearers') responses. It is this dual attention to narrative shape and readers' response that has informed the present writer's assessment of Markan discipleship.

## THE PARABOLIC PATTERN OF DISCIPLESHIP

A flowering of recent publications by John D. Crossan,[57] Robert W. Funk,[58] and Paul Ricoeur[59] has forced attention upon parable as a hermeneutical category in its own right. These scholars prepared the ground for Donahue's seminal insight into the parabolic dynamic of Mark's narrative.[60] But whereas Donahue shunned application of parabolic logic to the one theme most deeply marked by it—that is, discipleship—Tannehill in effect undertook a parabolic reading of discipleship, without, however, explicitly invoking the hermeneutic of parable. Aided by the works of Crossan, Funk, Ricoeur, Donahue, and Tannehill, I have come to recognize the parabolic pattern of Markan discipleship.

In his first public act following the proclamation of the kingdom, Jesus calls upon four fishermen to follow him (Mark 1:16–20). This call is associated with a promise for the followers to become fishers of men. As the four leave their trade and families to join Jesus, a sympathetic bond is created between the faithful followers and the readers. Subsequently, the narrator promotes the readers' identification with the disciples by strengthening the impression of an essential consensus between Jesus and the disciples. The appointment of the Twelve (3:13–19) serves to confirm our confidence, for now it is obvious that the Twelve, and among them the three, have been selected to leadership positions. To be sure, the introduction of Judas as the one "who was to betray him" (3:19) causes a crack in the structure of expectancy. But it cannot undermine faith in the reliability of the eleven; for inasmuch as Judas is singled out negatively, his case appears to be exceptional, which reinforces our positive view of the eleven.

Following his public narration of the parable of the sower (4:1–9), Jesus withdraws from the crowds and positions the Twelve, together with a group of select ones, on the inside. As insiders they are privileged to participate in the mystery of the kingdom of God (4:10–11a). In addition to making the Twelve insiders, Jesus informs them in carefully measured terms of the characterizations of outsiders (4:11b–12). No sooner is the insider-outsider dichotomy affirmed, fully persuading us of the disciples' inside position, than Jesus questions their comprehension of the parable of the sower, and of parables in general (4:13). The sense of reproachfulness on the part of Jesus does not seem to accord well with their position as insiders. Yet it is precisely at the point when the structure of expectancy is at its peak that the disciples' drift toward the outside is subtly set into motion.

Subsequently, Jesus, in a series of boat trips (4:35; 5:21; 6:32; 6:45; 8:10; 8:13), opens the frontier toward the Gentiles, without abandoning Jewish land, and all the way expecting the disciples to learn the paradigm of his travels. At one point he sends them out on a journey of their own (6:7–13, 30), thus living up to his earlier promise to make them fishers of men (1:17) by initiating them into apostolic successorship. And yet the logic and the purpose of Jesus' trips eludes the disciples' comprehension. Following the second trip to the Gentiles (6:45), they are in a narrative aside charged with hardness of heart (6:52), an accusation directed earlier toward hostile people in the synagogue (3:5) and later toward a group of Pharisees (10:5). If at this stage our confidence in the disciples is shaken, it will be thoroughly undermined when after the second feeding Jesus himself applies the whole catalogue of outsider characteristics to the disciples: hardness of heart, lack of understanding, seeing and not seeing, and hence blindness, hearing and not hearing, and hence deafness (8:17–18). At this point the structure of expectancy is overturned.

On the way to Jerusalem, Peter's Christ confession (8:29) teases readers into taking it at face value. But as the unfolding story reveals Peter's opposition to Jesus' own confession—his first passion prediction (8:31)—Peter's confession is exposed as being less than adequate. Not only does Peter appear to reject a suffering Messiah but a false sense of presence also makes him, together with James and John, misjudge the proleptic nature of the transfiguration (9:2–8). The triumvirate, moreover, exhibits unusual obtuseness in regard to the resurrection (9:9–10). Unable to perform an exorcism, the disciples default on an obligation they had earlier been able to discharge successfully (9:14–29; cf. 6:7, 13). Jesus' second passion prediction is greeted with incomprehension and fear by the disciples (9:31–32). Contrary to Jesus' wishes, the disciples obstruct the work of an accomplished exorcist (9:38–41) and rebuke children (10:13–16). Shocked over Jesus' harsh treatment of the rich young man, the disciples under the leadership of Peter point to the sacrifices they have made in following Jesus (10:28). In response, Jesus promises a new community and life (10:29–30). But this reward has a "critical edge"[61] to it because it is promised "with persecutions." Moreover, Jesus' last word following the qualified promise is a warning aimed at Peter and the disciples: "But many that are first will be last, and the last first" (10:31). If, as a result of the ironically qualified promise and the warning, the reader feels ambiguous about the disciples, a negative judgment soon prevails as one approaches the third passion prediction (10:32–34). Directed specifically at the Twelve, it is met with

James's and John's request for positions of power (10:35–40). The author, it seems, has spared little effort to sharpen the conflict between Jesus and the disciples and to consolidate thereby the outsider position of the latter.

Above, we have reflected on the function of Mark 13 in relation to discipleship. Designed to correct false premises held by the disciples, the discourse predicts disaster as well as the coming of the Son of man, while it requests rather than promises a continuing role for the disciples. But before making a premature judgement on the disciples' postresurrectional status, it is well to remember that one "cannot judge the meaning of a story without attention to its outcome."[62] There is little evidence that the disciples heed this discourse more faithfully than Jesus' previous teachings. When, for example, Jesus tells the disciples that they must in the face of persecution and death endure (13:9–13) and not be caught asleep (13:33–37), he is in short-range terms anticipating a situation that the disciples can expect during his own passion. But at Gethsemane the three intimates fail to wake, and they fall asleep in view of Jesus' impending death (14:32–42). The immediate effect of Jesus' discourse on the disciples is therefore not encouraging. Far from strengthening their future leadership positions, it corroborates their role as outsiders.

If readers have retained a residue of confidence in the disciples, it is decisively crushed during the events surrounding the passion. Judas takes the initiative to deliver Jesus into the hands of his opponents (14:10–11). In his last words addressed to the Twelve, Jesus announces his death, the flight of the disciples, and also his return to Galilee, without, however, promising an actual Galilean reunion with the disciples (14:26–28). Peter protests Jesus' announcement of the disciples' flight, which leads Jesus to refute Peter's claim and to predict his (Peter's) imminent denial. In turn, Peter refutes Jesus. Far from denying Jesus, he (Peter) would suffer and even die with Jesus; "and they all said the same" (14:29–31). The triumvirate falters at Gethsemane (14:32–42), Judas delivers Jesus into the hands of his executioners (14:43–46), and all desert him at the moment of arrest (14:50). Peter, the last hope, denies Jesus while the latter makes his fateful confession before the high priest (14:53–72).

After the disciples' disappearance, the women serve as vital intermediaries. One last time, hopes are aroused that the broken connection might be repaired, the message of life delivered, and the disciples reunited with the risen Lord. But inasmuch as the appearance of the women rekindles hope, their performance makes sure that that hope is dashed. While the women are indeed commissioned to carry the message of life to the disciples, they fail to carry out this vitally important task. By Mark's relentless narrative logic, therefore, the Twelve are prevented from receiving the message that is designated to get them in touch with the risen Lord. With the demise of the Twelve the structure of expectancy is firmly and irrevocably reversed, and the narrative has found its proper parabolic ending.

Frank Kermode, a literary critic and virtual outsider to New Testament Gospel studies, has confronted the issue of Markan discipleship head-on and in full light of parabolic dynamics: "They [the disciples] are behaving exactly like the outsiders in the theory of parables."[63] Indeed, the precise narrative pattern of Markan discipleship is one of parabolic role reversal: the disciples' initial role of insiders is reversed to one of outsiders.

There remains, of course, the tempting assumption of a postresurrectional reunion between Jesus and the disciples. It owes as much to a historicizing harmonization of different Gospel stories as to our natural inclination "to prefer fulfillment to disappointment, the closed to the open."[64] But Mark's parabolic pattern intends to preclude, not promote, a postresurrectional reunion for the disciples. To postulate a closure in defiance of narrative openness is to trivialize the parabolic ending, which is designed to place the burden of unexpected outcome upon the readers (or hearers) of the Gospel.

## THE NARRATIVE WITHHOLDING
## OF EASTER

Earlier, we had reflected on Easter as the alleged key to the form of the Gospel and had refuted the thesis that the narrative was born out of Easter faith and moves inexorably—toward the revelation of the risen Lord. Here we must come to terms with the narrative withholding of Easter. We must learn to see the ending of the discipleship narration in connection with the form of gospel. When Jürgen Moltmann writes that "the gospels intentionally direct the gaze of Christians away from the experiences of the risen Christ and the Holy Spirit back to the earthly Jesus and his way to the cross,"[65] he has specifically described the Markan form of gospel; for what typifies this Gospel is its exclusive cast in a preresurrectional framework. All sayings and narrative materials are singularly bound to the earthly Jesus, converging in a story in whose form discipleship has a crucial stake; for insofar as discipleship culminates in the women's inability to communicate the message of life, the Gospel's ending allows but one conclusion: the inaccessibility of the risen Lord to the disciples. It is, however, precisely this nonreporting of the Lord's appearance to the disciples that sanctions the preresurrectional form of Mark. One may thus plausibly contend that the reversal of the disciples from insiders to outsiders, the women's complicity in depriving the disciples of the risen Lord, thus finalizing their outsider role, and the narrative retrieval of the preresurrectional Jesus are all complementary features in the making of the form of Mark's Gospel.

If we can agree, therefore, that Mark's ending at 16:8 is by design rather than accidental, and if we can further agree that the absence of a resurrection appearance is a deliberate withholding that accords with and indeed contributes to the form of gospel, we must concur with Moltmann that Mark's Gospel is composed to redirect christology away from the risen Lord toward the earthly Jesus. In that case, however, those who subscribe to Markan priority will be compelled to conclude that the orthodox gospel arose not out of Easter faith itself but out of concern to deflect attention away from it.

## THE FORM OF GOSPEL VERSUS APOSTOLIC TRADITION

Understanding the interior landscape of the text—the parabolic pattern of discipleship and its implication in the form of gospel—has brought us close to the source of Markan motivation. We saw that discipleship and its parabolic outcome were deeply connected with the narrative withholding of Easter. And yet why Mark chose this and not any other model of discipleship, and why he deflected attention from Easter, still begs the question. At this point we must attend to Mark's versional status—that is, to its rootedness in the depth of tradition—and consider its possible function to correct what preceded it; for the answer to Markan discipleship will in the last analysis come from the history of the tradition.

My recent publication, *The Oral and the Written Gospel*, attempted a tradition-historical explanation of the gospel as counterform to an oral tradition fraught with gnosticizing proclivities.[66] What is striking about Mark's Gospel is a remarkably reserved attitude toward sayings, a repossession of the earthly life of Jesus, that culminates in death rather than in resurrection, a withholding of the risen Lord from the disciples, and the banishment of the disciples, the initial insiders, toward the outside. Together these features appear to subvert a genre partial toward sayings, the primary unit of oral speech, and partial also toward the risen Lord, who continues speaking through apostolic, prophetic personalities. Keeping in mind Robinson's observation that "gnosticism's *Gattung* begins just as regularly after the resurrection as the orthodox *Gattung* ends there,"[67] the corrective function of the form of gospel almost leaps to the eye. For by withholding the resurrection, Mark undermines a crucial starting point for oral tradition; by narrating the earthly Jesus and his death he has countered a *Gattung* rooted in the risen Lord; and by relegating the disciples to the outside he has completed what amounts to an anti-genre to the genre of a sayings tradition.

One feels bound to revisit Weeden, who understood the tradition-historical implications of Mark's Gospel with an intuition unlike anyone I know. As noted above, he sensed in Mark's alienation of readers from the course set by the Twelve a narrative resolve to refute those who had invoked "an unimpeachable authority for their position: their kerygma was passed on to them by the disciples themselves."[68] Put simply, Mark was up against a tradition that perceived itself to be apostolic.

It is tempting to search for traces of the kind of tradition against which Mark appears to have directed his Gospel. Where in Mark do we encounter an oral genre that could invoke apostolicity? Among the sundry oral traditions Mark's text has absorbed, the spotlight inevitably falls upon 4:1– 33, the first of only two major sayings collections in Mark. The pre-Markan existence of the core of this collection is almost universally acknowledged.[69] Here we witness Jesus as speaker of parables and sayings and the Twelve as privileged recipients. If we extricate Jesus from Mark's historicizing framework, and replace him with the risen Christ, we have in fact arrived at the genre of the revelation dialogue, or, in Robinson's terms, at the "immediate precursor to the Gospel of Thomas," where much of this material recurs.[70]

In the revelation dialogue that lies embedded in 4:1–33, we have come closest to the tradition from which Mark took major cues and in refutation of which he composed the form of gospel. It is a tradition that sanctions the Twelve as apostolic recipients and guarantors of Jesus' *logoi*. The Jesus, moreover, who operates outside of Mark's preresurrectional framework, is in all likelihood the resurrected Christ. Empowered by his risen status, he communicates mystery in sayings and parables. Such will have been the tradition from which Mark learned specifically the insider role of the Twelve, as well as the riddling function of parabolic speech that may have a way of casting hearers to the outside. The gnosticizing proclivity of this revelation dialogue is immediately evident;[71] for as carrier of secret words disclosed to the Twelve at the exclusion of outsiders, Jesus approximates the role of a gnostic redeemer, the bringer of secrecy to a chosen few. Apostolic tradition is here synonymous with esoteric knowledge.

By anchoring the sayings tradition in a genre that sanctions the earthly Jesus, and by applying the outsider characteristics to the Twelve, the original insiders, Mark has defeated the authentic hermeneutical function of the sayings genre. Now the mystery of the kingdom of God no longer resides in the *logoi* of the risen Lord; for the genre of the orthodox gospel has transformed Jesus' whole life and, above all, his death into the mystery that is accessible not to the few but to all who read (or hear) it.

## NOTES

1. W. H. Kelber, *The Kingdom in Mark: A New Place and a New Time* (Philadelphia: Fortress Press, 1974); idem, "Mark 14:32–42: Gethsemane. Passion Christology and Discipleship Failure," *ZNW* 63 (1972) 166–87; idem, "The Hour of the Son of Man and the Temptation of the Disciples," in *The Passion in Mark* (ed. W. H. Kelber; Philadelphia: Fortress Press, 1976) 41–60; idem, *Mark's Story of Jesus* (Philadelphia: Fortress Press, 1979); idem, *The Oral and the Written Gospel: The Hermeneutics of Speaking and Writing in the Synoptic Tradition. Mark, Paul, and Q* (Philadelphia: Fortress Press, 1983) 90–139.

2. R. Bultmann, *The History of the Synoptic Tradition* (trans. John Marsh; New York: Harper & Row, 1963). In view of the noted difficulties pertaining to the translation, citations are offered in my own translation of the German original: *Die Geschichte der synoptischen Tradition* (FRLANT 29, NF 12; 8th ed.; Göttingen: Vandenhoeck & Ruprecht, 1970). B. Gerhardsson, *Memory and Manuscript: Oral Tradition and Written Transmission in Rabbinic Judaism and Early Christianity* (ASNU 22; Lund: C. W. K. Gleerup; Copenhagen: Ejnar Munksgaard, 1961).

3. Bultmann, *Geschichte der synoptische Tradition*, 347.

4. Ibid., 394.

5. E. A. Havelock, *Preface to Plato* (Cambridge: Harvard Univ. Press, 1963); idem, *The Greek Concept of Justice: From Its Shadow in Homer to Its Substance in Plato* (Cambridge: Harvard Univ. Press, 1978).

6. A. B. Lord, *The Singer of Tales* (HSCL 24; Cambridge: Harvard Univ. Press, 1960).

7. W. J. Ong, S.J., *The Presence of the Word: Some Prolegomena for Cultural and Religious History* (New Haven, Conn.: Yale Univ. Press, 1967; paperback ed.: Minneapolis: Univ. of Minnesota Press, 1981); idem, *Interfaces of the Word: Studies in the Evolution of Consciousness and Culture* (Ithaca, N.Y.: Cornell Univ. Press, 1977).

8. N. Perrin, *What Is Redaction Criticism?* (GBS; Philadelphia: Fortress Press, 1969); idem, "Towards an Interpretation of the Gospel of Mark," in *Christology and a Modern Pilgrimage* (ed. Hans Dieter Betz; Claremont, Calif.: The New Testament Colloquium, 1978) 1–71; idem, *A Modern Pilgrimage in New Testament Christology* (Philadelphia: Fortress Press, 1974); idem, "The Creative Use of Son of Man Traditions by Mark," *USQR* 23 (1967–68) 357–65; idem, "The Interpretation of the Gospel of Mark," *Int* 30 (1976) 115–24; idem, "The Christology of Mark: A Study in Methodology," *JR* 51 (1971) 173–87.

9. Perrin, *What Is Redaction Criticism?*, 51 n. 8.

10. E. Güttgemanns, *Candid Questions Concerning Gospel Form Criticism: A Methodological Sketch of the Fundamental Problematics of Form and Redaction Criticism* (trans. William G. Doty; PTMS 26; Pittsburgh: Pickwick Press, 1979) 307.

11. Ibid.

12. T. J. Weeden, Jr., *Mark—Traditions in Conflict* (Philadelphia: Fortress Press, 1971).

13. J. M. Robinson, "Kerygma and History in the New Testament," in *Trajectories Through Early Christianity* (Philadelphia: Fortress Press, 1971) 29.

14. Weeden, *Mark—Traditions in Conflict*, 50.

15. D. Georgi, *Die Gegner des Paulus im 2. Korintherbrief* (WMANT 11; Neukirchen-Vluyn: Neukirchener Verlag, 1964; Eng. trans.: Philadelphia: Fortress Press, 1985).

16. C. R. Holladay, *Theios Anēr in Hellenistic Judaism: A Critique of the Use of this Category in New Testament Christology* (SBLDS 40; Missoula, Mont.: Scholars Press, 1977).

17. Weeden, *Mark—Traditions in Conflict*, 160.

18. Ibid., 117, 121–22, 148.

19. K. Stock, *Boten aus dem Mit-Ihm-Sein. Das Verhältnis zwischen Jesus und den Zwölf nach Markus* (AnBib 70; Rome: Biblical Institute Press, 1975).

20. E. Best, "The Role of the Disciples in Mark," *NTS* 23 (1976–77) 377–401; idem, *Following Jesus. Discipleship in the Gospel of Mark* (JSNTSup 4; Sheffield: JSOT Press, 1981).

21. G. Schmahl, *Die Zwölf im Markusevangelium. Eine redaktionsgeschichtliche Untersuchung* (TTS 30; Trier: Paulinus Verlag, 1974).

22. Stock, *Boten aus dem Mit-Ihm-Sein*, 194.

23. Ibid., 195.

24. Best, "Role of the Disciples," 394.

25. Best, *Following Jesus*, 24–25.

26. Best, "Role of the Disciples," 399.

27. Ibid., 388.

28. Ibid.

29. W. Wrede, *The Messianic Secret* (trans. J. C. G. Greig; Cambridge, Eng.: James Clarke & Co., 1971) 92–114, 231–36.

30. Ibid., 106.

31. J. B. Tyson, "The Blindness of the Disciples in Mark," *JBL* 80 (1961) 261–62.

32. The disciples fail to come to terms both with death (8:31–33; 9:31–32; 10:32–35) and resurrection (9:10). Consequently, they are absent during Jesus' suffering and forfeit his resurrection.

33. Kelber, *Mark's Story of Jesus*, 81–83.

34. The term "Easter shift" was coined by J. M. Robinson, "On the *Gattung* of Mark (and John)," in *Jesus and Man's Hope* (2 vols.; ed. D. G. Buttrick and J. M. Bald; Pittsburgh: Pittsburgh Theological Seminary, 1970) 1:99–129, esp. 116; reprinted in idem, *The Problem of History in Mark and Other Marcan Studies* (Philadelphia: Fortress Press, 1982) 11–39, esp. 29.

35. P. Perkins, *The Gnostic Dialogue. The Early Church and the Crisis of Gnosticism* (New York: Paulist Press, 1980).

36. On the neglect of narrative, see the masterful work by H. W. Frei, *The Eclipse of Biblical Narrative. A Study in Eighteenth and Nineteenth Century Hermeneutics* (New Haven and London: Yale Univ. Press, 1974).

37. Best, *Following Jesus*, 20, 33–34, 164.

38. G. L. Bruns, *Inventions: Writing, Textuality, and Understanding in Literary History* (New Haven, Conn.: Yale Univ. Press, 1982) 17–59.

39. Ibid., 26.

40. N. R. Petersen, *Literary Criticism for New Testament Critics* (GBS; Philadelphia: Fortress Press, 1978); idem, "When Is the End not the End? Literary Reflections on the Ending of Mark's Narrative," *Int* 34 (1980) 151–66.

41. R. C. Tannehill, "The Disciples in Mark: The Functions of a Narrative Role," *JR* 57 (1977) 386–405; idem, "The Gospel of Mark as Narrative Christology," *Semeia* 16 (1979) 57–95.

42. T. E. Boomershine, "Mark, the Storyteller: A Rhetorical-Critical Investigation of Mark's Passion and Resurrection Narrative" (Ph.D. diss., Union Theological Seminary, 1974); idem, "Mark 16:8 and the Apostolic Commission," *JBL* 100 (1981) 225–39.

43. J. R. Donahue, "Jesus as the Parable of God in the Gospel of Mark," *Int* 32 (1978) 369–86, reprinted in *Interpreting the Gospels* (ed. J. L. Mays; Philadelphia: Fortress Press, 1981) 148–67.

44. Kelber, *Kingdom in Mark*; idem, *Mark's Story of Jesus*; idem, *The Oral and the Written Gospel*, 90–139.

45. David Rhoads and Donald Michie, *Mark as Story. An Introduction to the Narrative of a Gospel* (Philadelphia: Fortress Press, 1982).

46. Petersen, *Literary Criticism for New Testament Critics*, 56.

47. Ibid., 79.

48. William A. Beardslee, *Literary Criticism of the New Testament* (GBS; Philadelphia: Fortress Press, 1970) 28. I find it difficult to appreciate Mark as an "irenic" theologian intent on reconciling conflicting traditions in early Christianity; thus, W. R. Farmer, *Jesus and the Gospel: Tradition. Scripture. and Canon* (Philadelphia: Fortress Press, 1982) 172–76.

49. Petersen, *Literary Criticism for New Testament Critics*, 77.

50. Petersen, "When Is the End not the End?," 162.

51. Tannehill, "Disciples in Mark," 399.

52. Ibid., 402.

53. The function of Mark 13 is thus not different from many previous teachings of Jesus, which on the story level run up against the disciples' lack of comprehension, but on the discourse level serve to supply Mark's generation with vital information.

54. Boomershine, "Mark 16:8 and the Apostolic Commission," 233.

55. Ibid., 225.

56. Ibid., 238.

57. J. D. Crossan, "Parable and Example in the Teaching of Jesus," *NTS* 18 (1971–72) 285–307; idem, *In Parables: The Challenge of the Historical Jesus* (New York: Harper & Row, 1973); idem, *The Dark Interval. Towards a Theology of Story* (Niles Ill.: Argus Communications, 1975); idem, "A Form for Absence: The Markan Creation of Gospel," *Semeia* 12 (1978) 41–55; idem, *Finding Is the First Act: Trove Folktales and Jesus' Treasure Parable* (Semeia Studies 9; Philadelphia: Fortress Press, 1979); idem, *Raid on the Articulate: Comic Eschatology in Jesus and Borges* (New York: Harper & Row, 1976); idem, *Cliffs of Fall: Paradox and Polyvalence in the Parables of Jesus* (New York: Seabury Press, 1980).

58. R. W. Funk, *Language, Hermeneutic, and the Word of God: The Problem of Language in the New Testament and Contemporary Theology* (New York: Harper & Row, 1966); idem, *Jesus as Precursor* (Semeia Studies 2; Philadelphia: Fortress Press, 1975); idem, *Parables and Presence. Forms of the New Testament Tradition* (Philadelphia: Fortress Press, 1982).

59. P. Ricoeur, "Biblical Hermeneutics," *Semeia* 4 (1975) 27–148.

60. Donahue, "Jesus as the Parable of God."

61. Tannehill, "Disciples in Mark," 401.

62. Ibid., 392 n. 21.

63. F. Kermode, *The Genesis of Secrecy: On the Interpretation of Narrative* (Cambridge: Harvard Univ. Press, 1979) 46.

64. Ibid., 64.

65. J. Moltmann, *The Crucified God. The Cross of Christ as the Foundation and Criticism of Christian Theology* (trans. R. A. Wilson and John Bowden; New York: Harper & Row, 1974) 54.

66. Kelber, *The Oral and the Written Gospel*, 199–211.

67. Robinson, "On the *Gattung* of Mark (and John)," 114 (reprint: 27).

68. Weeden, *Mark—Traditions in Conflict*, 162.

69. W. Marxsen, "Redaktionsgeschichtliche Erklärung der sogenannten Parabeltheorie des Markus," *ZTK* 52 (1955) 255–71. J. C. Meagher, *Clumsy Construction in Mark's Gospel: A Critique of Form and Redaktionsgeschichte* (TorSTh 3; New York and Toronto: Edwin Mellen Press, 1979) 85–142.

70. J. M. Robinson, "Gnosticism and the New Testament," in idem, *Problem of History in Mark*, 47.

71. For connections between gnosticism and orality, see Perkins, *Gnostic Dialogue*, 7–9, 32–35, 196–204.

# 2

# Uncertain Faith: Matthew's Portrait
# of the Disciples

## RICHARD A. EDWARDS

### METHOD OF APPROACH

Discipleship in Matthew has been studied in different ways.[1] Almost all scholars assume that the author or redactor has a unified view of the disciples which is expressed consistently and evenly throughout the book. This assumption means that the Gospel of Matthew is viewed as an essay in story form—that is, as a static construction in which each statement and incident are given equal weight. Thus, it is argued, for example, that a careful comparison of all references to the disciples (descriptions, synonyms, etc.) would produce an accurate reconstruction of the author's understanding of the disciples. A redaction-critical approach, seeking to uncover the theology of the editor, would require, in addition, an analysis of the changes and/or additions made by the editor; the cumulative weight of these modifications becomes the direct evidence for the distinctive and consistent position that the author wanted to express. The result is Matthew's theology of discipleship.

Recently, however, we have been alerted to the fact that this assumption does not take seriously the fact that a gospel is a narrative.[2] Matthew, as a theologian, is primarily a storyteller; or to use the new terminology, the author has written a narrative that relates a story in a very definite and unique way. The story is told by a narrator who may or may not be identical with the author. In deciding to tell a story, rather than compose a speech or an essay, the author has chosen to influence his readers in a distinctive way. The most significant aspect of any narrative is its movement; it is "art in sequence," which means that we must take seriously its development and flow.[3] And since Matthew does not use the word "discipleship," we can only uncover his understanding of it from the narrative itself. It is because the Gospel is a story that I want to place primary emphasis on the portrayal of the disciples as characters in the narrative.

47

To adopt this approach means that certain traditional methods are rejected. For example, we could collect and correlate all that Jesus says about the disciples, or about *his* disciples, or about following, or what he says *directly* to his disciples. Or in a similar way, we could combine the characteristics of the disciples—both positive and negative. However, since the impact of the narrative on a reader is a cumulative one which takes place over a period of time and in a definite sequence, I am suggesting that the best way to pinpoint Matthew's understanding of discipleship is to concentrate on the distribution of the narrative material rather than its total effect.

This study, then, is an experiment in reader-response criticism.[4] As the term implies, this approach assumes that a literary work is not complete in itself—rather, a text becomes literature through the interaction of the text and the reader. That is especially significant with a narrative which by nature proceeds in linear fashion. As the reader progresses through the narrative, he responds both to the information presented and the information withheld—the so-called gaps. The reader is encouraged to develop hypotheses about what is lacking on the basis of what is given. Since the same story could be told in many different ways, the specific sequence and the data supplied by an author are designated the narrative. Thus, for example, the four Gospels each represent a different narrative of the same basic story of Jesus.

The importance of the reader-response method is its focus on the author's manipulation or guidance of the reader and, as a result, those moments when the reader is encouraged to fill in the gaps—that is, to integrate the information he or she is supplied. The concern is for both the text and the reader. Since the reader is envisioned as responding to a specific text, the overall effects of reading Matthew's narrative of Jesus will be quite distinct from the effect of reading Luke's narrative.

## GOSPEL AS NARRATIVE

Before taking up the specific question of discipleship, I want to point out briefly some of the basic features of a narrative and then of Matthew's narrative.

A primary influence on the reader is the narrator of the story, the individual who "tells" this particular narrative. The narrator might be the same person as the author, or one aspect of the author's personality, or perhaps a character within the story. It is important that we identify this narrator because he or she controls the basic information—just as the director of a movie determines from what angle the audience views an incident and, of course, what will not be shown.

As with most biblical narrative, the Gospel of Matthew is incident-based:

that is, the story is told with an apparent objectivity.[5] The narrator does not interject his or her own opinions very often, and we are seldom told what a character is thinking, although the narrator is close enough to see and overhear what is going on. He or she follows Jesus almost entirely. This perspective gives the reader the impression that the report is more lifelike, since in our own experience we do not have access to the thoughts or motives of those we meet or observe; we must make judgments on the basis of what we observe, on our own. Therefore, the reader has the impression of being a witness to events which are not clouded or modified by someone else's perspective. The reader's sympathy or antipathy is gained by the general perspective or point of view first established by the narrator at the beginning of the narration. This makes it imperative that we note carefully how the basic framework of the narrative is established at the outset: it will have a distinct and crucial importance as we move through the narrative toward the conclusion.

The narrator of Matthew is unobtrusive; the reader is encouraged to accept things as they are. But further, the exposition, or fundamental background of the narrative, which establishes the basic features of the narrative world, carries the added implication that the narrator is speaking from the point of view of "the Father," or at least that the narrator reflects the Father's point of view. Put spatially, we might think of the narrator as above the action, looking down. This impression is created by a number of features in the first few chapters.

First, the genealogy (Matt. 1:1–17) with its repetition not only establishes the pedigree of Jesus, it also instructs the reader about God's plan. The summary (v. 17) explains that the span of time from Abraham to Jesus is to be divided into three periods of fourteen generations each. Without being told outright, the reader is encouraged to view the story of Jesus from the perspective of the one who controls both people and events.

Second, the story of Jesus' birth (1:18–25) is really the story of Joseph's recognition of God's involvement. The reader is told at the start that Mary's child is "of the Holy Spirit," so that when Joseph accepts this explanation he is presented in a very favorable light.

Third, the number of fulfillment quotations (1:2; 2:5, 15, 17, 23) in these early chapters reinforces the reader's impression of the righteousness of Jesus and also of the reliability of the narrator. The angel of the Lord speaks to Joseph, and he listens. The fulfillment of the word of the Lord spoken by the prophet is just as impressive. It is clearly the Lord who is in control, and the reader, through the narrator, shares that perspective. The extensive use of fulfillment quotations in these first few chapters, then, helps to establish a framework for the rest of the story.

Perhaps enough has been said to give some indication of the importance of the opening chapters as exposition. The narrator presents a basic context to encourage the reader to assess and interpret the rest of the story. The narration in many ancient as well as contemporary narratives often begins in the middle of the story and then, using various devices to present the exposition, such as flashback, requires the reader to fill in the gaps.[6] It is crucial, then, to note that Matthew does *not* begin in the middle of the story. He orients the reader right from the start. There must be no misunderstanding of who Jesus is and what he represents. By the time the main action begins, the reader already knows his origins and credentials. The rest of the narrative is not intended to reveal anything more about his status but is designed in part to present the response of other characters.

Therefore, because I want to concentrate on the reader's response to the narrative, which is primarily the filling of gaps, the function of the exposition is crucial. Matthew's narrative, since it begins with an extended exposition which establishes a clear picture of Jesus' origins and of God's role in producing and controlling them, gives the reader an extensive base from which to interpret the specifics of the story. As the narrator reports the words and deeds of Jesus, the reader can determine their value and function. The narrator has created a common basis for evaluating the action not only of Jesus himself but of those who respond to him.

In direct contrast to Jesus, the absence of any exposition about the disciples and followers makes it difficult for the reader to interpret their action. Using the terminology of M. Sternberg,[7] the extensive exposition about Jesus creates no curiosity about his actions but does, of course, cause the reader to look ahead with suspense about how he will be received. Conversely, the absence of exposition for the disciples and opponents does elicit curiosity in the mind of the reader because he or she has no comparable basis from which to interpret them without positing a set of hypotheses— that is, filling in the gaps. There is both curiosity and suspense about the disciples. Any knowledge of the disciples, which is not in the exposition, must be supplied temporarily by the reader. The remainder of the story will confirm or deny the reader's supposition. The narrative of Jesus begins at the beginning with the exposition, while the disciples are presented abruptly, even though it is the beginning of their association with Jesus. This difference has a powerful effect on the reader because part of the exposition about Jesus shows how many of these events were determined by God himself. As a result, even if Jesus' fate, or certain of his actions, seem startling, they are not likely to be judged impossible or out of character. The disciples, not Jesus, are the mystery. Thus, at one level, after Jesus' baptism and temptation, the reader is not surprised when the disciples leave everything to follow Jesus, but he or she is not prepared to interpret their further action.

This is not to deny God and/or Jesus can act in mysterious ways; Jesus' death is something that we would not expect. But his death is not unacceptable because we have come to recognize the authority of Jesus and his narrator.

There is one further preliminary matter that should be mentioned—some of the details about the disciples that are distinctive to Matthew.

It has often been noted that Matthew's portrayal of the disciples is more sympathetic than Mark's. G. Barth[8] has collected the comparative data, and I will simply mention some of it here. The most striking thing is the understanding that they either claim or is reported about them. In addition, they are obedient at the end of the story when all eleven gather in Galilee after the resurrection. Many of Mark's critical comments about the disciples have either been removed or toned down. Thus, it is possible that the disciples could function as a positive example of the faithful followers of Jesus. But Matthew is not always positive: (1) he does describe them negatively; (2) he indicates that they do not at times understand what Jesus is saying; (3) he reports Jesus' criticism and rebuke; and (4) he is fond of describing them as "those of little faith." This apparent inconsistency has been variously ascribed to the sources, to a lack of editing skill, or even to a polemical attitude that is essentially inconsistent.

## THE READER'S INVOLVEMENT

How does one deal with this kind of evidence? The approach I am suggesting requires that we consider the entire story that Matthew has composed rather than isolated segments. This makes the task a bit unwieldy. The question should be: How does the narrative develop or flow? Where are the gaps or indeterminacies, and how are they filled?

The reader's involvement in the text is determined by the gaps, and therefore, they must be described. The gaps are not merely the openings in the plot where the narrator skips forward or backward in time. They are, in addition, those places in the narration where the reader must supply some information to make the incident comprehensible in the context of the story. For example, when a contemporary author begins a new chapter with an interior viewpoint—where we are privy to the character's thoughts— it is often not clear at first who is narrating or perhaps what the immediate situation is. The reader, as a result, will form a hypothesis about the character or the situation, built from the clues contained in the narration itself, which will be either substantiated or rejected as the narration continues.

The process of hypothesis formation, re-evaluation, and confirmation about the disciples in Matthew is more intense than it is for Jesus because there is less basic information to begin with. That is, there are more gaps relating to the disciples and the filling in of gaps stimulates reader activity to account for the new or missing information.

My thesis is that because of the absence of exposition about the disciples, the reader is encouraged to respond to them favorably when first introduced. This "primacy effect"[9] brings with it the related problem of the rationale for their action. Since the reader already knows a great deal about Jesus and is not at all well informed about the disciples, there is a tendency to suppose that the disciples know what the reader knows about Jesus. Once the gap has been closed by the hypothesis of the reader, he or she will expect confirmation or at least a continuation of consistent action on the part of the disciples. But that is not what happens. The reader is confronted with contradictory or puzzling details that will keep him or her on edge. Any evaluation of the disciples can never be secure; the narrator continues to keep the reader off-balance. This "both/and" technique of the narrator, especially in contrast to the information relayed about Jesus, will condition the reader to expect neither security nor certainty in the disciples. When, at the end of the Gospel, the disciples are told to "disciplize" the nations, this ambivalence will be part of the reader's expectation. The disciples never live up to Jesus' standards. Given the effect on the reader, discipleship will be viewed as a situation that is never completed, is likely to be in constant flux, and cannot be idealized. Nevertheless, it requires dedication and denial and especially a need to recognize the deeper significance of Jesus' teaching.

To verify this judgment, I want to sketch the flow of Matthew as it relates to the disciples.


## INCONSISTENT FOLLOWERS

As already noted, the opening exposition, which supplies detailed information about Jesus' background, emphasizes the consistent activity of the Father in orchestrating and directing the story. With no warning, the reader must bridge the temporal gap at Matt. 3:1 between Jesus' infancy and his confrontation with John the Baptist. The continuity is quickly established when John submits to Jesus' request and also when the Father confirms, at Jesus' baptism, that Jesus is indeed his Son. It is important to note that it is at the baptism when the reader first hears Jesus speak; he affirms that God is in control when he responds to John's reluctance to baptize him: "Let it be so now; for thus it is fitting for us to fulfil all righteousness" (3:15). Later, when tempted by the tempter himself, the Son of God demonstrates his purity and singleness of purpose. Then, after John's arrest, Jesus "dwells" in Capernaum, and the narrator informs us that Jesus' primary message is the same as the basic message of John the Baptist: "Repent, for the kingdom of heaven is at hand" (3:2 and 4:17). Immediately following, in the next independent section, Jesus calls the four fishermen to follow him. So the importance of the followers is quickly established, and their connection to the kingdom of heaven is implied. In addition, they are reported to follow him immediately by dropping everything. They are not yet called disciples.

This first report about the followers is especially important for the reader. The initial appearance of a character has a lasting impact on the reader because it establishes a base or context of information (Sternberg calls this the primacy effect) that can then be manipulated by the narrator as the story continues. Jesus' character is already rather firmly fixed, and although the specifics of his program have yet to be detailed, the question that confronts the reader is how people will react to him as he proceeds.

When the followers are first introduced, however, we are given a glimpse of four men whose positive reaction to Jesus is not explained. What they might know about Jesus and why they would take such extreme action are not explained. This gap creates one of the fundamental tensions of the narrative. The reader must cope with a substantial problem: it must be interpreted or filled in. This initial puzzlement about the followers and the basis for their immediate and unusual response creates part of the interest and curiosity for the reader. By the end of the narrative we hope to have an answer.

The importance of the disciples for Matthew is underlined when in the next narrated action Jesus sits down on the mountain to teach "his disciples"—the first time this phrase appears (5:1). The reader does not yet know definitely who they are; they could be the four fishermen, but the great crowds might also be included because they are said to follow him (4:25). This ambiguity is perhaps not accidental.

Jesus' first speech (Matthew 5—7: the Sermon on the Mount) is a repeated reminder of the importance of the kingdom of heaven. This phrase appears five times in the first eighteen verses (vv. 3–20) and seven times in the full discourse. The Sermon on the Mount is an inaugural address to the reader who already knows Jesus' true identity. But a discordant note about the disciples is sounded early when Jesus speaks of persecution (vv. 11–12). That Jesus' demands are hard is not necessarily unexpected. But the disciples are also warned in Matthew 6 about anxiety and its consequences, and they are then addressed: "O men of little faith" (6:30). The Sermon on the Mount not only establishes the basic rules for the seekers of the kingdom of heaven, it specifically anticipates some of the difficulties the followers will encounter. So the combination of persecution and "little faith" creates another gap.

The first major crisis that the disciples must confront is the threat of drowning during the storm (8:18–27). The narrator has made it obvious

53

how we are to read it by imbedding in the introduction two statements about "following" and the phrase "another disciple said." Although the disciples have been warned about anxiety (6:25–33), they are nevertheless worried even though they imply some confidence in Jesus by addressing him as "Lord" and by assuming that he can save them. For the second time we hear Jesus call them "men of little faith" (8:26). Indeed, having been warned about troubles, they still do not act with confidence, and our initial good impression is decidedly modified; we begin to see the reason for the epithet "men of little faith." We still do not know what motivates them to continue following Jesus, but this incident forces the reader to adjust his or her opinion; that is, the primacy effect will probably be lessened. Because there has been no expository material for the disciples, the reader must use incidents reported by the narrator to adjust and re-evaluate his or her image of them. The initial positive impression needs correcting.

Despite their failings, however, Jesus continues to demonstrate confidence in the disciples, and they are reported to continue to follow him. It is in Matthew 10 that the narrator first mentions that twelve disciples are singled out as a special group. The narration between the storm (8:27) and the selection of the Twelve (10:1–4) presents to the reader more extraordinary actions of Jesus, and he or she will imagine that part of the attraction is the wonderworking of Jesus. But a secondary theme is introduced at the end of Matthew 9, just prior to the mission call, when the Pharisees, who were first presented in very negative terms when John the Baptist characterized them as the "brood of vipers," are now reported to claim that Jesus' power comes from the prince of demons (9:34). Immediately after quoting the Pharisees, the narrator repeats a summary statement (9:35) that is almost identical to an earlier summary (4:23) reminding the reader of the basic message of Jesus. This summary is in turn followed by a rare statement about Jesus' feeling—that is, he has compassion for the people. Finally, he is quoted as recommending that his followers pray to the lord of the harvest for laborers. All this serves as an introduction to the "call" of the Twelve. It is not, of course, a call to follow him but a call to accept the authority that Jesus can bestow. This is the only time in Matthew when the disciples are called "apostles" probably because it is simply a functional term: that is, they are being sent out (10:2). The Twelve are then named. The four fishermen previously mentioned are included, along with Matthew, who has also been mentioned earlier (9:9). The last person named is Judas, who is designated "the one who turned him in." This description, of course, creates another problem or gap for the reader, forcing him or her to anticipate Jesus' fate, as well as to wonder about his choice of followers. But we know that the Twelve followers are recipients of the authority to act in Jesus' name: they are to preach, heal, raise, cleanse, and exorcize. The practical mission advice is short and curt. It is followed by an extended warning about the negative reaction they should anticipate. In fact, the bulk of Matthew 10 is a prediction of the persecution they should expect, the conflict they will produce, and even the possibility that they will die for the cause.

We are not told what happens on the mission. The narrator indicates, however, that the reputation of Jesus—and perhaps that of his followers/apostles—is spreading when John the Baptist hears about the "deeds of the Christ" while in prison (11:2). It is the end of Matthew 11 that is important for our concerns: after some indication of a negative reaction to Jesus, the narrator reports a rather peculiar saying of Jesus—the so-called "Johannine" thunderbolt (11:25–30). The reader is permitted first to over-hear Jesus thank the Father for revealing "these things" to babes, not to the wise. Jesus continues: the Son carries out the Father's will and com-municates his identity to whomever he chooses. Those chosen ones are, most likely, the disciples, who are then invited to come to him and accept the easy burden. The burden, however, has been repeatedly described as difficult or at least dangerous. This inconsistency or gap also demands some interpretation from the reader. Here is a word of Jesus that appears to contradict previous statements about the welfare and fate of his disciples. It is at the same time a very specific and heavy-handed reminder of the ultimate source of authority for the entire story: the Father is in control. The reader is encouraged to evaluate the disciples favorably but only be-cause of the Father's assistance.

The disciples remain in the foreground for the reader when the Pharisees attack them in Matt. 12:1. Their antagonism towards Jesus and his fol-lowers is emphasized by the narrator: "But the Pharisees went out and took counsel against him, how to destroy him" (12:14). Then they again accuse him of casting out demons by Beelzebub (12:24). As the antago-nism against Jesus builds, the positive value of the disciples is reasserted when Jesus calls the disciples "his mother and brothers" while his own natural family is at the door (12:46–50). The contrast with the opponents is striking.

At this point in the narrative, the opposition is clearly defined, while the disciples are presented in both favorable and negative terms. The favorable emphasis resumes when Jesus begins to teach parables in chap. 13. The disciples ask why. Jesus says that it is simply a matter of the disciples having something the others do not have: "To you it has been given to know the secrets of the kingdom of heaven, but to them it has not been given" (13:11). Indeed, Jesus compliments them with a beatitude—their eyes and ears are blessed because they see and hear (13:16). Jesus then explains the parable of the sower and relates a few more parables. Later, when Jesus and the disciples are alone, they ask him this time for an explanation of the parable of the weeds. After the explanation he adds some more parables and ends by asking them if they understand. They reply, "Yes."

For the reader this is a significant development. The twelve disciples are not praised for their outstanding preaching and healing but rather—after their situation is juxtaposed with that of the Pharisees—for their claim that they understand the parables. Although one might expect some minimal comprehension on the part of any followers (otherwise they would not follow at all), it is the word "understanding" that is now explicitly stated, repeated, and underlined. And because they understand, Jesus says: "Therefore every scribe who has been trained [disciplized] for the kingdom of heaven is like a householder who brings out of his treasure what is new and what is old" (13:52). The reader is encouraged to assume that the secrets of the kingdom, already given to them (13:11), have truly been received.

What will the reader make of this? The disciples have been highlighted, both in the narrative and in Jesus' words, as truly distinctive followers— they understand the parables of the kingdom. After the initial good impression, followed by the apparent inadequacy in crisis, they are presented favorably again—they comprehend parables. They should see the real significance of Jesus—that is, to interpret his teaching and his actions. What does it mean to understand? Both interpretations of the parables are allegorical. If the disciples do indeed understand, they would see the significance of his words. With the Father's help, they would comprehend both the immediate significance and the deeper meaning. They claim to see; can they also act consistently?

The first test of this new understanding is once again at the lake (14:22–33). This time they are on their own crossing the sea, when Jesus appears, walking on the water. After the initial fright, Peter walks on the water until he becomes afraid and begins to sink. Jesus calls him a man of little faith who is "of two minds" (διστάζω). After Peter and Jesus are both back in the boat, all the disciples "worship" him (v. 33) and say that he is the Son of God. They have definitely come a long way from the previous crisis; they now are portrayed as acknowledging the facts that the reader has been assured of from the beginning. But the note of difficulty is still there, and the reader is forced to account for it and to look forward to some further clarification.

The disciples remain in the spotlight when the Pharisees again accuse them of transgressing the law (15:1). Jesus does not defend them, but he does attack the Pharisees for being guilty of the same kind of offense. He tells the people: "Hear and understand" that what enters does not defile, but what comes out of a person does defile (15:10–11). In other words, we have another parabolic saying. Surely, the disciples could understand it. But Peter wants it explained; Jesus replies, "Are you also still without understanding?" (v. 16). Thus, the reader's positive evaluation of the ability of the disciples is once again disturbed. Jesus must again explain what the parable means, and once again, allegorical methods are used.

At this point the issue of understanding is directly before the reader. The present inability of the disciples to understand is then clearly contrasted in the next incident, when the Canaanite woman, who does understand Jesus' saying about the children's bread and the dogs, elicits Jesus' praise— in this case for her faith! (15:21–28).

The narrator continues to keep the question of understanding in front of the reader. After Jesus heals and feeds the crowd, the Pharisees and Sadducees come to him asking once again for a sign (16:1). They are told they will be given the sign of Jonah even though they probably won't understand it; just as these Pharisees do not know how to interpret the signs of the times, the disciples do not understand the saying about the leaven of the Pharisees and Sadducees (16:5–12). Thus, as a summary, Jesus refers back to the significance of the feeding as well as to the accusations of the Pharisees and Sadducees: "Do you not yet perceive?" (16:9). The *narrator* then informs us that the disciples finally did understand that the leaven was the teaching of the Pharisees and Sadducees.

What has happened? The reader is encouraged not only to contrast the Pharisees and Sadducees with the disciples but also to look for the deeper implications of what Jesus says and does. It is clear that it is important to Jesus that the disciples understand or perceive the deeper meaning of these sayings and actions. This section of the Gospel (15:1 — 16:12) prepares for the Caesarea Philippi event (16:13–20) that follows; it establishes the importance of the interpretation of Jesus' words and deeds.

With this buildup, the narrator now reports that Jesus asks the disciples a direct question about the Son of man (16:13). When Peter answers correctly, Jesus states that he can do this because of the Father's inspiration (16:17). Peter, the spokesman, called "rock" at this moment, is soon afterwards called Satan. It is obvious that Jesus' identity is only partially understood, and even this comprehension is aided by revelation. The disciples' problem continues to be in understanding what Jesus says because Peter is rebuked when he misinterprets Jesus plain saying about death and resurrection (16:23). The transfiguration (17:1–18) confirms what Peter said (by inspiration, see v. 17), and the truth of Jesus' status is confirmed before the three disciples by God's own words, with the significant addition: "Listen to him" (17:5).

The very next incident in the narrative continues to develop this theme. After a discussion about the coming of Elijah (17:10–12), the *narrator* tells us that the disciples understand that Jesus is speaking about John the Baptist. The entire sequence finally comes to a conclusion when the disciples, because of their "little faith" (17:20), cannot heal the epileptic boy. Nevertheless, we are told by the narrator that they are greatly distressed (v. 23) when Jesus once again predicts his passion and resurrection, a great improvement over their earlier reaction.

Although the disciples continue to be mentioned often in the remainder of the narrative, there is a definite shift in focus from the disciples to the opponents. The number and frequency of parables increase, but we are often not told how the disciples respond. There are a few more incidents that should be mentioned, however, because the pattern of alternation between a positive and negative view continues, albeit at a slower rate.

In Matthew 19, after Jesus advises the rich man to leave everything and follow him, Peter affirms that the disciples have indeed done just that and asks, "What then shall we have?" (v. 27). Jesus responds with the "twelve thrones" saying (v. 28), which leads to a familiar emphasis: following Jesus requires one to leave house, family, and land (v. 29). This issue was first stated in Matthew 10, and it is now followed by the parable of the vineyard (20:1–16). Since there is no word to the contrary, the reader will assume that the disciples do understand the parable. In the same vein, the two sons of Zebedee also claim to understand what lies ahead when Jesus speaks about the cup from which he must drink (20:20–28).

The final instance of understanding in this phase of the narrative is in Matt. 21:20 when the disciples marvel at Jesus' ability to wither the fig tree. Jesus replies that if one has faith, mountains can be moved. But, of course, the disciples do not have that kind of faith. They show signs of comprehension, but they are "of little faith." They vacillate from good intentions to immature reactions. They have committed themselves to follow Jesus, they have grown to understand much of what Jesus has been saying and doing, but they still have not reached a state of perfection. Despite their faults, however, Matthew has counterbalanced them with the more obstinate opponents who plot to destroy him. The reader will recognize how far they have come, even though they still lack full commitment of faith.

In the passion story, the disciples will be perceived by the reader as again failing to put together their newfound comprehension with Jesus' inevitable movement toward death. The reader's primary interest will be captured by the correspondence between his predictions and the action of the opponents to assure that what God has planned will indeed transpire. The disciples play a role, of course, but their failure seems assured, even though they have good intentions.

When we reach Matthew 28, the disciples are still present. The risen Lord calls them his brethren, and they respond to the final command to meet him in Galilee. Is this a new development—a miraculous change? No. The narrator is consistent to the end, for he says they worshiped him but doubted (διστάζω: "were of two minds," "were unsure"). The Greek here is ambiguous: οἱ δέ can mean "but some" if it is preceded by οἱ μέν which is not the case here (nor in 26:67). I am suggesting that the proper and consistent reading would be "they worshipped him but were not sure" (διστάζω is used both here and in chap. 14 with the word "worship"). There is no special indication here that this description is especially negative; it is the way they have been all along. Jesus' final command assures us that they are his disciples and will follow. But even more significant is his command (28:19) to "make disciples" or "disciplize" (μαθητεύσατε). Now that he has full authority, he commissions these vacillating followers to go and gather others like themselves. There is one major change, however; they are now told to teach, something they have never before been asked to do.

## CONCLUSION

In sum, this rapid, selective survey of the Gospel of Matthew was necessary to demonstrate the possible interaction between text and reader. I have tried to show how the preliminary exposition can affect the reader's response to the specific ordering of the narrative. Since the narrator is able to withhold as well as reveal information, the reader is inevitably influenced by this interaction. Thus, it was imperative that we pay close attention to the ordering of data, that is, to the narrative's flow.

By attempting to follow the reader's response to the narrative, I have suggested that a certain pattern emerges, a pattern which nudges the reader one way and then another. And because one specific issue is the matter of the disciples' understanding of Jesus' teaching, its location at the end of the Gospel helps to pull the entire issue from the background into the foreground of the reader's attention. The ambivalence of the disciples is contrasted to the stability of Jesus and his Father in heaven. Thus, the last two stories bring together (1) the disciples, (2) Jesus' teaching, (3) the affirmation about the Father's activity among men, and (4) the opponents, who are reduced to bribery to save face among their own people. Does the narrator expect the reader to try to understand the career and teaching of Jesus in the way that Jesus tried to educate his disciples? The narrator keeps the disciples in the forefront of the reader's mind from the opening call of the four fishermen (4:18–22) down to their "unsure worshipping" (28:17). Jesus himself tells them that their task is to "disciplize" (28:19).

I have concentrated on the disciples and, as a result, have neglected certain other features of Matthew that are usually mentioned in any study of this

Gospel. For example, the five major speeches (Matt. 5—7; 9:36—10:42; 13:1—53; 17:22—18:35; 23—25) which alternate with narration, usually associated with the name of B. W. Bacon, are indeed a major feature. But as Karen Barta has pointed out to me, the alternation of speech and narration produces an uneven pace for the story and is perhaps related to the oscillation that I have tried to describe. Another possible disciple-related issue is the distinctive emphasis on the importance of the performance of the will of God as opposed to merely advocating it. This application of reader-response criticism suggests, however, that such a factor must be viewed in a wider context.

What I am not yet prepared to do is to suggest how one can move from these literary matters to a judgment about the historical situation of the author, narrator, or reader. Perhaps in time such a leap can be made with some certainty. Even though W. Iser and others talk about the indeterminacy assumed by the method, they nevertheless act as though one interpretation is better than another. In the meantime, this trial probe seems fruitful enough to me to merit further consideration of Matthew's art of storytelling.

## NOTES

1. Among others: G. Barth, "Matthew's Understanding of the Law," in *Tradition and Interpretation in Matthew* (ed. G. Bornkamm, G. Barth, and H. J. Held; Philadelphia: Westminster Press, 1963) 105–24; E. Schweizer, *Matthäus und seine Gemeinde* (SBS 71; Stuttgart: Katholisches Bibelwerk, 1974); U. Luz, "Die Jünger im Matthäusevangelium," *ZNW* 62 (1971) 141–71.

2. N. R. Petersen, *Literary Criticism for New Testament Critics* (GBS; Philadelphia: Fortress Press, 1978); E. McKnight, *Meaning in Texts: The Historical Shaping of a Narrative Hermeneutics* (Philadelphia: Fortress Press, 1978); David Rhoads and Donald Michie, *Mark as Story: An Introduction to the Narrative of a Gospel* (Philadelphia: Fortress Press, 1982); R. Fowler, *Loaves and Fishes: The Function of Feeding Stories in the Gospel of Mark* (SBLDS 54; Chico, Calif.: Scholars Press, 1981); B. Uspensky, *A Poetics of Composition: The Structure of the Artistic Text and Typology of a Compositional Form* (trans. V. Zavarin and S. Wittig; Berkeley and Los Angeles: Univ. of California Press, 1973).

3. S. Chatman, "Towards a Theory of Narrative," *New Literary History* 6 (1975) 295–318; idem, *Story and Discourse: Narrative Structure in Fiction and Film* (Ithaca, N.Y.: Cornell Univ. Press, 1978); idem, "The Structure of Narrative Transmission," in *Style and Structure in Literature, Essays in the New Stylistics* (ed. R. Fowler; Ithaca, N.Y.: Cornell Univ. Press, 1975) 213–57; G. Genette, *Narrative Discourse: An Essay in Method* (Ithaca, N.Y.: Cornell Univ. Press, 1980).

4. S. Suleiman, "Varieties of Audience-Oriented Criticism," in *The Reader in the Text: Essays on Audience and Interpretation* (ed. S. Suleiman and I. Crosman; Princeton, N.J.: Princeton Univ. Press, 1980) 3–45; J. P. Tompkins, "An Introduction

to Reader-Response Criticism," in *Reader-Response Criticism: From Formalism to Post-Structuralism* (ed. J. P. Tompkins; Baltimore: Johns Hopkins Univ. Press, 1980) ix–xxvi; W. Iser, "Indeterminacy and the Reader's Response in Prose Fiction," in *Aspects of Narrative* (ed. J. Hillis Miller; New York: Columbia Univ. Press, 1971) 1–45; idem, "Interaction Between Text and Reader," in Suleiman and Crosman, *Reader in the Text,* 106–19; idem, *The Act of Reading: A Theory of Aesthetic Response* (Baltimore: Johns Hopkins Univ. Press, 1978).

5. Cf. esp. R. Alter, *The Art of Biblical Narrative* (New York: Basic Books, 1981).

6. M. Sternberg, *Expositional Modes and Temporal Ordering in Fiction* (Baltimore: Johns Hopkins Univ. Press, 1978) esp. 56–89.

7. Ibid.

8. Barth, "Matthew's Understanding of the Law," 105–25.

9. Sternberg, *Expositional Modes,* 93–97.

# 3

# Discipleship in Luke-Acts

## CHARLES H. TALBERT

Our intention is to describe the Lukan understanding of discipleship after Easter.[1] This aim does not restrict us to an examination of Acts alone because Luke's Gospel foreshadows the post-Easter situation. A proper reading of Acts rather requires using Luke as a commentary on it, while a correct interpretation of Luke necessitates employing Acts as a commentary on it. With this methodological guideline recognized, we can pursue our aim.

In the Acts, "disciple" (6:1–2, 7; 9:10, 26; 11:26; 15:10; 16:1) is used for believers in Christ. The term is employed as a synonym for Christian (11:26; 26:28), for saint (9:13, 32, 41), and for Nazarene (24:5). The usage in Luke's Gospel foreshadows that in Acts (6:13; 8:9; 9:54; 10:23; 11:1; 14:26; 19:37, 39). Taking Luke-Acts as a whole, one finds discipleship described in various ways. (1) It involves a detachment from all other allegiances and a total allegiance to Jesus (Luke 14:26–27). This allegiance is described as "coming after Jesus" (Luke 14:27; 9:23). It is illustrated by the Lukan modification of the Simon of Cyrene pericope where Simon carries the cross "behind Jesus" (Luke 23:26). But since the death of Jesus put an end to the practice of a physical walking with Jesus, the church rarely used the language of "following" (only Rev. 14:4 outside the Gospels, to my knowledge); rather, other language was chosen. (2) It involves repentance and baptism in the name of Jesus (Acts 2:38)—that is, detachment from old ties and attachment to a new authority.[2] (3) It involves submission to the will and purpose of the living Lord, whose power is irresistible (Acts 9:1–19; 22:6–16), and obedience to the heavenly vision (Acts 26:12–19).

What does this attachment to Jesus, however described, involve? Two dimensions of the Lukan answer must be explored in their interrelationships. On the one hand, discipleship consists of being molded by a tradition, being empowered by an experience, and being a participant in a community. On the other hand, it involves both a way to walk and a mission to fulfill. It is in the interactions of these components that the Lukan view of discipleship becomes clear.

62

## SHAPED BY A TRADITION

The Lukan principle that a tradition shapes the lives of disciples is reflected in several strands of evidence. In the first place, one must remember the basic architectural pattern that controls Luke's two-volume work. It is that remarkable series of correspondences between what Jesus does and says in Luke's Gospel and what the disciples do and say in the Acts. Not only is the content similar but often the sequence is the same.[3] This can only be explained if the evangelist is consciously narrating the story of the followers of Jesus so as to have them embody the substance of what he has already said about the earthly Jesus. What better way to say that Jesus' disciples are shaped by the tradition about him?

In the second place, there is the evidence from the genre of Luke-Acts. Does Luke-Acts belong to any known literary genre of antiquity? Until recently, critical orthodoxy's answer had been a negative. All of the canonical Gospels were regarded as literarily, as well as theologically, sui generis. In recent times, there has been a recognition that an absolutely unique literary form would not have been intelligible to its readers/hearers. Hence, there has been an effort to locate the Gospels, including Luke-Acts, within their proper literary milieu in Mediterranean antiquity. Various options have been proposed, both from the Jewish and from the Greco-Roman environments of early Christianity. The alternative that has seemed most convincing to me for Luke-Acts is the one suggested years ago by H. von Soden.[4] Luke-Acts is similar to the biographies of certain founders of philosophical schools, that contained within themselves not only the life of the founder but also a list or brief narrative of his successors and selected other disciples.[5]

Charting the trajectory of this type of biographical writing is helpful in our grasping the place of Luke-Acts within this subgenre of biography. (1) The earliest evidence, to my knowledge, that we have for this A-plus-B form is in a pre-Christian biography of Aristotle.[6] Here the life of Aristotle is followed by a succession list. Among the Herculaneum papyri, moreover, there may be evidence for lives of other philosophers written in the same way.[7] (2) In Diogenes Laertius certain lives of philosophers reflect this pattern.[8] In some of them, not only is there the life of the founder (A), followed by a brief narrative of his successors and selected other disciples (B), but also an extensive statement of the teaching of the philosopher (C). Examination of Diogenes Laertius's references to the sources for his lives shows that the material in the C component comes from a different origin than that in A plus B. This allows one to conclude that in his *Lives of the Philosophers* Diogenes Laertius took over individual biographies of some founders that were written in terms of an A-plus-B pattern and added the

C component himself.[9] Either he or his sources sometimes filled out the B component with anecdotes and sayings of the founder's successors, so that B is not a list but a brief narrative. (3) In *The Life of Pachomius* we find a Christian appropriation of this subgenre of ancient biography.[10] It is fitting because this biography deals with both the father of cenobitic monasticism and his successors in the community. The early part of the biography deals with the career of Pachomius. In section 117, in language that may be regarded as the technical terminology of succession characteristic of the philosophical schools, he appoints Orsisius to succeed him. In the sections that follow we are told what Orsisius did and said (118–29), zealously emulating the life of Pachomius (119). Then Orsisius appoints Theodore (130). Subsequently, we are told what Theodore did and said. This biography confirms not only that such biographical types existed well into our era but also that, when appropriate, there was no obstacle to Christian appropriation of this subgenre of biography. (4) In Hilary of Arles's *Sermon on The Life of St. Honoratus,* we meet an encomium praising Honoratus, the founder of the monastery, that fits into the A-plus-B subgenre.[11] In chap. 8, Hilary says he is Honoratus's successor and that his task is to do what the founder had done. This piece shows what a biographical task would look like when performed according to the rules of epideictic or encomiastic oratory.[12]

When one has charted the development of the A-plus-B biographical pattern from pre-Christian times to its later Christian appropriation, certain things are obvious. First of all, the subgenre has a long life. Second, it is appropriate only where the hero is a founder of a community (e.g., philosophical school or monastery) whose death demands successors. Third, the material about the successors can be given briefly in a list or more extensively in a narrative. The narrative tends to expand in length over the lifetime of the subgenre. It is longer in Christian circles than in non-Christian ones. Fourth, in the second component (B), when a narrative is given, the emphasis is on the successor(s) emulating the founder.

It now remains to ask where Luke-Acts might fit into this trajectory. Luke-Acts tells the story of the life of Jesus in such a way that he is depicted as the founder of the Christian community who provides for its continuation after his departure. The narrative about the community led by his appointed ones portrays the Twelve and Paul in such a way that they reproduce in their careers the prototypical events of the career of the earthly Jesus. The B component is long, longer than that in the *Life of Pachomius.* It is expanded with novelistic elements throughout (e.g., the sea journey). Nevertheless, Acts remains within the general bounds of an A-plus-B biography within antiquity, both in terms of its pattern and in terms of its function. It deviates no more from the cultural pattern than do Paul's letters from the Greek letter or the *Apocalypse of John* from the genre of Jewish apocalyptic.

What is the significance of such a conclusion about the genre of Luke-Acts for the view of discipleship in the Lukan writings? In such biographies, the thrust is that the founder's life/values must be reproduced in those of his followers. Genre agrees with architecture, therefore, that disciples are shaped by the tradition about Jesus. A third line of evidence converges with these first two, that of Luke's portrayal of Jesus as ἀρχηγός and model.

In Luke 6:40, there is an explicit statement about Jesus as model: "A disciple is not above his teacher, but every one when he is fully taught will be like his teacher." It is in line with this expression that the evangelist repeatedly tells of Jesus' career in such a way that its events are seen as models for the disciples (e.g., Luke 4:1–13: the temptation; Luke 22:39–46: the prayer on the Mount of Olives). It is in this context that one should understand the reference to Jesus as ἀρχηγός in Acts (3:15; 5:31).[13] Jesus is not only the originator of a way of life but also an example for followers to emulate.[14] This example is set forth in Luke's Gospel and is shown to have been embodied in the careers of his successors in the apostolic age, those who are themselves models of how the Christian way is to be walked by later generations (e.g., Acts 20:17–35). In Luke-Acts disciples are shaped by a tradition. This formation, moreover, applies both to the way they are to walk and to the mission they are called upon to fulfill.

The Christian *way to walk* is set forth in the Gospel's depiction of the stages of the earthly Jesus' development.[15] Luke portrays the career of Jesus in developmental terms. First, this is shown clearly by Luke 2:52. Luke 2:41–51, the story of the twelve-year-old Jesus in the temple, is enclosed in a frame, vv. 40 and 52, focusing on the youth's growth and development. Verse 52—"And Jesus increased in wisdom and in stature, and in favor with God and man"—uses the term προκόπτειν ("to increase"). The Greek world used this term to depict an individual's process of moral and spiritual development between beginning and perfection.[16] Philo uses the term in the same way except that he regards the source of one's progress not as nature but as God. For example, he speaks of three stages of development: (1) ὁ ἀρχόμενος, the man who is just beginning; (2) ὁ προκόπτων, the person who is making gradual progress; and (3) ὁ τέλειος, the perfect or mature one (*Leg. all.* 3.159). In the New Testament's nine uses of προκοπή and προκόπτειν, two are very close to the widespread use in popular philosophy in speaking of the personal moral and spiritual progress of individuals (1 Tim. 4:15—Timothy; Luke 2:52—Jesus). In Luke 2:52 the emphasis is on the spiritual progress of the youth, Jesus. Later Christian writers used the term in the same way. For example, in the *Life of Pachomius* 2, we read: "He made progress [προκόψας] and achieved perfection [ἐγένετο τέλειος] as a monk." In section 9 we hear that he became apprehensive over his own progress (προκοπῆς), that is, his victory over evil desire. In

65

section 28 we are told that Pachomius took joy in those who made progress (τῶν προκοπτόντων) in virtue and increased (αὐξανομένων) in faith (cf. Luke 2:40).

Second, in 13:31–35 Luke offers further evidence for the developmental pattern of Jesus' career in his Gospel. There Jesus says: "Behold, I cast out demons and perform cures today and tomorrow, and on the third day I am being perfected" (au. trans.; "and the third day I finish my course," RSV), τελειοῦμαι—first person singular, present indicative passive. This completion refers to his death, as the context makes clear. This is very much the same thing that is said in Heb. 2:10 and 5:8–9 where Jesus' being made perfect (τελειῶσαι and τελειωθείς) refers to his having learned obedience through suffering. In Philo's terms, Jesus will then have reached the third stage of development (ὁ τέλειος, the perfect or mature person). Similarly, in his *Life* Pachomius was considered perfect (τέλειον) by his fellows (106). In section 2 we are told that this perfection *followed* his making progress (προκόψας). Section 43 speaks of brothers who have not yet attained perfection (εἰς τελειότητα). By his choice of words, Luke has indicated that he is depicting the life of the earthly Jesus in terms of the traditional Hellenistic development between beginning and perfection.

This picture of a developing *way* shows the reader five stages in the career of the Lukan Jesus:[17] (1) dedication to God as an infant (Luke 2:22–24), where his parents do not redeem the firstborn but give him totally to God; (2) youthful agreement with the parental decisions made about him by his parents at birth (2:41–52); (3) empowering for service (3:21–22), where in a prayer scene after his baptism the Lukan Jesus sees a vision, hears an audition, and experiences the anointing necessary for his mission that is coming (cf. 4:16–21); (4) acceptance of rejection, suffering, and death (chaps. 9—23), where after two sessions of prayer (9:18–27; 9:28–29) the Lukan Jesus comes to an awareness that his way now involves a new departure the content of which will be rejection, suffering, and death; and (5) resurrection, ascension, and exaltation (Luke 24—Acts).

That this tradition was intended to shape the disciples seems certain in view of the fact that the two major components of *the way* are reflected in Acts: that is, empowering (e.g., Acts 2) and suffering (e.g., Acts 14:22; also Paul's passion journey to Jerusalem, that is analogous to that of Jesus in Luke's Gospel).[18] The components that are not reflected in Acts are missing because of their inappropriateness to the narrative (e.g., there is no need for an infancy dedication or for youthful commitment; there is no place for a resurrection that is still future). In sum, the principle that a disciple's life is shaped by a tradition in the way he or she walks is seen to be applied through the depiction of Jesus' earthly career in developmental terms. For Luke, these are the five stages of the Christian disciple's *way*.

The Jesus tradition in Luke-Acts also shapes the mission a disciple is called upon to fulfill. This is made clear in two ways: (1) in the prophecies of the risen Jesus, and (2) in the foreshadowing of the mission in the life of the pre-Easter Jesus. In the first place, there is an explicit prophecy by the risen Jesus about his disciples' mission. Luke 24:44–49 gives this instruction in the context of a resurrection appearance in Jerusalem. Jesus says, "Repentance and forgiveness of sins should be preached in his name to all nations, beginning from Jerusalem. You are witnesses of these things." Acts 1:8 repeats the prophecy in another resurrection appearance setting: "You shall receive power when the Holy Spirit has come upon you; and you shall be my witnesses in Jerusalem and in all Judea and Samaria and to the end of the earth." Disciples have a mission to fulfill: they are to be witnesses for Jesus.

In the second place, there is a foreshadowing of this mission in Luke's Gospel.[19] First, this can be seen in 5:1–11 where the evangelist uses a commissioning story form instead of a call story form for the call of Peter and others. In harmony with the commissioning form, the story ends with Jesus' words: "Do not be afraid; henceforth you will be catching men." Second, Luke 5:27–29 also foreshadows the disciples' future mission in the career of the Lukan Jesus. As soon as Levi left all and followed Jesus, he made a great feast in his house to introduce his associates to Jesus. Third, there is Luke 8:38–39. These verses are part of the climax of the healing of the Gerasene demoniac. The healed man begs Jesus that he might be with him. Jesus, however, sends him away with these words: "Return to your home, and declare how much God has done for you." Luke adds: "And he went away, proclaiming throughout the whole city how much Jesus had done for him." Implicit in being a disciple is bearing witness. Fourth, there is Luke 9:1–6, the story of Jesus' dispatch of the Twelve to preach and heal, after giving them power and authority. This echoes Acts 1:8 for sure. Fifth, there is Luke 10:1–16, the account of the mission of the Seventy who were sent out ahead of Jesus to the places he was about to come, foreshadowing most likely the Gentile mission of Acts. In all of these instances, Luke's Gospel is foreshadowing the evangelistic outreach of the post-Easter disciples. Whether it is through explicit prophecies of the risen Jesus or through the implicit foreshadowing in the narrative about the pre-Easter Jesus, there is a tradition which shapes disciples in the mission to be fulfilled just as much as the same tradition shapes *the way* disciples are to walk. A disciple, in the Lukan view, is shaped by a tradition of Jesus.

## ENABLED BY AN EXPERIENCE

In saying that a disciple, in the Lukan perspective, is enabled by an experience, it is necessary to note that this includes both *the way* walked and the mission fulfilled. Let us examine these two dimensions in order.

In the first place, one walks *the way* of a disciple of Jesus only if he or she is called by Jesus. This is made clear in the Acts' accounts of Paul's conversion (Acts 9, 22, 26). The first of these may be analyzed as representative (9:1–31). The narrative about Paul's conversion in 9:1–31 is composed of two commissioning stories[20] that, when joined, have a formal parallel in 2 Maccabees 3.[21] In both Acts and 2 Maccabees, (1) an enemy sets out to do an act against God's people or house; (2) there is a divine intervention resulting in the enemy's falling to the ground and being in darkness; (3) a devout person intervenes on the enemy's behalf, and the enemy is relieved of his afflictions; (4) the enemy becomes a believer in the God who overpowered him and bears witness to him. This is the form of a story about a god overpowering his enemy.

The first twenty-five verses of the conversion account are chiastically arranged.[22]

A. Paul plots against the Christians in Damascus (Acts 9:1–2)
  B. Paul sees a vision, is blinded, and fasts (vv. 3–9)
    C. Ananias sees a vision, is commanded to go to Paul (vv. 10–14)
      D. Paul's mission is foretold by Christ (vv. 15–16)
    C.' Ananias goes to Paul and reports his vision (v. 17)
  B.' Paul's sight is restored, he is baptized and eats (vv. 18–19a)
A.' Paul preaches Christ in Damascus; Jews plot to kill him (vv. 19b–25)

The significance of this surface structure is that its centerpiece focuses the item of central significance for the evangelist: Paul's commission.

The narrative involves two geographical settings: Damascus (vv. 1–25) and Jerusalem (vv. 26–30). There are parallels between the end of the first geographical unit and the entirety of the second.[23]

| | |
|---|---|
| Ananias hesitates to believe Paul has been converted (vv. 13–14) | (1) The disciples in Jerusalem fear Paul; they did not believe he was a disciple (v. 26) |
| The Lord assures Ananias (vv. 15–16) | (2) Barnabas assures the disciples in Jerusalem (v. 27) |
| Ananias goes to Paul and does as he was told (vv. 17–19a) Paul is with the disciples in Damascus (v. 19b) | (3) Paul was with them, going in and out among them in Jerusalem (v. 28a) |
| Paul preaches immediately in the synagogue (vv. 20–22) | (4) Paul speaks freely in the name of the Lord (vv. 28b–29a) |
| The Jews plot to kill Paul (vv. 23–24) | (5) The Hellenists seek to kill Paul (v. 29b) |
| Paul escapes (v. 25) | (6) Paul escapes (v. 30) |

The very pattern (cf. item 1 for an explicit statement of the issue) indicates that the issue is whether or not Paul's conversion/commission is genuine. The narrative functions as a confirmation of Paul's experience in a number of ways: (1) the vision to Ananias (vv. 10–12) with its reassurance (vv. 15–16);[24] (2) Paul's preaching (vv. 20, 22, 28–29) in obedience to the commission of v. 15; (3) Barnabas's vouching for Paul (v. 27); (4) Paul's sufferings (vv. 23–25, 29–30) in fulfillment of the prophecy of v. 16.

In Acts 9:1–31, then, we have a narrative in which the Lord Jesus overpowers his enemy, Saul, the persecutor of *the way*. The christophany involves both Paul's call to discipleship and his commissioning as a chosen instrument to bear witness. Various means are employed to give confirmation to the genuineness of Paul's experience. For our purposes, this story says quite clearly that a disciple is one enabled by an experience. Paul's participation in *the way* was not as a "walk on" but as one overpowered by the summons of his call by Jesus.

The same emphasis is foreshadowed in two narratives in Luke's Gospel: 5:1–11 and 5:27–28. The first is a commissioning story, the second a call narrative. A call story like the call of Levi in Luke 5:27–28 involves the following: (1) Jesus comes; (2) he sees the person; (3) he calls; (4) the person leaves all and follows him (cf. Mark 1:16–20; 2:13–14). A commissioning story like that of Peter in Luke 5:1–11 includes the following:[25] (1) an introduction describing the circumstances (v. 2); (2) the confrontation between the commissioner and the one to be commissioned (v. 3); (3) the commission, in which the recipient is told to undertake a specific task (v. 4); (4) a protest in which the person questions in some way the word of the commissioner (v. 5); (5) a reaction of fear, amazement, unworthiness in the presence of the august commissioner (vv. 8–9); (6) reassurance to the individual, providing confidence and allaying misgivings (v. 10b); and (7) the conclusion, usually involving the beginning of the commissioned one's undertaking the assignment (v. 11). Although there are overtones of a call story in v. 11 ("they left everything and followed him"), the dominant thrust is that of a commissioning of Peter (v. 10) for his mission: "Henceforth you will be catching men." Whether it is the one form or the other, the emphasis is the same. A disciple of Jesus is such because he or she has received a summons/call. Without this experience, there is no discipleship.[26]

What is true about the Lukan conviction that the divine initiative is determinative in one's walking *the way* is also present in the dimension of mission. In Luke-Acts, one fulfills the mission only as one is empowered, guided, and protected through an ongoing experience.

Empowering is the prerequisite for mission in Luke-Acts. This is made clear in the speeches of the risen Jesus in Luke 24:44–49 and in Acts 1:8, in the narratives of Acts 2 and 4, and is foreshadowed in Luke's Gospel at 9:1–6 and 10:1–16. (1) In Acts 1:8 the risen Jesus tells his followers: "But you shall receive power after [RSV: when] the Holy Spirit has come upon you; and you shall be my witnesses. . . ." (RSV revised). In 1:4 he charged them not to depart from Jerusalem "but to wait for the promise of the Father. . . ." Luke 24:48–49 makes the same point: "You are witnesses of these things. And behold, I send the promise of my Father upon you; but stay in the city, until you are clothed with power from on high." (2) The narrative of Acts 1–5 falls into two parallel units: 1:12—4:23 and 4:24—5:42.[27] There are correspondences in content and sequence between these two sections. In both there is an account of the outpouring of the Holy Spirit on the disciples (2:1–13 and 4:31b) followed by their powerful witness (2:14–41 and 4:31c). The witness follows the empowering just as the risen Jesus said it would. (3) That effective mission follows the experience of being empowered is foreshadowed in Luke 9:1–6 and 10:1–16. The first of these pericopae is the climax to a larger thought unit that runs from 8:22 to 9:6.[28] In Luke 8, Jesus is portrayed as one who possesses power and authority (Lord of nature—vv. 22–25; Lord of the evil powers—8:26–39; Lord over death—vv. 40–42, 49–56; and Lord over disease—vv. 43–48). In Luke 9:1–6 "he called the twelve together and gave them power and authority over all demons and to cure diseases, and he sent them out to preach. . . ." The authority Jesus possesses he gives to his disciples. Their mission follows this experience of empowering. The same emphasis is found in the sending out of the Seventy in Luke 10:1–24. They return with a testimony of victory because of the power they experienced (10:17–19).

The disciples of Jesus are not only empowered by an ongoing experience, they are also guided. Acts contains numerous examples of this. In Acts 8:26 we read that "an angel of the Lord said to Philip, 'Rise and go toward the south to the road that goes down from Jerusalem to Gaza.'" As a result Philip evangelizes the Ethiopian eunuch. Afterwards, v. 39 says, "The Spirit of the Lord caught up Philip; and the eunuch saw him no more." In Acts 10, God prepares Peter for his encounter with the Gentile Cornelius through a vision and an audition (10:9–16). Then Peter is led to accept Gentiles as equals because the Holy Spirit fell on all who heard the word (10:44). When called to account by the circumcision party in Jerusalem (11:2–3), Peter can only say, "Who was I that I could withstand God?" (Acts 11:17). In 13:1–3 the Gentile mission of Paul is initiated through a word of prophecy while the Christians are worshipping in Antioch. The Holy Spirit says, "Set apart for me Barnabas and Saul for the work to which I have called them" (Acts 13:2). Acts 16:6–10 tells us that Paul was forbidden by the Holy Spirit to speak the word in Asia, that the Spirit of Jesus did not allow them to go into Bithynia, but that through a vision they were led into Macedonia. Acts 20:22, in the midst of Paul's farewell speech to the Ephesian elders at Miletus, has the apostle say that he is "going to Jerusalem, bound in the Spirit. . . ." In the midst of a defense speech before the Jews in Jerusalem

(Acts 22:17–18), Paul tells of an early experience he had: "When I had returned to Jerusalem and was praying in the temple, I fell into a trance and saw him saying to me, 'Make haste and get quickly out of Jerusalem, because they will not accept your testimony about me.'" Throughout Acts the disciples are portrayed as guided by an ongoing experience with God.

This guidance is foreshadowed in Luke 5:1–11, where Jesus tells Peter to "put out into the deep and let down your nets for a catch" (5:4). Although they have toiled all night and caught nothing, Peter obeys Jesus' word. "And when they had done this, they enclosed a great shoal of fish" (v. 6). Successful fishing follows the guidance of the Lord.

Jesus' disciples are not only empowered and guided in their mission by an ongoing experience of God, but they are also protected when the mission demands it. Three visions of Paul point in this direction. In Acts 18:9–10 the Lord says to Paul in Corinth one night in a vision, "Do not be afraid . . . for I am with you, and no man shall attack you to harm you. . . ." Acts 23:11 says that in Jerusalem the Lord stood by Paul and said, "Take courage, for as you have testified about me at Jerusalem, so you must bear witness also at Rome."[29] Finally, in Acts 27:23–24, in the midst of a storm at sea, Paul tells his sailing companions to take heart, for there will be no loss of life. "For this very night there stood by me an angel of [God] . . . and he said, 'Do not be afraid, Paul; you must stand before Caesar; and lo, God has granted you all those who sail with you.'"

This protection of the messenger is foreshadowed in Luke's Gospel both in the experience of Jesus, the prototype of Christian existence, and in that of his disciples. In Luke 4:16–30 the Nazareth episode ends with the people rising up, putting Jesus out of the city, and leading him to the brow of the hill so they could throw him down (v. 29). "But passing through the midst of them he went away" (v. 30). Moreover, when Jesus sends the Twelve out in Luke 9:1–6, he tells them to take nothing with them (v. 3); so also with the Seventy in Luke 10:4. According to Luke 22:35, Jesus asks them, "When I sent you out with no purse or bag or sandals, did you lack anything?" They reply, "Nothing." Not only are the messengers provided for, they are also protected from harm. "Behold, I have given you authority to tread upon serpents and scorpions, and over all the power of the enemy; and nothing shall hurt you" (Luke 10:19). In multiple ways, then, a disciple fulfills his or her mission in Luke-Acts because of an ongoing, enabling experience.

## PARTICIPANT IN COMMUNITY

In Luke-Acts, the disciple who is shaped by the tradition of Jesus and enabled by an ongoing experience of the Lord is no solitary individual but a participant in a community. The communal dimension of discipleship is seen both in *the way* one is called to walk and in the mission he or she is commissioned to fulfill.

The communal dimensions of the Christian *way* are accented in Acts from the first. Each of the two parallel panels (1:12—4:22; 4:23—5:42) of the Jerusalem narrative has a summary that speaks of the unity of the disciples in their communal existence.[30] Acts 2:44 puts it this way: "And all who believed were together and had all things in common. . . ." Acts 4:32 states, "Now the company of those who believed were of one heart and soul, and no one said that any of the things which he possessed was his own, but they had everything in common." In 6:1–6 the church acts to see that no one is neglected among the widows. In 11:27–30 and 12:25 the new Gentile church in Antioch sends relief to famine-stricken Christians in Judea as an expression of their solidarity with the one community. The Jerusalem sessions of 11:1–18 and 15:1–35 point to the existence of accountability of individuals within the larger community. Both events are climaxed by communal decisions (11:18; 15:22–29). Acts 21:17–26, moreover, tells of Paul's actions to allay suspicions of the Jewish Christians about him and to bring unity to the larger fellowship. Throughout the Acts, the involvement of disciples in community with other disciples is highlighted.

This communal aspect of discipleship is foreshadowed in Luke's Gospel in numerous ways. Luke 8:1–3 speaks of the group traveling with Jesus which includes not only the Twelve but also some women.[31] Luke 9:1–6 and 10:1–24 tell of the Twelve and the Seventy whom Jesus sent out. This implies that these persons were with him in some type of communal existence. In 11:1 we hear that, as Jesus was praying, one of his disciples said to him: "Lord, teach us to pray, as John taught his disciples." Luke 18:31–34 pictures Jesus traveling with the Twelve toward Jerusalem. Luke 22:28–30 has Jesus, at the last supper, say to the disciples: "You all are those who have continued with me" (RSV revised). Luke 24:50–53, the last pericope of the Gospel, tells how after Jesus' departure the disciples return to Jerusalem together. The communal existence of Jesus' disciples after Easter is foreshadowed by the corporate life of the disciples throughout the Gospel of Luke.

The mission a disciple is called to fulfill, no less than the way he or she is summoned to walk, is corporate in nature. Several threads running through Acts make this clear. (1) In Acts one must reckon with the participation of Ananias in Paul's conversion (9:10–19; 22:12–16). Though this is alien to Paul's own account of his conversion in Galatians 1, it is characteristic of Luke. Not even the most dramatic inbreaking of God's power into one's life is devoid of its corporate dimensions in Acts. (2) In Acts, Jerusalem is linked with missionary outreach. In 8:14, Peter and John come to pray that the Samaritans might receive the Holy Spirit. In 9:27, Barnabas, a Jerusalem Christian, brings Saul to the apostles and vouches for him. In 11:1–18, the

Jerusalem church checks on the conversion of Cornelius. In 11:19–23, Barnabas is sent by the Jerusalem church to Antioch to oversee the new church there. In Acts 15, Paul and Barnabas go to Jerusalem to settle the issue of Gentile acceptability in the church. A Jerusalem letter is sent to Antioch to confirm the decision made. In Acts 21, the decision of Acts 15 is repeated as a way of confirming it by Jerusalem. Furthermore, on Paul's missionary outreach in Acts 13—14, he is accompanied by a member of the Jerusalem church, Barnabas. On his missionary journeys in Acts 16—20, Paul is accompanied by yet another member of the Jerusalem community, Silas. That Jerusalem is the umbrella under which Paul's mission is carried out testifies to the communal character of the Christian mission. Moreover, when Paul goes out in Acts 13—14, he is sent by the church at Antioch (13:1–3); the same thing happens in 15:40b prior to the journeys of Acts 16—20. The Lukan Paul does not act as an individual but as the emissary of the corporate bodies to which he belongs.

The corporate nature of the disciple's mission is foreshadowed in Luke 9 and 10. In 10:1, Jesus sends out the Seventy two by two. Luke 9:1–6, in contrast to Mark 6:7–13, where the Twelve are sent out two by two, seems to imply that the Twelve are sent out as a group (cf. v. 4, "into whatever house you all enter"; v. 5, "wherever they do not receive you all, when you all leave that town" [au. trans.]). Fulfilling Jesus' mission is a communal venture, just as is walking Jesus' *way.*

We are now in a position to look back over our description of discipleship in Luke-Acts and see it as a whole. When this is done, it becomes clear that Luke resists the type of reductionism so characteristic of much contemporary Christianity. On the one hand, in Luke-Acts discipleship cannot be reduced to mission: it also involves formation. But neither can it be reduced to formation: it involves mission. It is not either formation or mission in Luke-Acts; it is both/and. On the other hand, the Lukan view of discipleship has no place for a Robinson Crusoe Christian: discipleship is communal. Neither does Luke have room for an "enthusiastic" Christian (that is, one with an over-realized eschatology). Discipleship is lived out in this world and is shaped by the tradition of Jesus and the apostles. Nor does the evangelist have any conception of Christian life devoid of the experience of the numinous. The community of disciples shaped by the tradition of Jesus lives out of the power, direction, and protection of the numinous that is experienced directly and regularly in their lives. Only when all of these components are held together as part of a balanced whole do we grasp the distinctively Lukan view of discipleship.

## NOTES

1. On discipleship in general, see: H. Crouzel, "L'imitation et la 'suite' de Dieu et du Christ dans les premiers siècles chrétiens, ainsi que leurs sources gréco-romaines

et hébraïques," *JAC* 21 (1978) 7–41; H. D. Betz, *Nachfolge und Nachahmung Jesu Christi im Neuen Testament* (BHT 37; Tübingen: Mohr/Siebeck, 1967); M. Hengel, *The Charismatic Leader and His Followers* (trans. J. Greig; New York: Crossroad, 1981); E. Schweizer, *Lordship and Discipleship* (SBT 28; London: SCM Press, 1960).

2. J. Dupont, "Conversion in the Acts of the Apostles," in *The Salvation of the Gentiles* (trans. J. R. Keating; New York: Paulist Press, 1979) 61–84; F. X. Hezel, "Conversion and Repentance in Lucan Theology," *TBT* 37 (1968) 2596–2602; W. S. Udick, "Metanoia as Found in the Acts of the Apostles," *TBT* 28 (1967) 1943–46.

3. C. H. Talbert, *Literary Patterns. Theological Themes. and the Genre of Luke-Acts* (SBLMS 20; Missoula, Mont.: Scholars Press, 1974) 15–18.

4. H. von Soden, *Geschichte der christlichen Kirche. 1: Die Entstehung der christlichen Kirche* (Leipzig: Teubner, 1919) 73.

5. Talbert, *Literary Patterns.* chap. 8; idem, *What Is a Gospel? The Genre of the Canonical Gospels* (Philadelphia; Fortress Press, 1977); idem, "The Gospel and the Gospels," in *Interpreting the Gospels* (ed. J. L. Mays; Philadelphia: Fortress Press, 1981) 14–26.

6. I. Düring, *Aristotle in the Ancient Biographical Tradition* (Göteborg, Swed.: Göteborgs Universitets Arsskrift, 1957).

7. W. Scott, ed., *Fragmenta Herculanensia* (Oxford: At the Clarendon Press, 1885); A. Traversa, ed., *Index Stoicorum Herculanensis* (Genova: Instituto di Filologia Classica, 1952).

8. Socrates, Aristippus, Plato, Zeno, Pythagoras, Epicurus. At no time have I ever claimed that Diogenes Laertius's work as a whole reflected this pattern, only these six biographies within the whole.

9. Talbert, *Literary Patterns.* 131, 138 n. 39.

10. A. N. Athanassakis, ed. and trans., *The Life of Pachomius* (SBLTT 7; Missoula, Mont.: Scholars Press, 1975).

11. *The Fathers of the Church: Early Christian Biographies* 15 (Washington, D.C.: Catholic Univ. of America Press, 1952).

12. If the thesis of P. L. Shuler in *A Genre for the Gospels: The Biographical Character of Matthew* (Philadelphia: Fortress Press, 1982) were true, this would be what the canonical Gospels ought to look like. This also shows that the A-plus-B pattern is not incompatible with encomium. This is a lesson Shuler needs to learn.

13. G. Delling, "ἀρχηγός," *TDNT* 1 (1964) 487–88.

14. Luke's view corresponds to what J. M. Gustafson ("The Relation of the Gospels to the Moral Life," in *Jesus and Man's Hope* [ed. D. G. Miller and D. Y. Hadidian; Pittsburgh: Pittsburgh Theological Seminary, 1971] 2:110–16) means when he says the Jesus of the Gospels functions as a "paradigm."

15. C. H. Talbert, "The Way of the Lukan Jesus: Dimensions of Lukan Spirituality," *PRS* 9 (1982) 237–49.

16. G. Stählin, "προκοπή, προκόπτειν," *TDNT* 6 (1968) 703–19.

17. Talbert, "Way of the Lukan Jesus," 237–49.

18. Talbert, *Literary Patterns.* 16–18.

19. C. H. Talbert, *Reading Luke: A Literary and Theological Commentary on the Third Gospel* (New York: Crossroad, 1982).

20. B. J. Hubbard, "The Role of Commissioning Accounts in Acts," in *Perspectives*

*on Luke-Acts* (ed. C. H. Talbert; Danville, Va.: Assoc. of Baptist Professors of Religion, 1978) 187–98.

21. J. Roloff, *Die Apostelgeschichte* (NTD 5; Göttingen: Vandenhoeck & Ruprecht, 1981) 145.

22. J. Bligh, *Galatians* (London: St. Paul Pubs. 1969) 95.

23. D. Gill, "The Structure of Acts 9," *Bib* 55 (1974) 546–48.

24. G. Lohfink, *The Conversion of St. Paul* (trans. B. J. Malina; Chicago: Franciscan Herald Press, 1976) 73–77.

25. B. J. Hubbard, "Commissioning Stories in Luke-Acts; A Study of Their Antecedents, Form, and Content," *Semeia* 8 (1977) 103–26.

26. Dupont, "Conversion in the Acts," 74–76.

27. Talbert, *Literary Patterns.* 35–36.

28. Talbert, *Reading Luke.* 95–101.

29. G. W. MacRae ("Whom Heaven Must Receive Until the Time: Reflections on the Christology of Acts," *Int* 27 [1973] 151–65) points out the inadequacy of an "absentee christology" model for Acts.

30. J. Dupont, "Community of Goods in the Early Church," in idem, *Salvation of the Gentiles*, 85–102.

31. B. Witherington, III, "On the Road with Mary Magdalene, Joanna, Susanna, and Other Disciples—Luke 8:1–3," *ZNW* 70 (1979) 243–47.

# 4

# "Peace I Leave with You;
# My Peace I Give to You":
# Discipleship in the Fourth Gospel

## FERNANDO F. SEGOVIA

In the last decade or so, perhaps the most fertile area of New Testament studies—and certainly the most fertile within Gospel studies—with respect to the nature and character of Christian discipleship has been that of Markan scholarship. Most influential and most fruitful in this regard have been the development and the continued use of what represents, in effect, a new vantage point on the question of discipleship in that work, as well as in Gospel studies in general: namely, a study of the way in which the disciples function in the development of the Gospel narrative. The emergence of this new approach has given rise to a rather lively and ongoing debate within Markan scholarship.

In the earliest stages of this approach, the proponents argued on behalf of what might be called a polemical view of Jesus' disciples in the Markan narrative. Thus, as the narrative unfolded, the Gospel was seen as presenting an increasingly negative view of the disciples and their relationship with Jesus. Indeed, the climax of this relationship was said to be their rejection and abandonment of Jesus in Jerusalem and Jesus' subsequent rejection of them after the resurrection. Furthermore, this polemic against the disciples in the narrative was seen as pointing to and reflecting a polemic by the author of the Gospel against fellow Christians in the community. The grounds for such a polemic were variously identified: both christology[1] and eschatology[2] were proposed as the main issue of contention.

There were two main reactions against these conclusions from within the approach itself. Both pointed to and emphasized the more positive aspects of the disciples and their relationship with Jesus and called into question the proposed polemical purpose behind the admittedly stark portrayal of the disciples' failure in the Markan narrative. Such a failure, it was argued, was used by way of example—that is, to show what true discipleship means and entails. However, the exemplary aspect of the disciples' failure in the narrative was variously interpreted: it was seen as having a precise historical application[3] or a solely literary one.[4]

It is not my purpose here to render judgment on the validity of all or any of these specific proposals but, rather, to point to the vitality that research into the theme of discipleship enjoys in a specific area of Gospel studies and to the central role that the study of the characterization of the disciples in the narrative has played in the growth of that research.

## RECENT JOHANNINE SCHOLARSHIP

By way of contrast, almost exactly the opposite situation may be said to prevail in Johannine studies. Although some attention has been paid within Johannine scholarship to the implicit or explicit ecclesiology of the Johannine community,[5] the question of discipleship per se has been largely by-passed. Such an omission is even more surprising when one compares the incidence of the term "disciple" (μαθητής) itself in the four Gospels: it is in fact the Fourth Gospel that provides the highest number of such occurrences.[6]

Recently, there have been some major contributions to the topic, and these do represent a wide variety of exegetical approaches. Two such approaches may be found in a 1971 article by R. Moreno Jiménez.[7] In the first part of the study, Moreno Jiménez selects two individual verses (8:31; 13:35) and a full unit (15:1–12) as the key to the concept of discipleship in the Gospel.[8] Then, in the second part, the concept of discipleship is examined on a more theological level from the point of view of the ideal disciple's relationship to the Father, to Jesus, and to the Spirit in the text.[9]

Four years later, in the last volume of his commentary on John, R. Schnackenburg devoted a full excursus to the subject of discipleship in the Gospel.[10] Two different approaches may be found here as well: on the one hand, Schnackenburg uses representative texts to outline what he considers to be the basic aspects of the concept of discipleship in the Gospel; then, he turns to specific expressions and images from the text to point out and emphasize the strong, underlying, ecclesial dimension of this concept.[11] Two years after Schnackenburg's excursus, M. de Jonge, in a new study introducing a collection of earlier essays on the Gospel, approached the question of discipleship from the point of view of a hermeneutical perspective found within the Gospel itself—namely, texts in the narrative that comment specifically on the differing understanding of the disciples before and after Jesus' departure.[12]

Most recently, in a wide-ranging study of the Johannine community, R.

Brown shed further light on the meaning of discipleship within this community by using, to some extent, the sequence of the Gospel narrative itself as a key to the historical and theological development of the Johannine circle.[13] In addition, Brown proceeded to identify and distinguish several other groups of Christian disciples known to the Johannine community by means of different characters in the narrative: namely, crypto-Christians, Jewish Christians of inadequate faith, Christians of apostolic churches.[14]

These recent studies begin to clarify and outline through their respective exegetical approaches the meaning and nature of Christian discipleship from the Johannine perspective. The results have not been at all dissimilar; indeed, general agreement may be said to prevail with respect to certain fundamental aspects of discipleship in the Johannine community: namely, the central role of belief for such discipleship, the evolving character of belief itself, and the sustained contrast between believers and unbelievers.

## THE ROLE OF THE DISCIPLES

I aim to contribute to this ongoing investigation of discipleship in the Fourth Gospel, and in the community situation presupposed and reflected therein, by turning to a specific vantage point which is referred to in passing by some of these previous studies but which has not yet been systematically employed in the analysis of this theme.[15] I refer to that vantage point mentioned earlier which has proved to be so influential and fruitful within Markan scholarship—that is, an analysis of the way in which the disciples function in the development of the Markan narrative.

In the introduction to his study on the narrative role of the disciples in Mark, R. Tannehill argues that such a study presupposes and is made possible by the continuing role of such a group in the Gospel and the presence—despite possible variations in the size of the group—of some common characteristics which define the group.[16] Given the continuity of persons and characteristics, developments can be observed not only from scene to scene but also in terms of an overall significant movement toward an end or conclusion. On the basis of these requirements, there is no reason whatever why the same kind of study cannot be applied to the Fourth Gospel.

On the one hand, it is quite clear that there is a group of Jesus' companions or "disciples" which plays a continuing role in the development of the Fourth Gospel. This group begins to be formed quite early in the Gospel narrative, is given the name of "disciples" already by the time of Jesus' first visit to Cana (John 2:1–11), and is then presented as following Jesus wherever he goes in his ministry.[17] Similarly, although their number or makeup is seldom specified and the focus of attention may differ from scene to scene,[18] it is also quite clear that they have all—with the sole exception of Judas—accepted Jesus' claims and remain bound to him in a continuing bond.

In what follows, therefore, I will turn to the characterization of Jesus' disciples in the Fourth Gospel as a way of probing further the concept of discipleship present in the Gospel and the community situation which it reflects and presupposes. The precise way in which the disciples as a character function in the narrative, Markan scholarship has taught us, proves to be of considerable help in determining more closely what discipleship means and entails for the author of the narrative. Characterization, however, is a complex phenomenon. It is my purpose in this study, given its nature as a preliminary inquiry into such a phenomenon, to forgo detailed discussion of individual scenes or specific development between individual scenes and to concentrate instead on the overall development of the narrative as a whole.

Given this specific focus for the inquiry, however, certain methodological comments are in order:

1. It is now general scholarly consensus that the present conclusion of the Gospel—that is, John 21—represents a later addition to the Gospel narrative and its original conclusion (20:30–31).[19] Thus, I propose to leave this chapter out of consideration in this study.

2. Similarly, there is growing scholarly consensus that a large part of the present farewell discourse of Jesus in the Gospel (John 15—17) also represents a later addition or series of additions to the original farewell discourse (13:31—14:31).[20] Thus, I propose to leave these chapters out of consideration as well in the present study.

3. In addition, earlier research has led me to identify two other texts in the Gospel, both of which are directly related to the question of discipleship, as later additions: 13:34–35[21] and 13:1b–3, 12–20.[22] Consequently, these two texts will also be left out of consideration.

In what follows, therefore, I will attempt to trace the overall development of the disciples in the narrative according to the original sequence of that narrative, thus excluding all of these sections that I myself accept as additions to the text. These additions may, and indeed do, develop the concept of discipleship present in the earlier edition of the Gospel along new and different directions. Thus, I deliberately limit myself to the characterization of the disciples in the earlier edition.[23]

Finally, I see this characterization as taking place in four basic stages, and I propose to follow these stages in the development of the present study. The four stages may be described and delineated as follows: (1) the gathering of the elect and the initial incomprehension of "the world" (John 1—3); (2) the elect on "the way" and the growing rejection of "the world" (John

4—12); (3) the farewell to the elect and the exclusion of "the world" (John 13—14); (4) the vindication of the elect and the judgment of "the world" (John 18—20). The proposed outline may be said to constitute a further subdivision of the traditional division of the Gospel into what may be called a "Book of Signs" (1:19—12:50) and a "Book of Glory" (13:1—20:31),[24] since each of these overarching divisions is seen as, in effect, containing two basic stages of the process of characterization (1—3, 4—12 / 13—14, 18—20).[25]

## The Gathering of the Elect and the Initial Incomprehension of "the World" (John 1—3)

The first stage of the characterization is directly delimited, I believe, by an *inclusio* consisting of two major sections dealing with the testimony of John the Baptist: first of all, in 1:19–34, the Baptist, baptizing in the vicinity of Bethany in the Transjordan (1:28), points forward to the coming of one greater than he (1:19–28) and then proceeds to identify Jesus as such a one (1:29–34); then, in 3:22–36, while baptizing in the vicinity of Aenon near Salim (3:23), not far from where Jesus himself is said to be baptizing after his departure from Jerusalem, the Baptist welcomes the reported success of Jesus' mission compared with his own and explicitly acknowledges the fulfillment of his own role and the end of his own mission (3:25–30).

Within this *inclusio,* a deliberate contrast is created and developed by the juxtaposition of two other major sections of this first stage. The first of these presents the early formation of the circle of Jesus' disciples, a process which is started by the Baptist himself (1:35–42) and is then continued by Jesus in the area of Galilee (1:43–51; 2:1–12). In the second, the first journey of Jesus to Jerusalem is described, a journey which evokes a demand for a sign (2:13–22) as well as an insufficient response to Jesus' signs and claims (2:23–25; 3:1–21) on the part of the Jews of Jerusalem. The group of disciples appears not only within the first section of the contrast but also in the first unit of the second section (2:13–22).

The very beginnings of the circle of Jesus' disciples is presented in the narrative as a series of individual callings leading up to a climax consisting of Jesus' first miraculous sign in the Gospel, a work performed in Cana of Galilee and witnessed by the entire fledgling group of followers (2:1–11). Two separate sequences may be discerned in the series.

The first sequence (1:35–42) is begun by the Baptist himself: on the basis of his now-open testimony concerning Jesus (1:35), two of his own disciples begin to follow Jesus.[26] Thus, in effect, the circle of Jesus' disciples quite clearly begins from within the Baptist's own ranks of disciples. A third disciple is added when one of these two, Andrew, searches out his brother, Simon Peter, and brings him to Jesus. The second sequence (1:43–51) is begun by Jesus himself: a fourth disciple, Philip, is called directly by him, and then, he, too, proceeds to search out and bring an additional disciple to Jesus—Nathanael, the fifth. Both of these sequences give rise to a series of christological confessions on the part of these disciples, all of which represent traditional Jewish messianic expectations: the messiah (1:41); the one written about in the Mosaic law and the prophets (1:45); the Son of God and the king of Israel (1:49).

Both sequences of callings come to a close with Jesus' declarations of 1:50–51: namely, a promise addressed not only to Nathanael but to the other disciples as well. The promise presents two fundamental aspects: on the one hand, it points to the fact that Jesus' revelation has barely begun, that there are "greater things" yet to come; at the same time, it also makes clear that, in the light of this outstanding revelation, the preceding confessions must give way to and be understood solely in terms of a further acceptance of Jesus' claim as the Father's unique representative. Both of these aspects begin to be developed immediately in the following climax to the entire first major section (2:1–11): in Cana, Jesus manifests his "glory" (δόξα), and his disciples believe in him—that is, accept him as the one who comes from the Father.[27]

The initial formation of Jesus' circle of disciples is followed by Jesus' first journey to Jerusalem. Two asides from the narrator in the very first unit of this journey (2:17, 22) indirectly inform the reader that the disciples, after a brief stay in Capernaum with him (2:12), do follow Jesus to Jerusalem as well.[28] Although this first journey does not give rise to the violent hostility which characterizes the later journeys,[29] the reception is nonetheless far from satisfactory and thus provides an immediate contrast to the preceding positive response of the circle of disciples.

At the same time, however, the two asides also qualify, quite unexpectedly, this earlier response of the disciples and thus, to some extent, the intended contrast as well. The asides do make it quite clear that, despite their previous acceptance of him as the one sent by the Father, the disciples' perception of Jesus remains incomplete. It is only after the resurrection that the disciples (1) recall the saying of 3:19 and interpret it correctly as a reference to the events of "the hour"; (2) further recall a text from Scripture (Ps. 69:9) and perceive it correctly as a reference to the sign performed at the temple. Thus, the ultimate reference of Jesus' action and saying to the events of "the hour," as well as their own status as fulfillment of prophecy, are not understood until after "the hour."

In sum, the first stage of the characterization provides the reader with a very definite contrast between an emergent group of disciples and the Jews of Jerusalem. The former, unlike the latter, not only responds to Jesus immediately with a variety of messianic titles but also proceeds quickly to a further acceptance of him as the Father's unique representative. At the same time, the contrast is somewhat qualified by the disciples' stated inability to comprehend fully the nature of Jesus' action and saying at the temple: neither their reference to "the hour" nor their status as prophetic fulfillment is said to be perceived until after "the hour." Thus, the disciples' perception of Jesus, while correct and adequate, remains nonetheless incomplete prior to "the hour."[30]

## The Elect on the Way and the Growing Rejection of "the World" (John 4—12)

The second major stage of the characterization presents a series of journeys on Jesus' part which give rise to a consistent and mounting rejection of his claims and/or violent opposition. Five major sections may be discerned: (1) a second journey to Galilee with a brief stop in Samaria (chaps. 4, 6); (2) a second journey to Jerusalem with a retreat to Galilee for safety (chaps. 5, 7:1–9); (3) a third journey to Jerusalem with a retreat to Bethany in the Transjordan for safety (7:10—10:39, 10:40–42); (4) a cycle of events connected with Lazarus and involving a return to the immediate area of Jerusalem (11:1—12:11); (5) a fourth and final journey to Jerusalem (12:12–50).[31] (6) The summary statement of 12:36b–43 (and 44–50) brings to a close not only this second major stage but all of the public ministry as well. The disciples appear in varying degrees in all of these sections except the second one (5, 7:1–9).

*1. A Second Journey to Galilee (John 4, 6).* The disciples appear prominently in this first section. The journey consists of a general introduction (4:1–3), a sojourn in Samaria (4:4–42), the arrival in Galilee (4:43–45), a series of miraculous signs (4:46–54; 6:1–15; 6:16–21), and a long conversation with the Galilean multitude that has followed him since his arrival (6:22–71). The disciples are mentioned in the unit on Samaria, in the last two signs, and at the very end of the conversation.[32]

Within the Samaritan story, the disciples play a minor but important role. Their journey into town to buy food, reported indirectly through the aside of 4:8, not only allows the conversation at the well between Jesus and the Samaritan woman to proceed without interruption (vv. 7, 9–26) but also paves the way directly for Jesus' subsequent exchange with them regarding the proper meaning and nature of "food" (vv. 31–38).

In the course of this exchange, both misunderstanding and a broader lack of understanding are quite evident on the part of the disciples. To begin with, the disciples clearly misunderstand the intended level of Jesus' discourse: they fail to see that Jesus' food is none other than the mission entrusted to him by the Father (v. 34). In addition, it is clear both from their initial astonishment and their given silence upon their return from town (v. 27) that the disciples fail to grasp altogther the fundamental meaning and significance of the witnessed encounter. It is Jesus who must tell them: the encounter is part of the mission given to him (vv. 37, 38b); they themselves are called to take an active part in this mission (v. 38) and thus to rejoice with him (v. 36); this mission of theirs is already very much at hand (v. 35).

The next two appearances of the disciples reveal a continuing lack of understanding on their part. Thus, for example, in 6:1–15 Jesus deliberately "tests" (πειράζων) the disciples on the subject of "feeding" the approaching crowds; in response, two of them affirm the impossibility of such a feeding on the grounds of either the cost involved ( = Philip) or the lack of available food ( = Andrew). In effect, the disciples fail the test because, despite their previous exchange with Jesus on the subject of "food," they do not see the present gathering in terms of mission.[33] Then, in 6:16–21, on their way back to Galilee, when they see Jesus walking on the sea and approaching the boat, their reaction is one of fear.

As in the case of 4:27, 31–38, where lack of understanding gives way to teaching, the disciples' failure is also immediately counterbalanced: in 6:1–15 they are assigned a role both before and after the feeding; they are asked to make the people recline (v. 10) and then to gather up the remaining fragments (vv. 12–13);[34] in 6:16–21, after Jesus' self-identification and exhortation, they welcome him into the boat (v. 21).

The last appearance of the disciples in this first section provides a direct counterbalance to these three successive examples of lack of understanding on their part. After the Galilean crowds completely reject Jesus' claims and abandon him (6:60–66),[35] the disciples,[36] who had remained completely in the background during the long and increasingly hostile conversation and are now addressed directly by Jesus, openly declare their intention to remain with him (vv. 67–68c), fully and explicitly accept the claims presented (v. 68d), and reaffirm their previous belief in him (v. 69).[37] The section thus ends with a sharp and dramatic contrast between large numbers of Jews (6:41, 52) who reject and a small group of elect who do believe.

*2–3. A Second and Third Journey to Jerusalem (John 5 and 7:1–9; 7:10— 10:42).* The circle of disciples is almost completely bypassed in the narrative during the course of Jesus' second and third visits to Jerusalem: they are not mentioned at all during the second journey (5, 7:1–9) and only once during the third (7:10—10:42), where they appear briefly at the very beginning of the second cycle of events within this journey (9:1–7).[38]

Within the miraculous sign that begins and largely controls this second cycle of events, the disciples are used very briefly (9:2–5) to introduce the

83

question of sin into the cycle. Once again, a lack of understanding is quite obvious on their part: their proposed association of physical blindness with sin (v. 2), despite the previous definition of sin as unbelief in 8:21–30 (a definition which they, too, have presumably heard), shows that they fail to grasp the real meaning of sin and thus remain very close indeed to the position held by the Pharisees themselves (v. 34).

In response, Jesus first calls directly into question their given conception of sin—later redefined once again as unbelief in vv. 39–41—and then proceeds to present the blind man to them as yet another occasion, despite the immediate danger involved, for his own mission (vv. 3, 5) as well as theirs (v. 4) to be made manifest.[39] Thus, the disciples have also failed to see the illness at hand in terms of the ongoing harvest.

4. *The Lazarus Cycle of Events (John 11:1—12:11).* After leaving Jerusalem for safety in the vicinity of Bethany beyond the Jordan (10:40–42), word comes to Jesus that Lazarus is dying (11:1–16). Thus, he returns to the immediate area of Jerusalem, Bethany (11:17–44), withdraws to Ephraim for safety (11:54), and then returns to Bethany once again (12:1–8).[40] In this section the disciples appear once, while the group is still in Bethany beyond the Jordan (11:5–16).[41]

When Jesus announces to them his decision to return to Judea, a conversation immediately ensues which reveals yet again the disciples' lack of understanding. Indeed, such failure to understand underlines every step of the conversation. To begin with, the disciples attempt to dissuade Jesus from undertaking the proposed journey because of the danger involved (v. 8); then, they directly misunderstand the nature of Lazarus's condition and consequently the very reason for the journey (v. 12); finally, when a decision is made (through Thomas) to follow him, it is clear that they have not yet grasped the real purpose for the journey but believe instead that it will lead to their own deaths (v. 16).

As in the previous case of 9:2–5, Jesus' responses directly counterbalance their failure to understand: the return, with all of the dangers involved, is presented once again in terms of the mission entrusted to him and to them (v. 9);[42] the fact of Lazarus's death is fully disclosed to them (v. 14); the journey, given its real purpose, is presented explicitly as an occasion for their own belief to develop further (v. 15)—that is, Lazarus's raising is meant to be an anticipation for his own approaching glorification.[43]

5. *The Final Journey to Jerusalem (John 12:12–50).* The second major stage comes to a close with Jesus' fourth and final journey to Jerusalem. The section consists of three main units: the triumphal entry (12:12–19); the proclamation of "the hour" (12:20–36a); a summary of the entire public

**84**

ministry (12:36b–43, 44–50). The disciples are mentioned indirectly in the first unit (12:16) and appear directly at the beginning of the middle unit (12:20–26). Both references continue the theme of lack of understanding on their part.

First of all, as in the earlier case of 2:17 and 22, the aside of 12:16 points out that it was only after Jesus' resurrection that the disciples were able to see the triumphal entry both as a prophetic action pointing to the events of "the hour" (19:19–22) and as a prophetic fulfillment of a text from Scripture (Zech. 9:9). Thus, once again, neither the ultimate reference of this entry to the events of "the hour" nor its own status as prophetic fulfillment is understood by them until after "the hour." In the second place, the hesitation shown by both Philip and Andrew with respect to the coming of the Greeks to see Jesus seems to indicate a failure to interpret such a request in terms of the mission or harvest.[44]

In response, Jesus first identifies for them this request from the Greeks as the beginning of "the hour" (v. 23). Then he proceeds to explain by means of two antithetical parallelisms that "the hour" necessarily involves his own death (vv. 24–25). He concludes by explicitly pointing out that the same possibility applies to all disciples (v. 26);[45] "serving" or "following" him may indeed demand and entail death: the believer, like Jesus, will be glorified by the Father and thus will be where Jesus is, that is, with the Father.[46]

6. *Summary*. First of all, in the second stage of the characterization, the contrast between the emergent group of disciples and the Jews of Jerusalem introduced in the first stage is considerably broadened and intensified. The earlier insufficient response recorded in the course of Jesus' first journey to Jerusalem is now clearly developed, with each subsequent journey to the city, into a series of outright rejections of his claims and direct attempts against his life (5:16–18; 8:59; 10:31; 12:27–36a). Outright rejection, but not violence, is also recorded among "the Jews" in Galilee (6:60–66). Yet in the midst of this sustained and mounting opposition, the circle of disciples continues to follow him and to reaffirm their earlier belief in him (6:67–71).

In the second place, it should be noted that the disciples' lack of understanding, first introduced in 2:13–22, is also considerably broadened and intensified in the course of the second stage, thus becoming, in effect, a major theme of the characterization. At the same time, however, this continuing failure to understand is also directly and systematically counterbalanced in the course of the stage.

This lack of understanding is variously portrayed in the narrative, where one finds: (a) another example of the disciples' inability to see a certain

**85**

event in terms of its ultimate reference to "the hour" and its own status as prophetic fulfillment prior to "the hour" (12:12–19); (b) an explicit reference to their need for further belief, specifically with respect to Jesus' glorification (11:5–16); (c) a repeated lack of awareness with respect to the mission and their own role in it (4:31–38; 6:1–15; 9:2–5; 11:5–16; 12:20–26); (d) a failure to understand the essentially christological meaning of sin (9:2–5); (e) a reaction of fear to a miraculous sign (6:16–21); (f) two instances of strict misunderstanding (4:31–33; 11:11–13).

The process of counterbalancing this sustained failure to understand is twofold. On the one hand, practically every instance in which lack of understanding is found gives way directly to further action or teaching on Jesus' part. Such action or teaching serves to place the pronouncement or event in question in its proper perspective. On the other hand, a scene in which the disciples reaffirm their earlier acceptance of Jesus' claims is given a highly climactic position within the stage (6:67–71). Nevertheless, it is quite clear that the disciples' perception of Jesus remains incomplete prior to "the hour" (12:12–19).

### The Farewell to the Elect and the Exclusion of "the World" (John 13—14)

Unlike the previous two stages, the third stage of the characterization is solely concerned with the circle of disciples. Three main units may be discerned, all of which take place during a meal in the city of Jerusalem: (1) the footwashing (13:1–20); (2) the identification and departure of the betrayer (13:21–30); (3) the farewell (13:31—14:31). In all three units the disciples' failure to understand continues to play a major role in the characterization.

Within the original version of the footwashing in the Gospel narrative (13:1a, 4–11),[47] the disciples (through Peter) fail to grasp altogether the real meaning of Jesus' action.[48] Then in the following unit, despite the earlier announcement of a betrayer (v. 21; see also vv. 10–11) and the immediate identification of Judas as the betrayer (vv. 22–26), the disciples clearly misunderstand the nature of Jesus' command to Judas (v. 27), failing to connect it altogether with the act of betrayal itself (vv. 28–29).[49] Finally, the disciples' individual responses and questions in the course of Jesus' farewell discourse show that, despite repeated explanations within the discourse itself, they fail to perceive entirely what Jesus' announced departure and return mean or entail;[50] indeed, their reaction of fear (14:1a, 27d) is specifically described as unbecoming (14:28).

The process of counterbalancing observed in the previous stage is very evident in this third stage as well, specifically in the first and third units, the footwashing and the farewell address. I have argued elsewhere that in its original version the washing is presented as a sign of Jesus' impending glorification and that it is precisely its character as a sign that the disciples are unable to comprehend.[51] At the same time, Jesus' responses to Peter make it quite clear that the disciples are already "clean" (= have already believed) except for the feet (= belief in the glorification; v. 10) and that such belief is impossible until after the glorification (v. 8). To some extent, therefore, the disciples' failure to understand in this unit is similar to the previous examples of 2:13–22 and 12:12–19.

In addition, the farewell discourse presents not only similar references to the certainty of future understanding on the part of the disciples but also a number of specific promises made to the disciples *qua* disciples. Thus, on the one hand, the discourse fully reaffirms the position that complete understanding is in fact impossible for the disciples prior to "the hour."[52] On the other hand, the discourse also extends various promises and privileges to the disciples for the time after "the hour."[53] In fact, one of these promises—the sending of another Paraclete—finally explains to the reader why the belief of the disciples cannot but remain incomplete prior to the completion of "the hour."[54]

In sum, the third stage may be said to continue and develop even further the central theme of the disciples' lack of understanding, as well as the closely related process of counterbalancing this given failure. However, a major difference may be noted between the second and third stages in the development of these two themes: quite unlike the second stage, in the third stage both themes are solely concerned with the events of "the hour"— that is, the meaning and nature of Jesus' departure and return.

The reason for this much narrower focus is not hard to ascertain: with the announced arrival of "the hour" at the conclusion of the second stage (12:20–26), the third stage may be seen as deliberately and exclusively centering on, developing, and counterbalancing that one aspect of the disciples' varied failure to understand from the second stage (11:5–16). Nevertheless, in the process of counterbalancing this much more precise focus, the fundamental reason for the disciples' observed general lack of comprehension is explicitly revealed: the Spirit has not yet been given.

Furthermore, despite the exclusive focus of this stage on the circle of disciples, the other central theme of the characterization—namely, the contrast with "the Jews"—is further continued and developed within it as well, specifically within the farewell address.

Thus, at the very beginning of the farewell (13:31–33, 36–38), the situation of the disciples after Jesus' departure is described as being quite unlike that of the Jews: whereas the latter will not find Jesus (v. 33; 7:23–26) and will die in their sin (8:21–24), the former are promised that they will indeed follow him at a "later" time. In addition, all of the subsequent promises made to the disciples in the discourse are also explicitly and repeatedly denied to "the world" (vv. 17b–d, 18–20, 22, 27a–c), a category which in the light of 13:31–33 can only mean the Jews. The contrast is perhaps best summarized by the designation accorded to the disciples in the discourse: "little children" (13:33).[55]

## The Vindication of the Elect and the Judgment of "the World" (John 18—20)

Four major sections may be discerned in the fourth and final stage of the characterization: (1) Jesus' arrest and appearance before the high priest (18:1–27); (2) Jesus' appearance before Pilate (18:28—19:16); (3) the death and burial (19:17–42); (4) the resurrection (20:1–29). John 20:30–31 provides a conclusion to the entire original Gospel narrative. The disciples appear sparingly in the first three sections (18:1–12) and rather prominently in the fourth (20:1–10, 11–18, 19–23, 24–29).[56]

In the first two of these units (18:1–12; 20:1–10), the disciples' failure to understand is once again quite obvious.[57] First of all, in the course of Jesus' arrest (18:1–12), Peter's armed resistance (v. 10), despite Jesus' repeated willingness to be apprehended (vv. 4–8b), shows that he (as well as the others) still does not realize what Jesus' "hour" means and entails and, in effect, tries to prevent it.[58] Similarly, the aside of v. 9 within the empty tomb story (20:1–12) makes it clear that neither Peter nor the Beloved Disciple (nor the others) connects either Mary Magdalene's report (v. 2) or their own findings at the tomb (vv. 4–7) with Jesus' previously announced glorification.[59]

As in the case of the second stage, the process of counterbalancing the disciples' incomprehension is twofold. Counterbalancing does take place within both of these units. With regard to 18:1–12, the aside of v. 9 explains, first of all, that Jesus' request that his disciples be allowed to go free is in keeping both with their status as the chosen ones and with the mission entrusted to him—namely, not to lose a single one of these chosen ones;[60] in addition, in the conclusion of v. 11c, Jesus explains after Peter's armed resistance that the arrest is also part of his mission. With regard to 20:1–10, Jesus specifically asks Mary Magdalene in the sequel of 20:11–18 to go and tell the disciples—who are now called his "brothers" (ἀδελφοί)—of his glorification and return to God the Father, who is now described as *their* God and Father as well.

Counterbalancing also takes place on a more general level through the first resurrection appearance of Jesus to his disciples (20:19–23).[61] In fact, counterbalancing at this point becomes correction: the unit serves to counterbalance not only the disciples' incomprehension within this stage but also to counterbalance and correct the disciples' incomprehension in all four stages.

It is through Jesus' appearance that the promises of the farewell discourse and of the Gospel narrative in general begin to be fulfilled: Jesus does return to his disciples (v. 19); he bestows upon them the Holy Spirit (v. 22), and extends to them his own function and role in and toward "the world". Their own mission is formally inaugurated (v. 21), and sin is now redefined in terms of this mission and this charge (v. 23). As a result, complete understanding concerning not only the events of "the hour" but also their own role after "the hour" is now possible for the disciples: thus, Jesus' return to them is now greeted with the proper attitude and reaction— namely, "joy" (v. 20b; cf. 14:28).[62]

In sum, it may be said that the fourth stage of the characterization continues to develop the interrelated themes of incomprehension and counterbalancing solely, as in the case of the third stage, with respect to the ongoing events of "the hour." A major difference, however, may be noted between the process of counterbalancing in this stage and that of the previous stages: with 20:19–23, counterbalancing becomes explicit and deliberate correction—that is, the fundamental reason for the disciples' incomprehension, previously disclosed in the third stage, is now explicitly corrected. Jesus bestows the Spirit upon the disciples.

As a result, the theme of incomprehension is completely reversed: finally the disciples do see the meaning and significance of "the hour" and do perceive Jesus' full status as God's unique representative. At this point in the narrative, therefore, both aspects of Jesus' programmatic promise of 1:50–51 begin to be fully developed: in the light of the "greater things" now revealed (= "the hour"), complete understanding on the part of the disciples also begins to take place.[63]

The theme of contrast is further developed in this fourth stage as well. Such contrast may be observed, first of all, at the scene of Jesus' arrest (18:1–12), where the disciples and the arresting crowd of chief priests and Pharisees stand opposite one another, but above all, in Jesus' resurrection appearance (20:19–23), where the disciples are said to be behind closed doors for fear of "the Jews" (v. 19) and are given the Spirit whom "the world" will never see, know, or receive.

## CONCLUSIONS

I have noted that previous studies on discipleship in the Johannine tradition have yielded—different approaches and perspectives notwithstanding— similar results with respect to certain fundamental aspects of this theme. I find that my study of the characterization of the disciples not only confirms but also further refines and sharpens these results as well: (1) to be sure, the narrative does present a sustained and deliberate contrast between disciples and nondisciples; (2) central, indeed exclusive, to this contrast in the narrative lies belief or acceptance of Jesus' claims vis-à-vis the Father; (3) in the development of the narrative, such belief is portrayed as necessitating and undergoing a process of gradual understanding and perception.

I have also noted that the reaction to the polemical view of the disciples' characterization within Markan scholarship was divided over the question of the possible historical applicability of such a characterization. Exactly the same question may be asked with respect to the portrayal of the disciples in the Fourth Gospel: Is such a characterization meant to be primarily literary in character, or does it presuppose and reflect as well a definite historical context?

Although proper caution should always be exercised in reconstructing community history from a gospel narrative, recent Johannine scholarship has shown that the search for such a historical context has been most useful and helpful in the interpretation of the Gospel narrative.[64] In what follows, therefore, I will examine the main aspects of discipleship delineated above—that is, the central themes of the disciples' characterization in the narrative—in terms of the *Sitz im Leben* they reflect and presuppose in the history of the Johannine community.

The first two main aspects of discipleship are very much interrelated: the narrative presents and develops a thorough and systematic contrast between the disciples as believers and all those who reject Jesus' claims. As the proposed outline for the characterization clearly shows, each stage serves to differentiate and separate further the circle of disciples from the unbelieving "world."

The very structure of the first stage of the characterization (John 1—3) introduces the contrast: whereas the disciples do perceive Jesus immediately not only in terms of traditional Jewish messianic expectations but also in terms of his status as God's unique representative, the subsequent journey to Jerusalem shows that no such understanding takes place among the Jews of Jerusalem, although no violence or outright rejection is recorded at this point.

In the second stage (John 4—12), the contrast is considerably intensified: while the disciples continue to follow Jesus and do reaffirm their belief in him, a series of journeys gives rise to outright rejection of his claims by the Jews of Galilee, as well as to repeated rejections of the claims and acts of violence by the Jews of Jerusalem. In the third stage (John 13—14), the contrast is extended to the period after "the hour" as well: unlike the Jews, the disciples are promised, as believers, that Jesus will return to them.

In fact, the farewell discourse contains a number of specific promises made to the disciples, all of which are directly associated with Jesus' return and are explicitly and repeatedly denied to the unbelieving "world."

The fourth stage of the characterization (John 18—20) brings to a distinct climax this process of differentiation and separation: immediately after the ultimate rejection of and violence against Jesus by the Jews in Jerusalem, his appearance to the disciples signals and begins not only the fulfillment of the earlier farewell promises but also the disciples' new perception of Jesus' full status as God's unique representative. At the same time, their reported attitude of fear toward the Jews at this point in the narrative clearly indicates that violence and rejection are by no means a thing of the past but continue past "the hour" as well.

Essential to the understanding of the historical and social factors behind this deliberate and sustained contrast, both prior to and after "the hour," between the circle of disciples and the unbelieving "world" is the precise identity of this latter term. It is clear, I believe, from every stage of the characterization that insufficient belief, outright rejection, and overt violence are consistently ascribed to "the Jews." Thus, although by definition the category "the world" would include anyone who rejects Jesus' claims,[65] in the narrative that category becomes practically synonymous with that of "the Jews" and thus gives rise to a very specific contrast between the believing disciples and the unbelieving Jews.

This systematic and thorough contrast between the disciples and the Jews points, in my opinion, to a Christian community or group of communities engaged in a process of self-definition and self-assertion over against a much larger Jewish "world." Different elements of the contrast help to delineate more precisely this process of self-definition.

Thus, the centrality of belief in the contrast points to a fundamental dispute concerning the validity of claims about Jesus' relationship with the Father. Similarly, the disciples' initial perception and acceptance of Jesus in terms of traditional Jewish messianic expectations show that the origins of the community as well as of the dispute are to be sought primarily in the synagogue itself. Finally, the violence ascribed to the Jews in the narrative, as well as the disciples' fear of the Jews after Jesus' death, indicate that the dispute was and continued to be a most bitter and acrimonious one.[66] In sum, a dispute that had its origins within the synagogue regarding claims concerning Jesus led to a bitter separation from the parent synagogue(s) and an ongoing, acrimonious confrontation with that parent synagogue(s).

Furthermore, the contrast also reveals a very strong and sharp hostility toward this larger Jewish "world": the Jews' ruler and father is said to be Satan, and they are pointedly denied all of the privileges which the community claims to possess, including access to the Father. At the same time, the community members clearly think of themselves as "the elect," those whom the Father has given to Jesus and whom Jesus has chosen. Both the community's antagonism toward "the world" and its profoundly exclusivistic self-conception point to a community which, undoubtedly on the basis of the circumstances surrounding its separation from and its ongoing confrontation with the synagogue, possesses a highly sectarian self-consciousness.[67]

The proposed social and historical factors underlying the first two aspects of the disciples' characterization are very similar indeed to those generally ascribed to the Gospel in contemporary Johannine scholarship: a prolonged and bitter confrontation between a Christian community and a parent synagogue(s) from which most of the former's present members have been forced to separate because of their belief in Jesus;[68] an elect community thoroughly alienated from "the world" and rejecting the values of that "world."[69] Thus, it may be said that the disciples' characterization in the narrative reflects, confirms, and reinforces the generally accepted *Sitz im Leben* of the Gospel.

These first two main aspects of discipleship are qualified to some extent by the third: although from the very beginning of the narrative the disciples are differentiated from "the world," and although belief in Jesus' claims constitutes the sole basis for such a separation, belief itself is presented as requiring and undergoing a process of gradual understanding and perception. This process, which consists of both a failure to understand and a direct counterbalancing of that failure, is developed in all stages of the characterization and presents several distinct foci.

The sole and initial failure of the disciples in the first stage to see a certain event in Jesus' ministry in terms of its reference to "the hour" is considerably broadened in the second stage to include—besides a similar example concerning another event in Jesus' ministry—misunderstandings, fear in response to a miraculous sign, a failure to see sin in the context of Jesus' mission, a persistent lack of awareness concerning their own call to and role in that mission, and a failure to grasp the fact, nature, and meaning of the approaching "hour." In the third and fourth stages, then, this last element becomes the exclusive focus of attention: despite the arrival and identification of "the hour," the disciples still fail to see and understand the nature and meaning of Jesus' glorification.

This consistent and varied failure to understand is directly counterbalanced in all stages of the characterization. The process of counterbalancing takes several distinct forms: (1) within units displaying incomprehension: further teaching or action on Jesus' part; explicit references to the fact that complete understanding is impossible prior to "the hour"; similar references to the effect that full understanding will and does take place after "the

92

hour"; (2) units that emphasize the understanding, albeit limited, of the disciples. One of these units, the first resurrection appearance, not only counterbalances but corrects all previous incomprehension as well: with the reception of the Spirit, the disciples finally see Jesus' full status as Son of God.

This third main aspect of discipleship sheds further light on the historical and social factors outlined above underlying the first two aspects of the characterization. My remarks are limited to what I consider to be the two most important elements within this third aspect: the disciples' failure to integrate the events of "the hour" into their belief prior to "the hour," and their persistent lack of awareness concerning their own role in the context of Jesus' mission.

First of all, since the disciples' failure to understand the nature and meaning of Jesus' departure and return is presented as unavoidable prior to "the hour" and the concomitant bestowal of the Spirit, their situation in the narrative in this regard can in no way presuppose and reflect directly a similar situation in the community at the time of writing. For the community it is clear that "the hour" has passed, the Spirit has been received and abides in the community, and Jesus' full status as God's unique representative has been grasped and accepted in spite of the momentous social consequences.[70]

I therefore propose that the disciples' failure to understand the events of "the hour" should also be seen in the context of the community's confrontation with the synagogue. This failure would then point to a fundamental issue in that confrontation: namely, the tremendous difficulty and substantial objection that Jesus' death on the cross represents for any claims concerning his origin, mission, and goal (see, e.g., 6:61–62; 12:30–31; 20:21). Yet at the same time, the narrative would also point to, reflect, and reinforce, in the face of rejection and active opposition, the community's conviction that it is precisely this event that constitutes the key to life, joy, and peace.

In the second place, since it is only at "the hour" and in conjunction with the bestowal of the Spirit that the disciples receive the formal mission charge from Jesus, their repeated lack of awareness in the narrative concerning their own call to and role in that mission can in no way presuppose and reflect directly a similar situation in the community at the time of writing. For the latter it is clear that they do represent and continue, under the tutelage of the Spirit, the mission entrusted to Jesus by the Father insofar as they continue to hold and present, regardless of the consequences, Jesus' claims to "the world."[71]

Once again, I propose that this lack of awareness should be seen in the context of the confrontation with the synagogue. This failure would then point, given the strong rejection and hostile opposition encountered in the course of the Jewish mission, to a certain despondency among the disciples and perhaps even to a growing reluctance to engage in such a task. At the same time, the narrative would also point to, recall, and reaffirm the community's conviction that its mission, like that of Jesus, must go on regardless of circumstances or consequences and must actively and deliberately reach out to Samaritans and Gentiles as well, because only through the mission will the sheep of all folds come to life, joy, and peace.

As the title for this study on discipleship, I have chosen Jesus' statement of 14:27 because I believe that its promise of "peace" reflects and captures very accurately the basic understanding of discipleship in both the community and its Gospel. Thus, on the one hand, the peace of the disciples is a peace which comes from knowing that *they and they alone* have and provide access to the Father through Jesus and the Spirit. On the other hand, this peace is also a peace which implies and entails rejection, open hostility, and even the possibility of death. It is, therefore, in every way possible, a peace "not of this world."

## NOTES

1. See, e.g., W. Kelber, *The Kingdom in Mark. A New Place and a New Time* (Philadelphia: Fortress Press, 1974); idem, "The Hour of the Son of Man and the Temptation of the Disciples (Mark 14:32–42)," in *The Passion in Mark* (ed. W. Kelber; Philadelphia: Fortress Press, 1976) 41–60; idem, *Mark's Story of Jesus* (Philadelphia: Fortress Press, 1979).

2. See, e.g., T. J. Weeden, Jr., "The Heresy that Necessitated Mark's Gospel," *ZNW* 59 (1968) 145–58; idem, *Mark—Traditions in Conflict* (Philadelphia: Fortress Press, 1971); idem, "The Conflict Between Mark and His Opponents Over Kingdom Theology," in SBLASP, 1973 (2 vols.; ed. G. MacRae; Cambridge, Mass.: Society of Biblical Literature, 1973) 2:203–41; idem, "The Cross as Power in Weakness (Mark 15:20b–41)," in Kelber, *Passion in Mark*, 115–34.

3. See, e.g., E. Best, "Discipleship in Mark: Mark 8.22—10.52," *SJT* 23 (1970) 323–37; idem, "The Role of the Disciples in Mark," *NTS* 23 (1976–77) 377–401; idem, *Following Jesus: Discipleship in the Gospel of Mark* (JSNTSup 4; Sheffield: JSOT Press, 1981).

4. See, e.g., R. C. Tannehill, "The Gospel of Mark as Narrative Christology," *Semeia* 16 (1979) 57–92; "The Disciples in Mark: The Functions of a Narrative Role," *JR* 57 (1977) 386–405.

5. In more recent times see, e.g., E. Schweizer, "Der Kirchenbegriff im Evangelium und den Briefen des Johannes," *SE* I (TU 73; Berlin: Akademie-Verlag, 1959) 363–81; J.-L. d'Aragon, "Le caractère distinctif de l'Église johannique," in *L'Église dans la Bible* (Studia 13; Paris: Desclée, De Brouwer, 1962) 53–66; C. F. D. Moule, "The Individualism of the Fourth Gospel," *NovT* 5 (1962) 171–90; H. van den Bussche, "L'Église dans le quatrième Évangile," in *Aux origines de l'église* (RechBib 7; Paris: Desclée, De Brouwer, 1964) 65–85; S. Pancaro, " 'People of God' in St. John's Gospel," *NTS* 16 (1967–68) 114–29; G. Baumbach, "Gemeinde

und Welt im Johannesevangelium," *Kairos* 14 (1972) 121–36; K. Haacker, "Jesus und die Kirche nach Johannes," *TZ* 29 (1973) 179–201; S. Pancaro, "The Relationship of the Church to Israel in the Gospel of John," *NTS* 21 (1975–76) 395–405; J. F. O'Grady, "Individualism and Johannine Ecclesiology," *BTB* 5 (1975) 227–61.

6. The term may be found seventy-eight times in the Fourth Gospel, forty-six in Mark, seventy-three in Matthew, and thirty-seven in Luke (as well as twenty-eight times in Acts). See R. Morgenthaler, *Statistik des neutestamentlichen Wortschatzes* (Zürich: Gotthelf-Verlag, 1958).

7. R. Moreno Jiménez, "El discípulo de Jesucristo, según el evangelio de S. Juan," *EstBib* 30 (1971) 269–311.

8. Ibid., 276–88.

9. Ibid., 288–311. Moreno Jiménez refers to this theological orientation as a "proyección teológico-trinitaria."

10. R. Schnackenburg, "Exkurs 17: Jünger, Gemeinde, Kirche im Johannesevangelium," in *Das Johannesevangelium* (3 vols.; HTKNT 4; Freiburg: Herder Verlag, 1967–75) 3:231–45.

11. Ibid., 3:233–37 and 237–41, respectively.

12. M. de Jonge, "The Fourth Gospel: The Book of the Disciples," in *Jesus: Stranger from Heaven and Son of God. Jesus Christ and the Christians in Johannine Perspective* (SBLSBS 11; Missoula, Mont.: Scholars Press, 1977) 1–27.

13. R. E. Brown, *The Community of the Beloved Disciple: The Life, Loves, and Hates of an Individual Church in New Testament Times* (New York: Paulist Press, 1979) 25–28.

14. Ibid., 71–88.

15. Moreno Jiménez, "El discípulo," 270–76; Schnackenburg, "Exkurs 17: Jünger, Gemeinde, Kirche," 3:233–36; de Jonge, "Fourth Gospel: Book of the Disciples," 12–17. See now in this regard the recent study by R. Alan Culpepper, *Anatomy of the Fourth Gospel. A Study in Literary Design* (Philadelphia: Fortress Press, 1983), esp. chap. 5: "Characters." Unfortunately, Culpepper's work reached me after the completion of the present study; for his treatment of the disciples, both as a group and as individuals, see 115–25 therein.

16. Tannehill, "Disciples in Mark," 388–89; see also David Rhoads and Donald Michie, *Mark as Story: An Introduction to the Narrative of a Gospel* (Philadelphia: Fortress Press, 1982) 101–3; David Rhoads, "Narrative Criticism and the Gospel of Mark," *JAAR* 50 (1982) 417–19.

17. See 2:2, 11–12, 17, 22; 3:22; 4:2, 8, 27, 31, 33; 6:3, 8, 12, 16, 22, 24; 9:2; 11:7–8, 12, 54; 12:4, 16; 13:5, 22–23; 18:1–2, 15–17, 25; 19:26–27; 20:2–4, 8, 10, 18–20, 25–26, 30. There are also references to other "disciples" or groups of "disciples": in 4:1 (with reference to 3:22–36) Jesus is said to have made and baptized (cf. 4:2) more "disciples" than John in the land of Judea; in 6:60–66 many of the "disciples" who had followed him in the land of Galilee (with reference, I believe, to 4:45; 6:2, 14–15, 22–24, 25) are said to abandon him because of the christological claims he is making; in 7:3, while seeking refuge in Galilee, his brothers ask him to go back to Judea and to show his signs to his "disciples" there (with possible reference to 2:23–25 and/or 3:22–24; 4:1); in 9:27–28 "disciples" of Jesus are alluded to by both the man who had been born blind and his questioners; in 19:38 Joseph of Arimathea is described as a secret "disciple" of Jesus. Thus, in

addition to the group that follows him, the term may also be used of those who accept his claims but do not follow (9:28), of secret believers (19:38), of those who can only go so far in accepting the claims (6:60–66), as well as of many whose precise response or status is impossible to ascertain (4:1; 7:3; 9:27; 18:19).

18. Thus, for example, on the basis of the preceding episode, five would seem to be present at Cana (2:1–11), and "the twelve" play a major role in Galilee (6:67–71). Different individuals are also singled out from the group: Andrew (1:35–40; 6:8–9; 12:22); Simon Peter (1:40–42; 6:68; 13:4–11, 24, 36–38; 18:10–11, 15–18, 25–27; 20:1–10); Philip (1:43–46; 6:5–7; 12:20–22; 14:8–11); Nathanael (1:45–51); Judas (6:70–71; 12:4–8; 13:21–30; 18:1–5); Thomas (11:16; 13:5–7); the beloved disciple (1:35–37[?]; 13:23–26a; 18:15–16[?]; 19:26–27; 20:1–10). Although each of these disciples may also be examined as an individual character, I believe that they are all, by and large, with the salient exception of Judas and to a lesser extent that of the beloved disciple as well, representative or typical of the entire group.

19. See, e.g., D. Moody Smith, "Johannine Christianity: Some Reflections on Its Character and Delineation," *NTS* 21 (1974–75) 222–48, esp. 235.

20. For the development of this exegetical position and its many variations, see F. F. Segovia, "The Theology and Provenance of John 15:1–17," *JBL* 101 (1982) 115–28; idem, "John 15:18—16:4a—A First Addition to the Original Farewell Discourse?" *CBQ* 45 (1983) 210–30.

21. F. F. Segovia, *Love Relationships in the Johannine Tradition: 'Αγάπη/'Αγαπᾶν in 1 John and in the Fourth Gospel* (SBLDS 58; Chico, Calif.: Scholars Press, 1982) 121–25, 129–31. See also idem, "The Structure, *Tendenz*, and *Sitz im Leben* of John 13:31—14:31," *JBL* (forthcoming: 1985).

22. F. F. Segovia, "John 13:1–20, The Footwashing in the Johannine Tradition," *ZNW* 73 (1982) 31–51.

23. This delimitation is already reflected in nn. 17 and 18 above, where all examples from these sections have been excluded.

24. See, e.g., R. E. Brown, *The Gospel According to John* (2 vols.; AB 29–29A; Garden City, N.Y.: Doubleday & Co., 1966) 1:cxxxviii.

25. The proposed outline also incorporates and reveals what I consider to be a fundamental aspect of discipleship in the Gospel: a thorough and systematic contrast of the disciples with their separation from an unbelieving and hostile "world." Thus, the title of each stage of the characterization includes the corresponding attitude of or toward "the world" within that stage.

26. To some extent, the action of "following" (ἀκολουθεῖν) becomes a *terminus technicus* for discipleship (1:37, 38, 40, 43; 8:12; 10:4, 5, 27; 12:26; 13:36, 37; 18:15); however, the term can also be used to refer to those who eventually reject Jesus' claims (6:2) as well as in a more neutral sense (11:31; 20:6).

27. For "glory" as Jesus' status as the Father's only Son, see, e.g., 1:14; 5:44; 12:41, 43. For the manifestation of "glory" through Jesus' signs, see also 11:4, 40.

28. This presence is confirmed by the information provided in the transition statement of 3:22: the disciples are portrayed as accompanying Jesus from Jerusalem to the land of Judea. From now on, I believe, the disciples should be seen as following Jesus wherever he goes, although their presence is not always explicitly acknowledged. See n. 17 above.

29. In addition to the *inclusio* mentioned above, this is another reason why I have

not included it in the second major stage of chaps. 4—12:there is no overt opposition or rejection during this first journey. Indeed, from quite a different perspective, this first journey may be said to be a foreshadowing of "greater things" to come as well. See n. 38 below.

30. Consequently, neither aspect of the promise of 1:50–51 mentioned above is fully developed until "the hour": neither the revelation of the "greater things" to come nor the disciples' full perception of what being the Father's unique representative means or entails.

31. The outline reflects an acceptance of the frequently encountered theory that John 6 originally preceded John 5 in the narrative, thus yielding an original sequence of chaps. 4, 6, 5, and 7. For a recent discussion of the literary problems involved and an acceptance of the displacement theory in the light of these problems, see R. Schnackenburg, *Das Johannesevangelium,* 1:34–35; 2:6–11. In the end, however, what original sequence one opts for does not affect in any major way the development of the characterization of the disciples.

32. The disciples are also mentioned in the general introduction of 4:1–3. In clear opposition to the information conveyed in the preceding unit (3:22–24), the aside of v. 2 explains that it was not Jesus but his disciples who baptized in the Judean countryside. In the light of this contradiction and the fact that their presumed baptismal activity is not pursued or developed elsewhere in the narrative, I accept the commonly held position that the aside represents a later addition to the text. See, e.g., C. H. Dodd, *Historical Tradition in the Fourth Gospel* (Cambridge: Cambridge Univ. Press, 1965) 285–86; D. Moody Smith, *The Composition and Order of the Fourth Gospel. Bultmann's Literary Theory* (New Haven, Conn.: Yale Univ. Press, 1965) 215 n. 5, 227.

33. Both the nature and purpose of Jesus' test, as well as the given response of the disciples in 6:1–15, should be seen, I believe, against the background of 4:31–38, especially given the close agreement between 4:35 and 6:5. The disciples fail to see the intended "feeding" in terms of Jesus' mission; they fail to realize, once again, that the fields are ripe for the harvest.

34. Again, in the context of 4:31–38, such roles should be seen as pointing to and anticipating the disciples' own call to active participation in the mission or harvest.

35. I take the μαθηταί mentioned in this section to refer to the crowds who have followed him in Galilee because of the signs (see n. 17 above) and who cannot accept the higher claims presented in the conversation of 6:22–66 (vv. 26, 30–31, 36, 41–42, 60–61, 62, 64, 66).

36. Quite unexpectedly, the disciples are now explicitly designated as "the Twelve" in this climactic scene; however, aside from 20:24, where Thomas is referred to as "one of the Twelve," the Twelve are not mentioned elsewhere in the narrative. Consequently, the μαθηταί who follow Jesus should in no way be limited to or even called "the Twelve." The latter group receives no specific or distinctive powers or tasks in this Gospel; indeed, its members are not even identified (with the exception of Peter, the spokesman in this scene; Judas, explicitly singled out as the betrayer; and Thomas). John 6:67–71 does imply that the Twelve do form part of the μαθηταί who follow Jesus.

37. Three rather important statements are made in 6:60–66 and 67–71 with respect to the disciples: (a) as believers (with the clear exception of Judas), they are

said to be "chosen" by Jesus (v. 70; vv. 64–65); (b) their acceptance of his claims as "words of eternal life" (v. 68) shows that they do not belong to the realm of "the flesh" but rather to that of "the life-giving Spirit" (v. 63); (c) verse 62 shows that there is another, far more scandalous claim that must also be accepted, namely, his coming glorification, but see already in this regard 2:13–22.

38. Both journeys lead to outright rejection and violent attempts against Jesus' life; furthermore, in both cases this violent hostility leads Jesus to seek safety away from the city. Thus, for example, the second journey gives rise to persecution and a desire to kill Jesus (5:16–18); safety is then sought in Galilee (7:1–9, esp. v. 1). Similarly, the third journey presents two largely independent cycles of events (7:10—8:59; 9:1—10:39) both of which give rise to violent attempts on his life (8:59; 10:31); safety is then sought in Bethany in the Transjordan (10:40–42; see esp. 11:8).

39. I believe that the readings ἡμᾶς δεῖ and πέμψαντός με are to be preferred on three counts: (a) somewhat superior attestation; (b) they constitute the *lectio difficilior* in the passage; (c) the proposed incorporation of the disciples into Jesus' own mission may be found elsewhere in the Gospel (e.g., John 4:31–38).

40. After each of these journeys, the scene shifts to Jerusalem (11:45–53; 11:55–57; 12:9–11) in order to describe the development of the plot to kill him in the city and thus prepare the reader for the tragic final journey to Jerusalem and its dramatic entrance into the city (12:12–19).

41. Judas does play a prominent part in 12:1–8; however, his objection and opposition to Jesus' action are in no way meant to be representative (see esp. vv. 4, 6).

42. Jesus' response of 11:9–10 is very similar to that of 9:3–5: the use of the indefinite pronoun τὶς in the conditional sentence of 11:10 shows that both missions are presupposed and included in this response as well.

43. The position of the disciples at this point in the narrative is quite similar to that of Martha and quite distinct from that of the attendant crowd (vv. 41–42): there is no question that she, too, accepts him as God's unique representative (v. 27), but her reaction at the tomb clearly shows that despite Jesus' earlier claims before her (vv. 23–26) belief does not yet include the very idea of death and resurrection (v. 39). For the disciples, therefore, the raising of Lazarus is meant to serve as a concrete preparation for Jesus' own glorification, a claim which they must also accept (v. 15; see also 2:13–22; 6:60–71, esp. v. 62).

44. Their reaction at this point is very similar to their previous reaction in 6:5–9 and consequently should also be seen against the background of 4:27, 31–38 (see n. 33 above): the disciples fail to see the coming of the Gentile proselytes to Jesus in terms of his—as well as their own—mission.

45. The remainder of the unit (12:27–36a) is not concerned at all with the disciples—or with the Greeks—but, rather, with the crowds that had witnessed or heard about the events at Bethany and had welcomed him into Jerusalem (11:18–19, 31, 33–37, 45–46; 12:9–11, 12–14, 17–19) and with their ultimate rejection of his claims. This rejection leads in turn to the very pessimistic summary of the ministry that follows (12:36b–43).

46. Although there have been earlier references to the dangers and difficulties connected with the mission of the disciples (e.g., 9:2–5; 11:5–16), this is the first explicit reference to the very real possibility of death in the mission.

47. See n. 22 above. As in the case of 13:34–35 and 15:1–17 (see nn. 20 and 21 above), I have argued that 13:1b–3, 12–20 presuppose and reflect the *Sitz im Leben* of 1 John, not that of the Gospel.

48. Peter is at first quite taken aback by Jesus' action, thus failing to understand the fundamental meaning of the washing (13:6b); this failure to understand is sharpened by his refusal to submit to the washing (13:8a); finally, faced with Jesus' severe threat of 13:8b, Peter proceeds to ask for a complete washing, again failing to understand—though from a different perspective—the character of the washing (13:9).

49. In this unit both the figure of the beloved disciple and the closely related theme of what appears to be a deliberate contrast between this figure and Peter (and thus, ultimately, with the others as well) are explicitly encountered in the narrative for the first time. (Both the figure and the contrast would already be present in 1:35–42 if the unnamed disciple were to be identified—as I believe he should be—as the Beloved Disciple.) To some extent the Beloved Disciple is representative of the group: it is clear from v. 28 that he himself, like all the others, misunderstands Jesus' command. (His appearance in 1:35–42 would also be representative insofar as his perception of Jesus would be no different than that of the others prior to 2:1–11.) To some extent, however, as the contrast does show, he is not representative. See n. 18 above. In the present study I should like to concentrate on the common characteristics rather than on the contrast itself. Finally, not only is Judas Iscariot explicitly identified as the betrayer in this unit, but his exit serves several important functions in the narrative: (a) it is a reminder that "the hour" has indeed arrived (13:30b); (b) it separates him completely from the other disciples; (c) it allows the farewell address with all of its promises to be delivered to the true circle of disciples.

50. First of all, Peter's two responses show that he has no idea whatever as to what Jesus' departure entails or where it is that he proposes to go (13:36–38). Second, after Jesus has identified the Father as "the whereto" of his journey and then proceeds to tell the disciples that they do know "the way" to where he is going, Thomas responds that they do not know "the whereto," much less "the way" (14:5). Third, a further identification of the Father as "the whereto" and of Jesus as "the way" leads Philip to ask for a vision of the Father (14:7). Finally, after Jesus' return and the sending of the Spirit to them have been explicitly announced, the other Judas asks how it is possible for Jesus to manifest himself only to them and not to "the world" (14:22).

51. Segovia, "John 13:1–20, 'The Footwashing,'" 31–35, 42–45. Jesus' action is closely tied to the theme and the events of "the hour": it is performed with the knowledge that "the hour" has come (v. 1a); it cannot be understood until the events of "the hour" have passed (v. 7); without it, a disciple can have no part of Jesus (v. 8).

52. First of all, within the introductory subsection (13:31–33, 36–38), Peter is told that he will indeed follow Jesus at a "later" time (v. 36). Second, within the subunit on departure (14:4–14), the disciples are told that "from now on" they have seen and do know the Father (v. 7). Third, within the subunit on return (14:15–27), the disciples are also told that "on that day" they will know that Jesus is in the Father (v. 20) and that they will "live" as he does (v. 19). Finally, within the concluding subsection (14:28–31), Jesus is said to tell the disciples about the impending

events so that, when they do take place, they may believe (v. 29). See also n. 54 below.

53.The disciples are told that they will be able to perform Jesus' own works and even greater works (v. 12); that they will be granted any request made in Jesus' name (vv. 13–14); that they will be given the Paraclete, the spirit of truth, who will stay with them forever (vv. 16–17a, 25–26); that they will be loved by both Jesus (v. 21c) and the Father (vv. 21b, 23c); that they will receive Jesus' self-revelation (v. 21c); and that they will become an abiding place for both Jesus and the Father (v. 23d).

54. All of the promises coalesce around that of the Paraclete. It is the Paraclete who will teach the disciples all things and will recall for them all that Jesus himself said to them (14:26–27). Belief and understanding on their part are thus necessarily incomplete prior to "the hour" and its concomitant bestowal of the Spirit. See also in this regard Jesus' declaration of 7:37–38 to the Jews of Jerusalem and the explanatory aside of 7:39.

55. According to 1:12, the children of God (τέκνα θεοῦ) are those who believe in Jesus and were begotten by God. On the other hand, the Jews, as those who reject Jesus' claims, may be said to be the children of Satan (8:39–48), who is, in effect—according to the discourse—the ruler of "the world," viz., those who will not find Jesus (13:33) and to whom the promises are completely denied (14:17b–d, 18–20, 22, 27a–c), i.e., the Jews.

56. In 18:13–27, Peter and an unnamed disciple, whom I take to be the Beloved Disciple, are portrayed as following Jesus to the house of the high priest after the arrest. However, neither the action of following nor the information given concerning the figure of the Beloved Disciple (which introduces the theme of contrast once again) nor Peter's denial (a fulfillment of 13:38) may be said to be representative of the group. Similarly, in 19:25–27 neither the figure nor the function of the Beloved Disciple at the cross is meant to be representative of the group. See nn. 49 and 18 above.

57. As in all previous appearances (1:35–42; 6:67–71; 13:1a, 4–11; 13:21–30, 31–33, 36–38), I take the figure of Peter in both of these units to be representative of the reaction and/or attitudes of the wider group. See nn. 18, 36, 48, 49, and 50 above. See, however, n. 56 above with regard to what I consider to be his atypical role in 18:13–27. Likewise, as in all previous appearances (6:67–71; 12:1–8; 13:21–30), Judas Iscariot is completely and explicitly differentiated from the others; indeed, 18:5 is particularly dramatic in this regard: during the arrest proceedings Judas is portrayed as standing with the crowd and facing Jesus and the circle of disciples. See nn. 18, 36, 37, 41, and 49 above.

58. This is the third time that Peter's response amounts (unknowingly) to a rejection of Jesus' "hour": in 13:8a he refuses to submit to the washing, thus bringing about a severe threat from Jesus (13:8b); in 13:37 he will not allow Jesus to depart without him, thus bringing about Jesus' prophetic statement concerning Peter's subsequent, threefold denial (13:38); in the present unit, Peter will not allow Jesus to be apprehended, thus giving rise to the rebuke of 18:11a.

59. As in the case of 2:13–22 and 12:12–19, the aside of v. 9 also shows that the disciples fail to see the events at the tomb in terms of prophetic fulfillment. To the extent that he, like Peter, does not understand at first either Mary Magdalene's discovery or his own findings at the tomb, the Beloved Disciple may be said to be

representative of the group. To the extent that he does understand precisely what has happened upon actually entering the tomb (20:8), he is not, and the contrast theme appears in the narrative once again. See nn. 18, 49, and 56 above.

60. The theme of the disciples as the chosen ones has already been encountered in 6:60–66, 67–71 (vv. 64–65, 70). See n. 37 above. The request is also presented as a prophetic fulfillment of a previous declaration of Jesus (e.g., 6:39, 10:28; see also 17:12, but this reference lies within the problematic chaps. 15–17 of the farewell discourse).

61. The second resurrection appearance (20:24–29) also concerns the circle of disciples; however, the main focus of the story is Thomas, who, given his absence at the time of the first appearance and his refusal to accept the testimony of his fellow disciples (vv. 24–25), is in no way representative of the group at this point in the narrative. Rather, as the climactic macarism of 20:29 indicates, Thomas now becomes representative of a different group altogether, namely, those who have not witnessed Jesus' return but are asked to accept it on the testimony of others.

62. Both their new understanding and their mission charge may already be seen at work in their immediate declaration to Thomas upon his return: "We have seen the Lord." (20:25).

63. See n. 32 above. Given the earlier promise of the Paraclete and his specific functions within the community of the disciples (14:25–26), the promise may be said to be programmatic as well for the period after "the hour": full development implies and entails the activity of recalling and interpreting anew, under the tutelage of the Paraclete, previous events and sayings in the light of the disciples' new perception of Jesus' full status as God's unique representative.

64. The works of J. L. Martyn (*The Gospel of John in Christian History: Essays for Interpreters* [TI; New York: Paulist Press, 1978]; and *History and Theology in the Fourth Gospel* [2d ed., rev. enl.; Nashville: Abingdon Press, 1979]) and Brown (*Community of the Beloved Disciple*) are, in my opinion, foremost in this regard.

65. For "the world" as the realm of active unbelief, see (in addition to its usage in the farewell discourse: 14:17, 19, 22, 27, 30, 31) 1:10c–11; 3:19; 7:4, 7; 8:23; 12:31; 18:36. For the position that "the world" also actively includes the Gentiles, see Brown, *Community of the Beloved Disciple*, 63–66; however, although anyone who does not believe is part of "the world," the fact remains that rejection by a Gentile is limited to Pilate in the narrative. Indeed, all of the above examples have an immediate Jewish context or reference.

66. This ongoing confrontation is also reflected in the teaching of 12:26; see n. 46 above. One of the later additions to the farewell discourse (John 15:18—16:4a) is meant to deal precisely with the continuation of this confrontation and its immediate effects on the circle of disciples; see F. F. Segovia, "John 15:18—16:4a—A First Addition," 225–30.

67. On alienation from and hostility toward "the world" as the main criteria for sectarianism, see B. R. Wilson, "An Analysis of Sect Development," in *Patterns of Sectarianism: Organisation and Ideology in Social and Religious Movements* (ed. B. R. Wilson; London: Wm. Heinemann, 1967) 22–45; idem, *Magic and the Millennium. A Sociological Study of Religious Movements of Protest Among Tribal and Third-World Peoples* (New York: Harper & Row, 1973) 9–30.

68. See, e.g., Martyn, *Gospel of John in Christian History*, 90–121; Brown, *Community of the Beloved Disciple*, 58–91.

69. See, for example, W. A. Meeks, "The Man from Heaven in Johannine Sectarianism," *JBL* 91 (1972) 44–72; Smith, "Johannine Christianity"; Segovia, *Love Relationships,* 204–13.

70. This is not to say that there is no further growth in perception and understanding within the community: both the tasks assigned to the Paraclete within the circle of the disciples and the self-reflections of the community in 2:13–22 and 12:12–19 clearly point in the opposite direction. See n. 63 above. Indeed, the entire literary posthistory of the Gospel should be seen in terms of this ongoing process of growth in perception and understanding.

71. In a previous work (*Love Relationships*, 204–19) I described, using Wilson's ideal typology (see n. 67 above, *Patterns of Sectarianism*), the Johannine community as a sectarian group with a predominantly introversionist orientation. Despite the fact that mission now emerges as a primary interest in the life of the community and the lack of a sense of mission in many introversionist sects, I still believe that this description remains fundamentally correct. First of all, the community, at least at the time of writing, should not be seen as a primarily conversionist group: the presupposition seems to be that not everyone can undergo a change of heart or perception. Second, mission within a predominantly introversionist perspective may be understood quite readily in terms of gathering "the sheep" out of "the world."

# 5

# Kenotic Imitation of Paul and of Christ in Philippians 2 and 3

## WILLIAM S. KURZ, S.J.

In many treatments of the Letter to the Philippians, few have given much attention to a very significant pattern in chapters 2 and 3 which proposes for imitation Christ's and Paul's parallel examples of renunciation of their own prerogatives.[1] Two methodological reasons and one presupposition seem to be especially responsible for this lack of attention in the literature. The approaches to Philippians 2 and 3 have been predominantly source and form criticism focused on the isolated Christ hymn in 2:6–11, as well as source criticism of the whole letter resulting in the currently dominant, multiple-letter hypothesis, with chaps. 2 and 3 belonging to fragments of different letters. With such emphases, it would be surprising if many would notice a parallelism between chaps. 2 and 3.

The presupposition that has contributed to neglect of this pattern of parallel imitation of Christ and of Paul is a fundamental bias against imitation of Christ in such seminal studies as W. Michaelis's *TDNT* article on *mimēsis* and E. Käsemann's analysis of the Christ hymn.[2]

### BEYOND SOURCE AND FORM CRITICISM

The methodological failure of form- and source-critical approaches to account for the present form and context of the canonical Letter to the Philippians raises the question whether Pauline studies need the same kind of methodological developments that have benefited research into the Synoptic Gospels and Acts. Recent approaches to the Synoptics and Acts have uncovered theological riches that had gone unnoticed during the earlier scissors-and-paste approach of exclusively form and source criticism. Redaction and composition criticism now focus on the whole Gospel (or the whole of Luke-Acts), including infancy narratives and postresurrection sequels that were once thought to be less amenable to synoptic comparison and source analysis. Study of the context of the entire work in its canonical form, its overall literary structure, and the narrative story line in which individual pericopes have been situated has clarified the literary and theological richness and individuality of Matthew, Mark, and Luke-Acts.

This study suggests that it is time for a similar move beyond form and source approaches to Philippians and other letters of the Pauline corpus. Even for letters that are held to be combinations of independent letter fragments (like 2 Corinthians and Philippians), their final "redacted" forms as they appear in the manuscript tradition and Christian canon need to be studied. If New Testament Gospel studies have anything to teach about method, they suggest the inadequacy of purely source explanations and scissors-and-paste approaches and the likelihood that the final redactor of the work had some personal literary and theological sensitivity and purposes. If someone so carefully interwove fragments of three of Paul's letters to the Philippians, as many suggest, then that person saw some overall purpose and unity to the finished product. This deserves explanation.

The letter as it now stands can be expected to have a message that goes beyond whatever purposes any possible fragments might have had. Ironically, the original occasions which scholars today work so hard to reconstruct proved to be a problem for the first-century churches that gathered Paul's letters into a collection.[3] Some of the original situations were not applicable to other or later churches. But the gathering of Paul's letters (whether into composite letters or as corpus of letters) provided the churches with a broad sample of Paul's pastoral responses to a variety of situations, which by being read together could give later churches insights on how Paul might answer their problems. If Philippians is a composite letter, it seems a priori likely that its major message would go beyond the purposes of its sources, as the theology of the Gospel of Luke goes beyond the traditions and sources it contains. Thus, the letter as it now stands (and as part of the Pauline letter corpus) gives strong encouragement in *any* situation of persecution, trials, and internal difficulties, and threats to sound teaching.

Further, for the history of exegesis and theology at least until the Enlightenment, and for the use of Paul's letters in the church's life, it has been the final canonical form of Philippians (the only form in the manuscript tradition) that is important and authoritative, not hypothetical, reconstructed sources or letter fragments. The lack of genuine unanimity among scholars on the details of these reconstructions and on most of the form- and source-critical questions pertaining to Philippians seems to add another reason for a renewed focus on the final, redacted canonical form for church life and use.[4]

My purpose here will be to apply some of these more redactional- and compositional-critical approaches to Philippians 2—3 in the context of the final form of the letter. It will argue that the present form of Philippians 2—3 is centered on the pattern of imitation of both Christ and of Paul in their self-emptying of prerogatives.

The imitation of Christ is indeed a central focus in the exhortation of Phil. 1:27—2:18.[5] The heart of this exhortation is the Christ hymn in 2:6–11, which in this context functions as an example of surrendering one's own prerogatives and letting God do the exalting. The section begins with a call for unity to a church facing persecution and sharing in Paul's sufferings on Christ's behalf (1:27–30). Philippians 2:1–4 then exhorts the community to have one mind: avoiding competition and vainglory, considering others better than themselves, and looking to the interests of others rather than just of themselves. The meaning of Phil. 2:5 is hotly debated, but the easiest reading in this overall context goes in the direction of the New American Bible: "Your attitude must be that of Christ."[6] This command to have a certain attitude in 2:5 further specifies those in 2:2 and will be echoed again in 3:15, 3:19, and 4:2 (for Euodia and Syntyche). The pattern of Christ Jesus is one of emptying himself and humbling himself in obedience even unto death on a cross (2:6–8). In response, God has exalted him to Lord of all "to the glory of God the Father" (2:9–11).

Philippians 2:12 follows from the example of Christ in 2:6–11: "for this reason, therefore" (ὥστε),[7] as they have always obeyed, so now they are to work out their salvation without grumbling and questioning, which destroy community harmony (2:12–15; cf. the rebellious Israelites in the desert). Thus, the overall immediate context for the Christ hymn is an exhortation to community harmony and unity through avoiding competitive self-promotion.

Philippians 3 offers a similar example of Paul's letting go of his own Jewish prerogatives in hope of being exalted in the resurrection, in a context at least initially dominated by the divisiveness of judaizers. Judaizing "mutilators" were tempting the Philippians to "trust in the flesh" (3:2–3). Paul responds with his own example of refusing to trust in the flesh through Jewish credentials, even though his Jewish credentials were the best (3:4–6). Trusting in the flesh at the beginning of chap. 3 clearly refers to desiring Jewish credentials and prerogatives through judaizing practices.

The verb ἡγοῦμαι provides an important verbal link from 3:7–8 back to 2:6.[8] As Christ in 2:6 did not "count" it something to be seized/clung to (οὐχ ἁρπαγμὸν ἡγήσατο) to be like God but emptied himself, so Paul now "counted" (ἥγημαι and ἡγοῦμαι) what had been his gain (his Jewish prerogatives) as loss, compared to knowing Christ without any judaizing justification on his own (3:7–11).

Thus, the pattern of imitating both Christ and Paul in their respective self-emptying of personal prerogatives dominates the central chaps. 2—3 in the present form of Philippians. This imitation pattern in Philippians 2—3 recalls Paul's call in 1 Cor. 11:1, "Be imitators of me, as I am of Christ." In chap. 2, Paul calls for community harmony through humility and the kenotic model of Christ. In light of chap. 2, Paul's self-emptying response to the judaizing threat in 3:2–11 has the appearance of imitating Christ's kenosis in the specific situation of judaizing. Since it follows the examples of Christ and of Paul in chaps. 2—3, Paul's call to be "imitators of me" (συμμιμηταί μου) in 3:17 has almost the same force as his call in 1 Cor. 11:1 to imitate him as he imitates Christ. This is true from the context, whether the phrase itself means that the Philippians should all together be imitators of Paul or should join him in being imitators of Christ.[9]

The argument to establish this thesis, that the present form of Philippians 2—3 provides a parallel pattern of imitation of both Christ and of Paul in their self-emptying of prerogatives, will have the following main steps: (1) to show the central importance of imitation in first-century exhortation with the help of previous studies; (2) to study the explicit calls to imitation in Phil. 2:5–8 and 3:17 (with 4:9) in their contexts and within the overall structure of the letter as a whole; (3) to confirm the thesis by briefly showing how two patterns in Phil. 2:1—4:2 also appear in other Pauline texts—(a) self-kenosis and subsequent exaltation, and (b) the ABA structure common to Phil. 2:3—4:2 and 1 Corinthians 8—10 and 12—14—and by recalling the vocabulary clusters that link the calls to imitation in Philippians 2 and 3.

## THE IMPORTANCE OF IMITATION OF EXAMPLES IN FIRST-CENTURY PARENESIS

In his unpublished dissertation of 1982, Benjamin Fiore gathers an extensive bibliography of secondary literature and collection of primary sources which document the critical importance of imitating personal examples in first-century exhortation, in rhetorical, philosophical and religious teaching, and in Paul.[10] Fiore demonstrates the importance of personal examples for imitation in such diverse sources as rhetorical treatises; handbooks and *chria;* hortatory literature; kingship literature by Isocrates, Plutarch, and Dio Chrysostom; official letters; philosophical and ethical hortatory letters by Seneca and others; the Socratic letters; the pastoral epistles; and Paul's letters.[11]

Greco-Roman pedagogical principles especially emphasize that the role of the teacher is not only to instruct by his words but to be an example of what he teaches. Thus, for example, Isocrates says, "And the teacher . . . must in himself set such an example of oratory that the students who have taken form under his instruction and are able to pattern after him will . . .

show in their speaking a degree of grace and charm which is not found in others."[12] Quintilian and Cicero have similar understandings of the teacher's role in the first century. Quintilian stresses the character of the teacher and the nonacademic cast of that relationship, for the teacher is to act *in loco parentis* and with a parental attitude.[13] Fiore concludes:

> This education by example (*non auribus modo, verum etiam oculis*) looks to various individuals for models; but the *parent's role is crucial* in proposing them when urging that some vice be avoided or that some course be chosen. The parents might propose someone from the family's ancestors as example, or might, like a rhetoric teacher in more institutionalized and technical education, be examples themselves.[14]

D. Stanley, W. P. De Boer, P. Gutiérrez, and others argue that the basis of Paul's call to imitate him (as in Gal. 4:12 and Phil. 3:17 and 4:9) is his special relationship as founding father of the community (1 Cor. 4:16).[15] Imitation is often linked with fatherhood, whether of God as father, one's ancestors or natural father, or teachers of noble living. The last category combines father and teacher and lies behind Paul's example (1 Cor. 4:15 and 17).[16]

Gutiérrez highlights these important uses of the image of fatherhood in the ancient Orient and during the Hellenistic period. "Father" is always a title of honor, signifying a sharing in God's life-giving activity and an immortalizing of oneself by projecting one's own existence on others. Calling someone "father" generally indicates some kind of dependence, unless it degenerates into formalism. The most common use for the image of fatherhood is the comparison of teaching activities to paternal duties. It envisages not merely formal teaching but the total formation of the disciple.

Another important first-century use of the fatherhood metaphor was by wisdom traditions. Because in the east wisdom and knowledge of life were passed on from father to son, sages were viewed as fulfilling a paternal function. The father was responsible for the total education of his children in the "way" that leads to a long, happy life. Upbringing had a religious dimension in its ideal of the just man walking in God's ways. Given this task, the sage viewed his disciples as his sons, and the more this way of wisdom encompassed the total religious life of the disciple, the more profound was the notion of pedagogical fatherhood. Both the Qumran and the New Testament texts indicate these ideas were current in Judaism in Paul's time. In addition, Philo of Alexandria attests the Hellenistic notion of teaching activity as analogous to giving life when he describes guides to perfection as fathers.[17]

Fiore shows the link in 1 Corinthians between exemplifying a way of life to be imitated and making that way explicit with precepts. That letter uses αἱ ὁδοί for Paul's way of life (1 Cor. 4:17; cf. 7:17; 11:16; 14:33, 36).

Precepts that make that way explicit appear at 1:10, 31; 3:21; 4:1, 5, 16; 5:9, 12–13; 6:18, 20; 7; 8:9; 10:10, 12; and many others. The letter also uses more general didactic reminders, such as the οὐκ οἴδατε ("Do you not know?") formula. Example puts life into the content and conduct of Christian life which precept and instruction delineate.[18]

This imitation focused especially on central attitudes of the Christian message, not on peculiarities of Paul's life.[19] In 1 Cor. 8—11:1, Fiore shows one of these central attitudes to be a self-effacement on behalf of "weaker" members of the community (esp. 11:1 specified by 10:31–33; cf. 9:19–23). This corresponds to Paul's own kerygmatic method in 1:26–29 and 2:1–5. The opening chapters of the letter help clarify what "as I am of Christ" in 11:1 means. In 2:3, Paul says he limited his knowledge to the crucified Jesus Christ and thus identified with the "weak" (like the Corinthians in 1:26–27). His kerygma was not in Greek wisdom but divine power (2:4–5). His own attitude in this was a pattern for the community (3:18–19), as also his example of voluntary curtailment in 9:19. Paul identified the word of the cross with the gospel (1:17), which was a proclamation of God's power.[20]

This illustrates the basic Pauline pattern that God's power is seen in human weakness, which fits both Christ's and Paul's examples in Philippians 2 and 3. In 1 Corinthians, for instance, Paul rejects the use of wisdom in preaching and in Philippians and Galatians the use of righteousness through the law, in order to rely on God's power alone. Philippians 2 applies this power-in-weakness pattern to Christ letting go his prerogative to be like God and letting God exalt him to be Lord. Philippians 3 shows the same pattern in Paul's example of letting go his Jewish prerogatives that he may know the power of Christ's resurrection.

Fiore isolates important elements and the form which Paul's exhortations to imitate his example share with other exhortations of his day. The use of both positive and antithetical examples was very important in exhortation. Paul contrasted himself and his teaching to people disturbing his churches (Gal. 1:10—2:21; 4:12–16; 5:11–26; 6:14–15; Phil. 3:3—4:1). Unlike the normal practice in exhortation of describing opponents as general types, Paul usually attacked specific known enemies, exposing their tactics and rejecting them directly (Gal. 1:6–9; 4:17; 5:7–10; 6:12–13; Phil. 3:2). Philippians 3:18–19 is the only text that stereotypes the negative examples (which is why mirror-reading to opponents there has led many exegetes astray). But 3:18–19 sets the stereotyped negative examples against an explicit call to imitation (3:16–17); the *context* is specific[21] and enables identification of these examples as judaizing enemies of Christ's cross who put stock in the flesh (3:2–4), versus those like Paul who did not trust in the flesh (3:4–11) but only in the cross. Other kinds of negative examples may be found in 1 Cor. 8:9–13 (harmful effects of bad human examples);

10:1–11 (the negative scriptural example of the wilderness generation—cf. 11:29–30); and 16:15–18 (the positive example of Stephanas and others).[22]

Philippians 3:12–16 uses another common approach in exhortations to imitate a teacher or leader. It is one of *synaskesis,* a call to imitate and share in the teacher's own striving for the perfection which he has not yet reached. It makes the call to imitate oneself seem a little less arrogant. Paul's claim to perfection in Judaism (3:4–6) had been already relativized in the light of Christ and his death (3:7–11). Christ and his cross lay behind Paul as model: "Allusion to the exemplary attitude of Christ was already made at 2:5 while the suffering first appears at 1:29–30 (here the word ἀγών is used)."[23]

Paul does not consistently use the common practice of filling out his example by virtue and vice lists and prescriptions.[24] Regarding the common use of both explicit and implicit examples, Paul explicitly calls for imitation of his example at Gal. 4:1–20 and Phil. 3:12—4:1. Philippians is unique in bolstering commands to rejoice (2:18; 3:1; 4:4) with the implicit example of Paul's joy in the most trying circumstances (1:4, 18; 4:10).[25]

Like the Socratic epistles, Paul uses other members of the community besides himself as examples, but their example is in explicit relationship to his example. Thus, in 1 Corinthians, Apollos's example is subordinate to Paul's and that of Stephanas is derivative from Paul's. Though Paul mentions the example of the suffering Judean churches in 1 Thess. 2:14, he quickly adds his own at 2:16, which echoes 1:7 where he mentions himself and Christ explicitly. Philippians 3:17b points to others insofar as they walk according to Paul's model, which 3:17a calls the readers to imitate.[26]

Let us end this consideration of the importance of imitation in first-century exhortation with Fiore's listing of the range of hortatory devices in Philippians 3. This passage resembles the Socratic and pastoral letters and other hortatory works "as it elaborates its exhortation with the cluster of devices specified for the development of the *chria.*"[27] These devices are negative example (vv. 2–4a), Paul's example (vv. 4b–11), a racing metaphor (vv. 12–14), the correct attitude (v. 15a), promise of its proof (v. 15b), restatement (v. 16), command (v. 17), contrast (vv. 18–19), gnomic saying and its elaboration (vv. 20–21), and concluding command (4:1).[28] But the aim of Philippians 3 is not purely hortatory. It includes polemic against false teachers and reasserts Paul's own authority.[29]

## CALLS TO IMITATION IN THE OVERALL LETTER CONTEXT

A major difference in a redaction and composition approach, from the usual form- and source-critical studies of passages from Philippians, is the importance of the structure and context of the *whole* letter for interpreting each passage. For the structure of ancient letters, this study will utilize the consensus in American scholarship.[30] Particularly significant is the function of the epistolary thanksgiving in foreshadowing the major themes and topics of the letter as a whole through vocabulary and other hints.[31]

Even if Philippians is a redacted letter, the thanksgiving section (1:3–11), as read in the light of the complete present form of the letter, does contain hints and verbal links with most of the complete letter, and thus provides a context for understanding chaps. 2 and 3. The note of joy in 1:4 is a striking characteristic running throughout the letter (1:4, 18, 25; 2:2, 17–18, 28–29; 3:1; 4:1, 4, 10). This joy is often an eschatological kind of joy in the midst of suffering or conflict (cf. esp. 1:17–18 with 3:1–2 and 4:1: joy in the same context as preachers Paul opposes).[32] The Philippians' "fellowship" with Paul for the gospel in 1:5 is re-echoed in his thanksgiving for their gift in 4:15 (cf. 2:1). The expressions "from the first day" (1:5) and "the one who began" (1:6) are recalled by "in the beginning of the gospel" (4:15). The notion of God "completing" at the day of Christ the good work begun in the Philippians (1:6) has echoes in "the day of Christ" of 2:16 and in 3:12–14, which emphasizes that Paul is not yet perfect (cf. 3:14 and 20).

The expression "to feel thus" (τοῦτο φρονεῖν) in 1:7 is echoed in 2:2, 5 and 3:15 (cf. 3:19), and "to feel thus about you all" (ὑπὲρ πάντων ὑμῶν) in 1:7 is reciprocated in 4:10, Paul's acknowledgment for their gift. That the Philippians were "partakers with [him]" (συγκοινωνούς μου) in 1:7 is echoed in his appreciation for their gift in 4:14.[33] Paul's longing for the Philippians in 1:8 has resonances in 4:1, at the end of his warning about the "dogs" (3:2). The word "affection" (σπλάγχνους) in 1:8 reoccurs as σπλάγχνα in 2:1.

Paul's prayer in 1:9–11, to the effect that their love may increase with knowledge and discernment so that they approve what is better, is quite general (cf. Rom. 12:2) but certainly applies to and prepares for the example of Paul's change of values in 3:7–11.[34] There Paul states that he counted as loss his Jewish credentials because knowledge of Christ was a greater good (3:8). Philippians 1:10b, "that they be pure and blameless for the day of Christ," reinforces 1:6 in foreshadowing 2:16, "the day of Christ." Paul's prayer in 1:11, that they would have completed the "fruit" (καρπόν) of the righteousness they received through Jesus Christ, has resonances both in 4:17 (Paul wants the "fruit" that increases to their credit) and 3:6–9, esp. 3:9 (Paul has righteousness not of his own from the law but through Christ). Philippians 1:11b, "to the glory and praise of God," is contrasted in 2:3, "do nothing from . . . conceit" (cf. not "trusting in the flesh" through Paul's Jewish credentials in 3:3–6). It is echoed in the doxologies to God in 2:11 (at the end of the Christ hymn) and in 4:20 (at the close of Paul's thanksgiving for their gift).

110

Thus, the thanksgiving and prayer in Phil. 1:3–11 call to mind the following themes as a context for the kenotic imitation of Christ and of Paul in Philippians 2—3: Paul's prayer with joy, thankful for the Philippians' fellowship for the gospel from the beginning, with forward-looking trust that God would finish at the day of Christ the good work he had begun in them. Paul has this mind about the Philippians because they were "partakers" with him in his chains and defense of the gospel (through their suffering and especially through their gift). Paul longs for them with the heart of Christ and prays that their love increases with knowledge and discernment to see through false teachings and approve what is better, and that they remain without offense until the day of Christ, producing the fruit of their justification through Christ (not through the law) for God's glory.

The structure of the *present* form of Philippians is relatively easy to delineate after the opening (1:1–2) and introductory thanksgiving and prayer (1:3–11): two major sections of exhortations and/or warnings (1:27—2:18 and 3:1—4:9) are interspersed with descriptions of Paul's situation (1:12–26), his plans for Timothy (2:19–24) and commendation of Epaphroditus (2:25–30), and his thanksgiving for their gift (4:10–20), followed by the closing (4:21–23). Thus, the order is: opening (1:1–2), thanksgiving (1:3–11), Paul's situation (1:12–26), exhortations (1:27—2:18), Timothy and Epaphroditus (2:19–30), exhortations and warnings (3:1—4:9), thanksgiving for their gift (4:10–20), closing (4:21–23).

Paul prepares for his exhortation to imitate the self-emptying of Christ by describing his own imprisonment, which seems to have led to the conversion of some of his jailers (cf. the Praetorium, 1:13; the saints of Caesar's household, 4:22). He refers to preachers emboldened by his captivity to preach from envy and rivalry and partisanship (1:17, cf. 2:3), thinking to afflict him. Paul responds with several expressions of his indomitable eschatological joy in the face of their spiteful efforts, refusing to give them the satisfaction of grieving him by rejoicing that, even if in pretense, Christ is proclaimed (1:18).

Paul continues to rejoice in his not being shamed, for Christ will be honored in either his life or his death (1:19–20). As Paul faces the two possibilities of either dying to be with Christ (his preference) or remaining to serve them, he trusts that he will return to them for their progress and joy (1:21–26).

This report of Paul's imprisonment and possible death introduces the first major section of exhortation (1:27—2:18), whose center is the kenotic example and exaltation of Christ (2:6–11).[35] Paul calls the Philippians to unity without fear of their persecutors, for they have the privilege of suffering for Christ as Paul does (1:27–30). He urges them to fill up his joy by being united in mind and love, doing nothing from self-seeking but looking to the needs of others in humility (2:1–4). Verbal preparations for the Christ hymn include "conceit" (κενοδοξίαν), "humility" (ταπεινοφροσύνη), and "count others better than yourselves" (ἀλλήλους ἡγούμενοι ὑπερέχοντας ἑαυτῶν) in 2:3. The verb "to look at" or "to mark" (σκοποῦντες) in 2:4 will recur in 3:17: 2:4 names the self-interest they are *not* to look to; 3:17, their true models.

The attitude Paul asks for in 2:1–4 is illustrated by the example of Christ in 2:5–8. Being "in the form of God" (ἐν μορφῇ θεοῦ), he "did not count equality with God a thing to be grasped" (οὐχ ἁρπαγμὸν ἡγήσατο) but "emptied himself" (ἑαυτὸν ἐκένωσεν), taking on "the form of a servant" (μορφὴν δούλου). Being found as a human, he "humbled himself" (ἐταπείνωσεν ἑαυτόν) and became obedient even unto death on a cross (a curse: Gal. 3:13).

In the Old Testament, self-abasement by a servant of God often leads to God's exalting that servant (cf. Isa. 53:10b–12 and the citation of Isa. 45:23 in Phil. 2:10–11). The Philippians hymn also culminates in God's exalting the self-abased Christ (2:9–11). The word "therefore" (διό) in 2:9 interprets this exaltation as God's vindication or reward for Christ's abasement.

This pattern of exaltation after self-abasement in Phil. 2:9–11 also corresponds to the promise of reward (or, in athletic terms, a prize) for exercising virtue in first-century parenesis, which was described above. The reward motif reoccurs in Phil. 3:10–11, being conformed to Christ's death so as to attain to resurrection, and in 3:12–16, pressing on for the prize. Philippians 3:21 repeats the humiliation-exaltation pattern of this hymn, even using the same verbal roots: "who [the Lord Jesus Christ] will change [μετασχηματίσει] our lowly body [τῆς ταπεινώσεως] to be like his glorious body [σύμμορφον τῷ σώματι τῆς δόξης αὐτοῦ]."[36] The cause of exaltation is God in 3:9–11 and God's power in 3:21.[37]

The conclusion and application of the hymn leads to further exhortation (2:12, 14, 15; cf. 3:6). Because of Christ's example, they should work out their salvation "with fear and trembling" (not complacently considering themselves "perfect," cf. 3:12–16). Avoiding the negative example of the wilderness generation who grumbled and questioned God, they should let their innocence shine as lights in a corrupt world, as they hold fast to the word of life (e.g., by refusing to judaize, chap. 3). The result will be Paul's pride on the day of Christ that he did not labor in vain for them (2:12–16). This recalls the constant eschatological perspective throughout the letter (e.g., 3:20–21 and esp. 1:6 and 10). The sacrificial language Paul applies to his possible death in 2:17 is very similar to the sacrificial imagery applied to their gift in 4:18 and recalls the context of possible martyrdom behind the letter as it now stands (1:7, 20–22). The exhortation section ends on the note of rejoicing in trials that is thematic for the whole letter (e.g., 1:17–18; 1:27—2:2; 3:1–2; 4:1–4).

Two short sections on Timothy and Epaphroditus have their setting in the canonical letter between the exhortation based on Christ's example and that based on Paul's in 3:1—4:9. This setting seems to imply some carry-over of Christ's example to Timothy and Epaphroditus and to prepare for Paul's presentation of his own example. Other preachers are antithetical examples, but Timothy exemplifies what Paul asked of the Philippians (not to seek their own interests but those of others, 2:4)—that is, other teachers look after their own interests (2:21), but Timothy looks after the interests of the Philippians (2:20). Timothy in turn is Paul's disciple and imitates Paul "as a son (τέκνον) with a father" (2:22). He worked as a slave with Paul (σὺν ἐμοὶ ἐδούλευσεν) for the gospel (2:22), as Christ had taken on the form of a slave (μορφὴν δούλου) and become obedient, even unto the slave's death on the cross (2:7–8).[38]

Plans to send someone and hopes to come oneself (as in 2:23–24 for Timothy and Paul) are commonplace in letters of that time.[39] Paul's praise of Timothy is also normal for letters of commendation, where the writer recommends someone by explaining their relationship and giving his or her credentials.[40]

Like that of Timothy, the commendation of Epaphroditus in 2:25–30 contains elements of a letter of commendation, and it also echoes significant phrases from the section on Christ's example. Many have wondered why Paul felt it necessary to tell the Philippians to receive and honor their own messenger, Epaphroditus (2:29). Perhaps part of the answer is the standard practice to have a letter of commendation for the letter carrier, who was probably Epaphroditus (2:25, 29). But because Epaphroditus had been sent to Paul by the Philippians, Paul deliberately modifies the usual commendation. He begins by calling Epaphroditus his brother, fellow worker, and soldier, as well as their messenger. The important role for this study on the example of Christ and Paul is the echo from the Christ hymn: that Epaphroditus had come "close to death" (μέχρι θανάτου, 2:30 as in 2:8) in Christ's work. By risking his life, Epaphroditus was another embodiment of Christ's self-sacrificing example in 2:7–8.

The letter returns to exhortation in 3:1—4:9 with "finally" (τὸ λοιπόν), as 1 Thess. 4:1 turns to two chapters of exhortation with λοιπόν after treating Timothy's news (3:1–8) and Paul's reaction to it (3:9–13).[41] Philippians 3:1 reiterates Paul's emphasis on rejoicing made in several earlier difficult situations of imprisonment, risk to life, and false teachers. Then the letter turns abruptly to a sharp warning against judaizers (3:2). Even if this is a seam between letter fragments, its redactor apparently did not think the transition impossible, for he left it as it was.[42]

Paul uses invective as he sharply warns against the antithetical examples of the "dogs," "evildoers" (often used by Jews against Gentiles), and "those who mutilate the flesh" (3:2, versus "circumcision," 3:3). He counters their bad example with "We are the true circumcision who . . . glory in Christ Jesus and put no confidence in the flesh" (3:3), and then with his own personal example in 3:4–21. Beginning with his Jewish credentials (3:4–6), Paul reverses his value judgments so that his Jewish "gains" he now considers "loss," compared to gaining Christ without justification from the law (3:7–9). His relationship to Christ echoes earlier language of the letter (3:10, cf. 1:7) and especially the Christ hymn (3:10; cf. 2:6–8). Paul chooses participation in Christ's death that he may attain to the resurrection (3:11; cf. Christ's exaltation, 2:9–11). Paul's example is not one of completed perfection but one of striving toward the goal (3:12–14), and he utilizes standard rhetorical admission of imperfection and athletic imagery, as mentioned earlier. As many as are "perfect" agree with Paul (3:15, recalling 2:5 and 2:2). Philippians 3:16 calls them to hold true to and follow what they have already attained.

The call to imitate Paul in 3:17, which is one of the main foci of this essay, forms an inclusion in the present form of the letter with the call to imitate his ways at the end of this exhortation section in 4:9. This inclusion is reinforced by another inclusion signaled by τὸ λοιπόν at the beginning and toward the end of this whole exhortation section (3:1 and 4:8).

Philippians 3:17 calls for imitation both of Paul and of "those who so live (περιπατοῦντας) as you have an example (τύπον) in us." Both περιπατέω and τύπος are technical terms in first-century exhortation, often applied to imitation of people as examples (e.g., 2 Thess. 3:19, 1 Tim. 4:12, Titus 2:7). The sentence extends imitation of Paul to imitation also of those at Philippi who follow Paul's way. In this context, these would presumably be those who refused to judaize, possibly including Epaphroditus and Timothy (when he arrives). The imperative "look at" or "mark" (σκοπεῖτε) of 3:17 points to positive examples for imitation (those in Philippi who follow Paul's way) in contrast to the antithetical examples they are to avoid (cf. βλέπετε three times in 3:2 and the many who "walk" as enemies of Christ's cross in 3:18).

Through the repetition of περιπατέω, 3:17 and 3:18 draw a sharp contrast between those walking according to Paul's "example" and the enemies of the cross of Christ (3:18) whose "minds [are] set on earthly things" (3:19). Philippians 3:18–19, 20–21 repeat this contrast between these enemies of Christ's cross and the "we" whose "commonwealth" (πολίτευμα; cf. πολιτεύεσθε in 1:27) is "in heaven," whence they await as their savior (versus saving themselves through judaizing) "the Lord Jesus Christ" (3:20, paralleling 2:11 at the end of the Christ hymn). The contrast between those whose heavenly hope is in Christ as savior, versus enemies of the cross of Christ whose minds are set on earthly things, is strong evidence that the latter refer to judaizers, not libertines as a mirror-reading of Phil. 3:19 might suggest.[43]

Against most commentators, Helmut Koester makes a convincing argument that there is only one situation throughout Phil. 3:2—4:1 and that 3:17 continues from 3:16 and what preceded. At least v. 17 as it now stands finds its most natural context in what precedes, with περιπατοῦντας in 3:17 recalling στοιχεῖν from 3:16. Moreover, Phil. 3:18 ("enemies of the cross of Christ") continues the themes of 3:3–4 (boasting in Christ versus trusting in the flesh) and 3:10 (sharing in Christ's sufferings and conformed to his death).[44]

If 3:17 continues what went before, then 3:2–16 specifies that in which Paul wants to be imitated: not trusting in the flesh (3:3–4) through judaizing efforts at perfection[45] but following his example of surrendering his Jewish credentials so as to gain righteousness in Christ, not of his own from the law (3:4–9), and being conformed to Christ's death that he may attain to the resurrection from the dead (3:10–11).

Those who walk as enemies of Christ's cross (3:18) are antithetical examples to Paul, who is conformed to Christ's death (3:10b) and who got that way by the change of attitude recorded in 3:7: "But whatever gain I had, I counted as loss for the sake of Christ." The same choice faces Paul in 3:7 and the enemies of Christ's cross in 3:18 to seek salvation in judaizing practices or in Christ alone. When Paul chooses the way of Christ's death, he willingly forfeits his accomplishments and standing as a Jew.

In turn, Paul's choice in 3:7 parallels Christ's in 2:6. We have seen that the use of ἥγημαι in 3:7 parallels that in 2:6, οὐχ ἁρπαγμὸν ἡγήσατο. Both Paul and Christ had a certain standing they were willing to consider expendable—Paul as the perfect Jew and Christ as "in the form of God" (2:6). Each of them made a kenotic choice, and both choices are held up for imitation.

Both Paul's choice and Christ's led to the cross, in contrast to the "enemies of the cross of Christ." If the context in the present form of the letter implies judaizing, then the negative examples are Christian enemies of Christ's cross for one of two reasons. Either their judaizing approaches to justification in effect nullify the cross of Christ, as Paul argues in Gal. 2:21: "I do not nullify the grace of God; for if justification were through the law, then Christ died to no purpose" (cf. Gal. 5:2–4). Or Christians are trying to mollify non-Christian Jews and avoid their persecution by making converted Gentiles into Jews. For example, in Gal. 6:12, Paul adds in his own hand, "It is those who want to make a good showing in the flesh that would compel you to be circumcised, and only in order that they may not be persecuted for the cross of Christ."

Perhaps the opponents mentioned in Phil. 1:28 are non-Christian Jews persecuting the church because of Gentile Christians. Philippians 1:27–30 would then be urging the Philippians to stand firm and united against Jewish pressure to circumcise Gentile Christians and not to be frightened by their opponents from suffering for Christ's sake, thus having the same conflict as Paul, who suffered from Jews because of his mission to Gentiles (cf. 2 Cor. 11:24: five times given thirty-nine lashes by Jews; 2 Cor. 11:26: "danger from my own people").

In the language of invective, "belly" could allude to food laws and "shame" to circumcision. As in Galatians (5:12, cf. 5:10–11), in Phil. 3:2, Paul twisted the term of Jewish pride, "circumcision" (περιτομή), to one implying the shame and ritual uncleanness of castration, κατατομή (cf. Deut. 23:2). Similar invective not related to libertinism appears in the warnings in Rom. 16:17–18 against those who cause division against received teaching: "Such men serve, not Christ our Lord, but their own bellies, and they deceive the simple-minded with smooth and flattering speech" (NAB).⁴⁶

The adjective "earthly" (ἐπίγειος) occurs in Paul only here in 3:19 and in 2:10, 1 Cor. 15:40, and 2 Cor. 5:1, always in juxtaposition with "heavenly." A similar contrast occurs in John 3:12, James 3:15, and in early Christian and other contemporary writings.⁴⁷ In an antijudaizing context, the adjective would correspond to trusting in the flesh (3:3–4) as a negative Christian evaluation of Jewish regulations like circumcision. Thus, Paul contrasts the "earthly things" of 3:19 to Christian citizenship (πολίτευμα, echoing the *hapax legomenon* in 1:27) in heaven, from where Christians await Jesus' return as savior. The basic contrast is between salvation through Christ or through "earthly" strivings of the "flesh."

Philippians 3:20b, "the Lord Jesus Christ," echoes 2:11, and 3:21 recalls several unusual key terms from 2:6–8 and 2:11. Paul's eschatological hope in 3:20–21 corresponds closely in vocabulary and structural pattern to the humiliation-exaltation of the Christ hymn in Philippians 2. In 4:1, the "therefore" (ὥστε) which follows 3:20–21 is the same as the ὥστε in 2:12 following the Christ hymn. Because of their eschatological humiliation-exaltation hope in 3:20–21, the Philippians should "stand fast" against enemies of the cross who would seek earthly solutions and await from heaven exaltation from their lowliness (4:1). Philippians 4:1 has several verbal echoes back to earlier parts of the canonical letter: the New Testament *hapax legomenon* ἐπιπόθητοι ("longed for") to ἐπιποθῶ πάντας ὑμᾶς ("I yearn for you all") in the thanksgiving at 1:8; χαρά ("joy") and στήκετε ἐν κυρίῳ ("stand firm thus in the Lord") to στήκετε ἐν ἑνὶ πνεύματι ("stand firm in one spirit") in 1:27 at the beginning of the first exhortation section.

In Phil. 4:2–3, Paul applies his more general calls to unanimity, especially those in 2:1–4, to asking that his co-workers Euodia and Syntyche "agree in the Lord" (4:2–3). He begins a last set of general exhortations in 4:4–9 with a twofold "Rejoice!" He sums up these exhortations and those of the whole letter with another call to imitate him in 4:9: "What you have learned and received [παρελάβετε, a technical term for receiving tradition] and heard and seen in me, do." The call to imitate Paul in 4:9 reinforces that in 3:17.

Paul's thanksgiving for their gift in 4:10–20 begins with "I rejoiced," which continues the theme of rejoicing that has pervaded the earlier parts of the canonical letter. Their concern for Paul in 4:10 reciprocates his concern for them in 1:7. Paul begins with the standard philosophical claim to be αὐτάρχης, content with what one has. For example, the Socratic letter "Antisthenes to Aristippus" begins: "It is not right for a philosopher to associate with tyrants and to devote himself to Sicilian tables. Rather, he should live in his own country and strive for self-sufficiency."[48] The verb "to be abased" (ταπεινοῦσθαι) in 4:12 illustrates this virtue of contentment and recalls the abasement that Christ underwent in 2:8 (ἐταπείνωσεν ἑαυτόν, cf. 2:3) and from which Paul hoped Christ would rescue him in 3:21 (ταπείνωσις), thus helping tie the major parts of the canonical letter together. In 4:14–20 the following expressions refer back to the epistolary thanksgiving: "to share my trouble" (συγκοινωνήσαντές μου τῇ θλίψει) in 4:14 to 1:7; "in the beginning of the gospel" (ἐν ἀρχῇ τοῦ εὐαγγελίου) and "entered into partnership" (ἐκοινώνησεν) in 4:15 to 1:5; "fruit" (καρπόν) in 4:17 to 1:11; "to God . . . glory" (τῷ δὲ θεῷ . . . δόξα) in 4:20 to 1:11. The sacrificial imagery for their gift, especially "sacrifice" (θυσία), recalls Paul's self-sacrifice in 2:17.

In the closing, the greetings from those of Caesar's household recalls the effect of Paul's chains on the praetorean guard in 3:13 and maintains to the very end of the canonical letter the self-sacrificial theme which has run throughout it.

Thus, in the context of the entire letter to the Philippians, the call to imitate the kenotic example of Christ in Phil. 2:5–11 and Paul in 3:4—4:1 and 4:9 dominates the two main sections of exhortation. In turn, the epistolary thanksgiving in 1:3–11 and Paul's acknowledgment of the Philippians' gift in 4:10–20 form an inclusion into which the parenetic sections in 1:27—2:18 and 3:1—4:9 are set. The inclusion emphasizes rejoicing in sufferings, mutual love and concern, communion through common suffering and their gift to Paul, appreciation of self-sacrifice, and abasement in the hope of eschatological exaltation, all to the glory of God.

The description of Paul's situation in Phil. 1:12–26 and remarks about Timothy and Epaphroditus in 2:19–30 add concrete details to the significance of the self-sacrificing examples of Christ and Paul, which the letter asks the Philippians to imitate. Paul can rejoice even facing death in prison.

He is willing to postpone his release in death for complete union with Christ in order to serve their needs. Timothy, too, unlike other teachers who seek their own interests by judaizing compromises to avoid Jewish persecution, shares Paul's concern for their needs and not his own. Epaphroditus risks his life and almost dies fulfilling the mandate the Philippians give him. The cumulative effect of all these personal examples is a powerful incentive to imitate their self-sacrifice for the interests of others.

## PATTERNS AND WORD CLUSTERS

A final, brief look at similar patterns in other letters of Paul can confirm the plausibility that this was the interpretation given to the final form of Philippians in the context of the Pauline letter corpus. A seminal suggestion for our thesis has been that the calls to imitate Christ and Paul, respectively, in Philippians 2 and 3 implicitly parallel 1 Cor. 11:1: "Be imitators of me, as I am of Christ." But the parallelism between Phil. 2:1—4:3 and 1 Cor. 8:1—11:1 goes further. Both contexts stress kenotic imitation of Paul and Christ, and both use an inclusion or A-B-A pattern.

The inclusion in Phil. 2:1—4:3 is caused by the parallel commands to community members in 2:2 and 4:2, "Be of the same mind" (τὸ αὐτὸ φρονεῖν). Though some have argued that the text would make more sense flowing directly from 2:2 to 4:2, that ignores the common practice of inclusions and A-B-A structures in New Testament writings and substitutes contemporary for first-century logic. Studies of the Gospel of Mark have benefited greatly from attention to its many A-B-A intercalations. Scholars now commonly recognize the A-B-A structure in 1 Corinthians 12—14 and 8—10, and how chaps. 13 and 9:1—10:13 add deeper perspectives (though seeming to digress) before returning to the original question in chaps. 14 and 10:14.

Whether the inclusion in Phil. 2:2 and 4:2 came from Paul or from a redactor, readers of the Pauline corpus would perceive it as an inclusion like other inclusions in Paul. And the structural similarity to the inclusion in 1 Cor. 8:1—11:1 is especially strong. Philippians 2:1–4 calls the community to unanimity through self-abasement and concern for others' interests. Before Phil. 4:2 applies this general admonition to Euodia and Syntyche, Phil. 2:5–11 grounds the call in Christ's example. Philippians 2:12–18 applies Christ's example to the community; 2:19–30 gives the examples of Timothy and Epaphroditus; 3:1—4:1 warns against judaizers and gives Paul's self-sacrificing example with an athletic metaphor to counter their judaizing attempts to avoid Jewish persecution.

A similar inclusion in 1 Cor. 8:1—11:1 occurs in the question of meat sacrificed to idols in 8:1–13 and 10:14—11:1. In 9:1–27, Paul deepens his preliminary answer about idol meat by his self-sacrificing example in letting go his apostolic prerogatives of support, also with an athletic metaphor (9:24–27). 1 Corinthians 10:1–13 adds a negative Old Testament example of idolatry to warn that baptism, eucharist, and community membership do not guarantee salvation. Only then does 1 Cor. 10:14–22 return to idol meat with a deeper reminder that idol worship has demonic aspects, even for a monotheist. Then 1 Cor. 10:23—11:1 returns fully to the original question from 8:1–13, ending with the call to imitate Paul as he imitates Christ (11:1).

Thus, in both Phil. 2:1—4:3 and 1 Cor. 8:1—11:1 there are inclusions of an original topic (unanimity and idol meat), deepened by further considerations of self-emptying examples of Paul and Christ contrasted to negative examples, before returning to the original question for a final statement or application. 1 Corinthians 12—14 have a similar inclusion, turning from spiritual gifts to how they function in Christ's body and to the generalized implied example of Paul in the love hymn before applying these insights to the gifts of tongues and prophecy in chap. 14.

Another pattern which Paul's other letters confirm as a plausible interpretation of Philippians 2—3 is Paul's self-sacrificing example for the sake of others. Some of these are mentioned in the first section on imitation in first-century exhortation and in Paul. They include the examples in 1 Cor. 8:1—11:1, esp. 1 Cor. 9:19, "For though I am free from all men, I have made myself a slave to all, that I might win the more." In 1 Corinthians 8, 9, and 14, Paul declines to use his knowledge, his apostolic right to support, and his strong gift of tongues, lest they hinder other Christians. (Cf. the same pattern in 2 Thess. 3:9, "It was not because we have not that right, but to give you in our conduct an example to imitate.") 1 Corinthians 1—4 focused on a call to unity and the example of Paul's refusal to rely on human wisdom or knowledge or rhetoric, but to preach only Christ crucified. 1 Corinthians 4:9–17 mentions Paul's sufferings, his call to imitate him as their only father, as Timothy his "son" reminds them of his ways in Christ which he teaches everywhere in every church.

Second Corinthians has a heavy emphasis on self-sacrifice and suffering as exemplary of true following of the crucified Christ. 2 Corinthians 8:9 refers to Christ making himself poor though rich so as to enrich others in his poverty, which is an example for their generosity to Paul's collection. 2 Corinthians 13:4 says that Christ was crucified from weakness but lives from the power of God. This has elements of both kenosis and exaltation. 2 Corinthians 1:7–9 hopes that "as you share in our sufferings, you will also share in our comfort" and tells how Paul felt as if under a sentence of death, "but that was to make us rely not on ourselves but on God who raises the dead" (cf. 4:10–14). 2 Corinthians 4:16–17 and 5:1 speak of the outer man corrupting but the inner man being renewed, slight affliction preparing for eternal glory, and the destruction of an earthly tent to receive an eternal building from God in heaven. The theme of divine strength in human weakness is important in 2 Cor. 11:30 and 12:9–10, with special reference to suffering persecution for Christ.

Though Paul has a lot of references both to self-sacrifice and suffering and to hope of resurrection, he does not have too much explicit combining of kenosis and exaltation as in Phil. 2:5–11 and 3:20–21. Nevertheless, this combination is common in Old Testament texts which Paul used, such as the servant of Isaiah, the suffering righteous person, and the rejected and vindicated prophet. Dying and rising with Christ is at the heart of baptism symbolism. The pattern is also current in the traditions of the sayings of Jesus about losing and finding one's life and humbling oneself to be exalted. Finally, it is related to Paul's strength-in-weakness motif and his common call to rely on God's power, not on human ways and resources.

The last confirmations for our thesis about the imitation of Paul and Christ in Philippians 2 and 3 are the vocabulary links between these chapters. They have been mentioned in the course of the argument, so here it is only necessary to list them all together for their cumulative effect. On the literary level of the manuscript tradition, the vocabulary evidence does support the theological parallelism now present in Philippians 2—3.

The parallel between ἡγεῖσθαι ζημίαν in 3:7 and ἡγεῖσθαι ἁρπαγμόν in 2:6 has struck many on both sides of the question concerning literary integrity. The verb occurs five times in Philippians, only three times in Paul's other letters. All five occurrences are in chaps. 2 and 3 (2:3, 6; 3:7 and 8).

The ταπειν-root appears only in Philippians and mostly in chaps. 2—3. ταπεινοφροσύνη appears only in Phil. 2:3 in the undisputed letters. It goes with ἡγεῖσθαι in the request, "in humility count others better than yourselves." The verb ταπεινοῦν occurs in Philippians only at 2:8 (Christ humbled himself) and 4:12 (in the acknowledgment of the gift). ταπείνωσις occurs in the Pauline letters only at 3:21 (transform our lowly body).

The links between Philippians 3 and 2 from using σχῆμα and μορφή and their compounds are quite strong. The words are almost peculiar to Paul in the New Testament and are concentrated mostly in these two chapters of Philippians. σχῆμα occurs only in 2:7 and 1 Cor. 7:31. μετασχηματίζω is only in 3:21 and four times in 1 and 2 Corinthians. μορφή appears in the New Testament only twice (Phil. 2:6–7; Mark 16:12). συμμορφίζω is a New Testament *hapax legomenon* at 3:10, and σύμμορφος occurs in the New Testament only in 3:21 and Rom. 8:29.

πολίτευμα in 3:20 is a New Testament *hapax legomenon*. It makes a strong verbal link with πολιτεύεσθε in 1:27 (in the New Testament, only there

120

and Acts 28:1), the beginning of the section of exhortation to which chap. 2 belongs.

Philippians has a heavy concentration of φρονεῖν (ten times in Philippians, eleven in the rest of Paul). They occur in 1:7 (Paul toward the Philippians); 2:2 twice and 2:5 (have one/Christ's mind); 3:15 and 19 (mature/worldly attitudes); 4:2 (between Euodia and Syntyche), and 4:10 (their thought toward Paul). The concentration of six of ten uses in chaps. 2—3 creates strong verbal links between those chapters.

In Phil. 2:7 and 3:9 one finds the only two uses of εὑρίσκω in Philippians. Less significantly, the only two instances of ὑπάρχειν in Philippians come at 2:6 and 3:20.

Finally, the thematic κοινων-root is found in the major sections of the letter (1:5, 7; 2:1; 3:10; 4:14—15) and strengthens the link between these two chapters. Philippians 2:1 mentions fellowship in the Spirit and 3:10, fellowship in Christ's sufferings.

## RECAPITULATION AND CONCLUSIONS

This study has shown the need to go beyond the scissors-and-paste approaches of source- and form-critical studies of Philippians and to explain the final redacted form of any composite letter, as the fruitfulness of recent studies in the Synoptics and Acts has demonstrated. It has studied the examples of Christ and Paul in Philippians 2 and 3 in the context of the whole canonical letter and in light of the importance of imitating personal examples in first-century exhortation. The kenotic examples of Christ and Paul ground the two main exhortation sections of the canonical letter and are in turn given the letter's setting of Paul's imprisonment and possible death.

The letter in its present form has a message that goes beyond the purpose of any sources it might contain. When the original problems were no longer of concern to the churches, the basic self-emptying models of Christ and of Paul maintained their relevance for imitation by Christians in any age. The letter as a whole provides a relatively unified situation of Paul writing from prison to urge a unified stand against persecutors and those who would compromise with persecutors by judaizing human means, instead of relying solely on God. It encourages Christians in any situation of external and internal trials and fortifies them against temptations to compromise to escape suffering.

This encouragement is based on an indomitable, eschatological joy amidst trials of all sorts, which pervades the whole document. The call to unanimity also runs throughout the letter. These themes and the call to reconciliation among respected members (4:2) have perennial validity for Christian communities, long after the readers might know who Euodia, Syntyche, and the "yoke-fellow" (4:3) were.

The letter's encouragement and exhortation revolve especially around the examples of Christ and Paul, who let go personal prerogatives that might have spared them suffering and trusted instead in God and not in the flesh to vindicate and exalt them. The main motivation to avoid human compromises like judaizing comes from Paul's example and that of those who follow Paul's nonjudaizing ways. Paul's example in Philippians 3 is in turn seen in light of Christ's example and cross in Philippians 2, an example which Paul himself embraced and taught to his followers.

The opening and closing chapters of the letter to the Philippians put these exhortations in the context of a community which has special fellowship with Paul, aiding him in his trials and imprisonment through Epaphroditus, who almost died in bringing this aid to Paul. The community is promised another link with Paul through Timothy, who is portrayed as a faithful son, like Paul, who puts others' interests before his own, as Christ and Paul did. For later churches reading this letter, all four personal examples embody the main message of letting go one's own interests for the sake of others. Those who imitate the kenotic example of Christ and Paul and their own leaders can expect the kind of eschatological joy the letter promises in even the worst of situations.

## NOTES

1. D. M. Williams, "The Imitation of Christ in Paul with Special Reference to Paul as Teacher" (Ph.D. diss., Columbia Univ., 1967) 2, 425–27; D. M. Stanley, " 'Become Imitators of Me': Apostolic Tradition in Paul," in *The Apostolic Church in the New Testament* (Westminster, Md.: Newman Press, 1965) 371–89, esp. 382.

2. W. Michaelis, "μιμέομαι, κτλ.," *TDNT* 4 (1967) 659–74; e.g., "The call for an *imitatio Christi* finds no support in the statements of Paul," 672; E. Käsemann, "Kritische Analyse von Phil. 2, 5–11," *ZTK* 47 (1950) 313–60. Käsemann denies example in Christ's kenosis (342), yet his closest analogy to it (2 Cor. 8:9) is clearly used as example for Corinthian generosity (335). B. Fiore ("The Function of Personal Example in the Socratic and Pastoral Epistles" [Ph.D. diss., Yale Univ., 1982] 309) sums up a thorough critique of Michaelis thus: "Consequently, on the basis of his own evidence . . . Michaelis' interpretation of 'imitating the example' in terms of obedience of authority is tendentious. Indeed, it is a usage which does not appear in the rhetorical treatises which treat example." Many agree with Stanley (" 'Become Imitators of Me' ") in his criticisms of Michaelis. See esp. E. Cothenet, "Imitation du Christ," in *Dictionnaire de Spiritualité* 7,2 (1971) 1536–1601, Part I, esp. 1536–37 on the Lutheran distrust of *Nachahmung* ("imitation") for *Nachfolge* ("following"); and R. Thysman, "L'Éthique de l'imitation du Christ dans le Nouveau Testament: Situation, notations et variations du thème," *ETL* 42 (1966) 138–75, esp. 155–56: though the New Testament generally keeps "following Christ" separate from "im-

itating Christ" on the literary level, yet the historical reality of following Christ must have implied the disciple would have a similar attitude.

Therefore, this study on imitation is included in a volume on discipleship, for though the vocabulary and corresponding backgrounds of *Nachahmung* and *Nachfolge* differ, they both refer from different perspectives to a common *res* ("reality, phenomena") in practice; for the application of imitation on which this study focuses is *pedagogical* practice, which lies behind both expressions.

3. See N. Dahl, "The Particularity of the Pauline Epistles as a Problem in the Ancient Church," in *Neotestamentica et Patristica. Eine Freundesgabe, Herrn Professor Dr. Oscar Cullmann zu seinem 60. Geburtstag überreicht* (NovTSup 6; Leiden: E. J. Brill, 1962) 261–71; and W. Kurz, S.J., "Inspiration and the Origins of the New Testament," in *Scripture and the Charismatic Renewal* (ed. G. Martin; Ann Arbor, Mich.: Servant Pubs., 1979) 29–58, esp. 51. For a similar comparison of redacted letters to the Synoptic Gospels, see W. Dalton, "The Integrity of Philippians," *Bib* 60 (1979) 97–102, esp. 102.

4. Though the currently most influential opinions in the debate over the unity of Philippians argue for up to three letters, scholarly challenges to the multiplicity theory continue to be published from a variety of perspectives, mainstream as well as conservative. This study will not enter the debate, except to point to the genuine evidence for unity in the letter at least on the redactional level. Whether Paul wrote one letter or a redactor combined three of Paul's letter fragments into one letter, the resulting document in either case has some unity and consistency of vocabulary and themes throughout. The arguments of this study for a redactional unity, even if there were originally three letters, would apply a fortiori under a unity hypothesis.

The more influential view for multiplicity is too well known to require documentation. A good bibliographical guide up to 1961 is H. Koester, "The Purpose of the Polemic of a Pauline Fragment (Philippians III)," *NTS* 8 (1961–62) 317–32. A convenient summary of the whole debate is in R. P. Martin, *Philippians* (NCB; Grand Rapids: Wm. B. Eerdmans, 1976) 10–22.

For recent arguments in favor of unity, see the following with their bibliographical references: Dalton, "Integrity of Philippians"; H. Gamble, Jr., *The Textual History of the Letter to the Romans* (SD 42; Grand Rapids: Wm. B. Eerdmans, 1977) Appendix 2, "Some Notes on the Literary Problems in Philippians," 145–46; P. T. O'Brien, *Introductory Thanksgivings in the Letters of Paul* (NovTSup 49; Leiden: E. J. Brill, 1977); G. Wiles, *Paul's Intercessory Prayers* (SNTSMS 24; Cambridge: Cambridge Univ. Press, 1974); H. R. Moehring, "Some Remarks on *Sarx* in Philippians 3,3ff," *SE* 4 (TU 102 [1968] 432–36); Williams, "Imitation of Christ in Paul,"; T. E. Pollard, "The Integrity of Philippians," *NTS* 13 (1966–67) 57–66; R. Jewett, "The Epistolary Thanksgiving and the Integrity of Philippians," *NovT* 12 (1970) 40–53; V. P. Furnish, "The Place and Purpose of Philippians III," *NTS* 10 (1963–64) 80–88; B. S. Mackay, "Further Thoughts on Philippians," *NTS* 7 (1960–61) 161–70.

5. E.g., I. Havener (*First Thessalonians, Philippians, Philemon, Second Thessalonians, Colossians, Ephesians* [CBC 8; Collegeville, Minn.: Liturgical Press, 1983] 35) entitles these verses "Christian Life as Imitation of Christ."

6. Against Käsemann, "Kritische Analyse."

7. BAGD, s.v., ὥστε.

8. Käsemann ("Kritische Analyse," 334) thanks R. Bultmann for this reference. See also Phil. 2:3.

9. On the meaning of συμμιμηταί, see Jewett, "Epistolary Thanksgiving," 52; Williams, "Imitation of Christ in Paul," 415–16, 427; J. B. Lightfoot, *Saint Paul's Epistle to the Philippians* (London: Macmillan & Co., 1913) 154.

10. For the importance and uses of imitation in Paul, see Fiore, "Function of Personal Example," chap. 7: "Example in the Letters of Paul," 304–55, esp. 305 n. 2. Especially important are W. P. De Boer, *The Imitation of Paul* (Kampen, Neth.: J. H. Kok, 1962); P. Gutiérrez, *La Paternité spirituelle selon Saint Paul* (Paris: J. Gabalda, 1968); D. M. Stanley, " 'Become Imitators of Me': The Pauline Conception of Apostolic Tradition," *Bib* 40 (1959) 859–77; H. D. Betz, *Nachfolge und Nachahmung Jesu Christi im Neuen Testament* (BHT 37; Tübingen: Mohr/Siebeck, 1967); and earlier works to which they refer. Also quite helpful is Williams ("Imitation of Christ in Paul") for gathering of sources and discussion of texts and literature.

11. Fiore, "Function of Personal Example."

12. Isocrates, *Against the Sophists*, 16–18; cited in Fiore, "Function of Personal Example," 58. See the other literature in Fiore, 58 n. 24, and A. Lumpe, "Exemplum," *RAC* 6:1229–57.

13. Fiore, "Function of Personal Example," 59–60. See also Pliny's *Letter* (to Titius Aristo) 8.14: "But in the olden time it was an established rule that Romans should learn from their elders, not only by precept, but by example. . . . The father of each youth served as his instructor, or, if he had none, some person of years and dignity supplied the place of the father. . . . Thus they were taught by that surest method of instruction, example, the whole conduct of a senator" (LCL; cited Fiore, 60–61).

14. Fiore, "Function of Personal Example," 61. (Italics Fiore's.) See sources and literature, 61–62 nn. 29–31; 329–30 nn. 34–35.

15. Stanley, " 'Become Imitators of Me' "; Gutiérrez, *La Paternité spirituelle*, 125, 172, 175, 178–81; De Boer, *Imitation of Paul*, 145–46, 153, 165, esp. 206–7; Fiore, "Function of Personal Example," 326, esp. nn. 27–29; 332–33, 337–43; B. Holmberg, *Paul and Power: The Structure of Authority in the Primitive Church as Reflected in the Pauline Epistles* (Philadelphia: Fortress Press, 1980) 77–79, esp. n. 97 about 1 Cor. 4:17 and Phil. 2:22 on children learning correct conduct by imitating their "fathers." For imitating a "father" as an example, see 1 Cor. 4:16; 10:33—11:1; 1 Thess. 1:6; Phil. 3:17; 4:9; Gal. 4:12. See O. Betz, "Die Geburt der Gemeinde durch den Lehrer," *NTS* 3 (1956–57) 314–26.

16. Fiore, "Function of Personal Example," 329–30, including nn. 36–38. For a treatment of "fatherhood" in antiquity, see Gutiérrez, *La Paternité spirituelle*, 15–83, on the title for priests and counselors of the king; on fatherhood of prophets, in wisdom schools, at Qumran, in the rabbis; and in Greco-Roman mystery religions. See also 116, 168.

17. Gutiérrez, *La Paternité spirituelle*, 81–83.

18. Fiore, "Function of Personal Example," 334.

19. Ibid., 335. Note 54 cites Gutiérrez, *La Paternité spirituelle*, 183, and Isocrates *Nicocles* 6 and *Philip* 114.

20. Fiore, "Function of Personal Example," 337–39, 342.

21. Ibid., 349–50.

22. Ibid., 343–44.

23. Ibid., 346; quotation is from n. 65.

24. Ibid., 351.

25. Ibid., 352.

26. Ibid., 352–53.

27. Ibid., 353.

28. Ibid., 353 n. 77.

29. Ibid., 353–54.

30. E.g., P. Schubert, *Form and Function of the Pauline Thanksgivings* (BZNW 20; Berlin: Alfred Töpelmann, 1939); W. Doty, *Letters in Primitive Christianity* (GBS; Philadelphia: Fortress Press, 1973); N. Dahl, "Letter," *IDBSup*, 538–41; H. Koester, *Introduction to the New Testament* (2 vols.; Philadelphia: Fortress Press, 1982) 2:52–56, esp. 55–56; J. White, ed., *Studies in Ancient Letter Writing* (*Semeia* 22; Chico, Calif.: Scholars Press, 1982), esp. J. White, "The Ancient Epistolography Group in Retrospect," 1–14, and idem, "The Greek Documentary Letter Tradition Third Century B.C.E. to Third Century C.E.," 89–106.

31. E.g., Doty, *Letters in Primitive Christianity*, 31–34; Jewett, "Epistolary Thanksgiving," 53: "Despite the abrupt transitions, the entire letter as it now stands is the product of the author's intention set forth in the epistolary thanksgiving." At least the thanksgiving can be read as preparing for the entire canonical letter, regardless of how the letter reached its present form. See Wiles, *Paul's Intercessory Prayers*, 195–97, and O'Brien, *Introductory Thanksgivings*, 19–46, esp. 37–41, on the epistolary purpose of the thanksgiving in Phil. 1:3–11.

32. See also Phil. 1:27—2:3, and see Koester's *Introduction to the New Testament*, 133, for eschatological joy amidst suffering in the "imprisonment letter."

33. Dalton ("Integrity of Philippians," 101) argues that the thanksgivings in chaps. 1 and 4 form an inclusion signaled by repetition of several key expressions.

34. See Wiles, *Paul's Intercessory Prayers*, 208–10, esp. 210 n. 2.

35. See Williams, "Imitation of Christ in Paul," 407; Quintilian *Institutio oratoria* 9.2.103; and R. P. Martin, *Carmen Christi: Philippians 2:5–11 in Recent Interpretation and in the Setting of Early Christian Worship* (SNTSMS 4; Cambridge: Cambridge Univ. Press, 1967) 42 n. 2.

36. N. Flanagan, "A Note on Philippians iii.20–21," *CBQ* 18 (1956) 8–9. R. P. Martin (*Philippians*, 150) and W. A. Meeks, ed. (*The Writings of St. Paul* [New York: W. W. Norton, 1972] 101 n. 7) both note the resemblance between 3:21 and 2:6–11 but exemplify the common failure to exploit it by relating the two passages, resorting instead to the source-critical explanation that they have common traditional material.

37. The word for "exalted" in the hymn (Phil. 2:9) is a typically Pauline compound beginning in ὑπέρ. Since the vast majority of compounds with ὑπέρ in the New Testament appear in the Pauline literature, the word here seems at least a Pauline retouching, if the verse was not originally by Paul. Against Käsemann's unsupported assertion that the Hellenistic age was especially partial to *composita* ("Kritische Analyse von Phil. 2, 5–11," 346). See Moulton-Geden, 974–75, and *Computer-Konkordanz*, 1836–38.

38. R. A. Culpepper ("Co-Workers in Suffering: Philippians 2:19–30," *RevExp* 77 [1980] 349–58) notes that Timothy and Epaphroditus were presented with Paul as examples of how the Philippians should imitate Christ in servanthood.

39. See White, "Greek Documentary Letter Tradition," 99, on stereotyped announcements of visits.

40. See ibid., 96.

41. Williams, "Imitation of Christ in Paul," 411. Gamble, in an appendix of his book on the ending of Romans (*Textual History,* 146), states flatly, "The τὸ λοιπόν of 3:1 cannot be called an immediate transition to the epistolary conclusion." Despite its similarity to 2 Cor. 13:11, the phrase is not common to Pauline conclusions and is used in contexts that precede by quite a bit epistolary conclusions in 1 Thess. 4:1 and 2 Thess. 3:1 (cf. 1 Cor. 7:29).

42. Caution must be exercised against arguing too much from a change in tone. First, the rejoicing in Philippians is usually set in a situation of trial and even hostile teachers, as mentioned earlier. Second, Paul's tone toward the recipients of the letter does not change here. His anger is directed toward outside judaizers, not to the Philippians themselves, as in Galatians. Besides, it is common in correspondence for one's tone to change according to the topic being discussed. In my own letters I have found drastic mood changes as I turned from happy topics to those that saddened or angered me. See also Furnish, "Place and Purpose of Philippians III," 83–84, 86–87, on verbal explanations by the letter carriers.

43. See Koester (*Introduction to the New Testament,* 134), who says the invectiveness of 3:2 and 3:18–19 is not against libertines but perfectionistic judaizers. On hazards of the mirror-reading that is so common in New Testament studies, see L. T. Johnson, "On Finding the Lukan Community: A Cautious Cautionary Essay," in SBLASP, 1979 (2 vols.; ed. P. J. Achtemeier; Missoula, Mont.: Society of Biblical Literature, 1979) 1:87–100.

44. Koester, "Pauline Fragment," 325. One can accept his arguments for an overall structure throughout Philippians 3 even if not fully persuaded by all the details of his reconstruction of the *Sitz im Leben.*

45. See Moehring, "Remarks on *Sarx,*" 434–36. A passage from the Jerusalem Targum on Gen. 40:23 blames Joseph for putting his confidence in the chief butler, trusting "in the flesh" rather than God. Moehring argues that trusting in the flesh refers to human means, even Jewish religious practices, in Paul.

46. See J. Behm ("κοιλία," *TDNT* 3 [1965] 788) on a context of judaizers rather than libertines, citing Theodore of Mopsuestia, Ambrosiaster, and Pelagius (n. 14). See Koester ("Purpose of the Polemic," 326–27) but without his parallel between ἀπώλεια, κοιλία, and αἰσχύνη; contra R. P. Martin (*Philippians,* 145) and many others.

47. BAGD, s.v., ἐπίγειος.

48. "The Epistles of Socrates and the Socratics," *Epistle* 8, in A. Malherbe, ed., *The Cynic Epistles: A Study Edition* (SBLSBS 12; Missoula, Mont.: Scholars Press, 1977) 245. See also 124 line 25, and 176 line 12.

# 6

## "Be Imitators of God":
## Discipleship in the
## Letter to the Ephesians

### ROBERT A. WILD, S.J.

A question that intensely preoccupied all of the Greek philosophical thought from the time of Plato onwards was that of the end, the purpose, the goal, or the *telos* of human living.[1] Discipleship as we encounter it in the pseudepigraphical, late first-century, Christian writing known as the Letter to the Ephesians may appropriately be investigated under that rubric since, as I shall argue, this New Testament text reveals significant links with Hellenistic philosophy and in particular with Middle Platonism.

Having said this, I wish to make my general perspective regarding Ephesians quite clear. Through and through, this letter is rooted in biblical and Jewish tradition. Biblical images and allusions are encountered everywhere, and there are numerous parallels in Ephesians to the language of other roughly contemporaneous Jewish texts.[2] If, for example, Karl Kuhn and Franz Mussner have not succeeded in demonstrating—as they have, at least to my satisfaction—a direct link between Ephesians and the Qumran scrolls, they have highlighted numerous expressions and images which the two traditions had in common.[3] So the point at issue is not whether Ephesians presents some sort of "Hellenistic Christianity" over against the "Jewish Christianity" of the primitive Church but, rather, to what degree Hellenistic categories of thought were used within a culturally Jewish setting to explain and elaborate the revelation of Christ.

Ephesians contains a number of statements that sum up the end or goal of Christian discipleship: "That we should be holy and blameless before him" (1:4); "We . . . have been destined and appointed to live for the praise of his glory" (1:12); "Until we all attain to the unity of the faith and of the knowledge of the Son of God, to mature manhood, to the measure of the stature of the fulness of Christ" (4:13); etc.[4] Consequently, a discussion of the end or finality of Christian ethical living could begin in this case at many different points. I have chosen Eph. 5:1–2 as a point of departure both because of the information it provides on the understanding of ethical finality in this letter and because of the important clues it offers for determining the precise background of Ephesians. The passage reads as follows: "Therefore be imitators of God, as beloved children. And walk in love, as Christ also loved us and handed himself over for our sake as an offering and a sacrifice to God for a sweet smelling aroma" (au. trans.; RSV: "and gave himself up for us, a fragrant offering and sacrifice to God").

Much of the vocabulary of this passage, particularly that used in v. 2, is deeply rooted either in the Scriptures or in the genuine Pauline letters. The verb "to walk" (περιπατεῖν), a word particularly favored by the author of Ephesians in speaking of the directionality of ethical activity, is a biblical commonplace, and the phrase περιπατεῖτε ἐν ἀγάπῃ ("walk in love") is similar to the language of Rom. 14:15: κατὰ ἀγάπην περιπατεῖς ("you are walking according to love").[5] Ephesians 5:2 follows the pattern of Gal. 2:20 in speaking of Christ's "handing himself over" on behalf of someone. The pleonastic reference in this same verse of Ephesians to "an offering and a sacrifice" may well be a reference to Ps. 39:7 (LXX) and, if so, is very appropriate to the context because of the obvious christological possibilities of this psalm. The final phrase in v. 2, "for an odor of sweetness," is utilized frequently in the Pentateuch and elsewhere in Scripture in sacrificial contexts.[6]

However, the opening command to "be imitators of God" (γίνεσθε . . . μιμηταὶ τοῦ θεοῦ) is quite another matter. μιμέομαι and its derivatives are of preternaturally rare occurrence in the Septuagint and are never used with reference to the imitation of God.[7] This set of words is found in the genuine letters of Paul but only with reference either to the imitation of Paul, other churches, or Christ.[8]

## "IMITATION OF GOD" IN THE WRITINGS OF PHILO

Although not providing exact verbal parallels, a series of texts from the exegetical treatises of Philo of Alexandria reveal, more than other writings prior to Ephesians, significant points of comparison with Eph. 5:1.[9] To begin with, Philo is conversant with the view that kings and rulers are imitators of God. In *Spec. Leg.* 4.187–88 he remarks:

> He [God] called the non-existent into existence and produced order from disorder, qualities from things devoid of quality, similarities from dissimilars, identities from the totally different, fellowship and harmony from the dissociated and discordant, equality from inequality, and light from darkness.

... These things good rulers must imitate [μιμεῖσθαι] if they have any as-
piration to be assimilated to God [εἴ γέ τις αὐτοῖς φροντίς ἐστιν ἐξομοιώσεως
τῆς πρὸς θεόν].[10]

Here Philo stands in a tradition already attested in Hellenistic Judaism. The
*Letter of Aristeas* tells kings that they are to imitate (μιμεῖσθαι) God in
being benefactors.[11] On the strength of this understanding of the ruler,
Philo can even in one place call Moses a "god" (θεός), since of all human
beings pre-eminently Moses is a king (*Moses* 1.158). Philo has a good biblical
basis for speaking this way about Moses, since in Exod. 7:1 God says to
Moses, "You will be a god [θεός] to Pharaoh." But Philo is also thinking
here of a Platonic archetype-copy relationship:[12] given Moses' vision of the
"paradigmatic essence" of God, Philo says that he was able in turn to display
himself and his life as a paradigm "for those wishing to imitate it."[13] Moses
here is allocated a position in the total order of things quite akin to that
normally assigned by Philo to God's *logos* or reason.[14]

Along with rulers, Philo also frequently refers to parents as imitators of
God: as God is the father and maker of the all, so parents imitate God's
nature by begetting particular persons (*Decal.* 51).[15] Philo did not originate
this perspective either, for it is clear that he knows of other thinkers who
even are ready to assert that parents are so like God that they, too, can be
termed "gods" (θεοί; *Decal.* 120). While the pre-Philonic sources that we
possess for this kind of statement are non-Jewish,[16] it is probable, since
Philo does *not* reject this point of view, that he is here citing a Jewish
source.[17] For his own part, however, he seems to prefer to say that parents
imitate God's nature or power "in so far as it is possible" (καθ᾽ ὅσον οἷον
τε).[18]

Beyond these limited statements about rulers and parents, Philo also
invites all human beings to an imitation of God. This he does not limit just
to an imitation of God's actions (as in *Leg. All.* 1.48) or of his virtue (*Det.*
160); he speaks more often of a direct imitation of God himself.[19] Thus,
he writes, for example, that "God's obedient children imitate their Father's
nature" in "doing what is excellent" and especially in honoring God (*Sacr.*
68). Elsewhere he adds: "What greater good is there than for creatures to
imitate the eternal God?" (μιμεῖσθαι θεὸν . . . τὸν ἀΐδιον; *Spec. Leg.* 4.73).
This same theme is also clearly enunciated in *Virt.* 168:

Especially does he [Moses] give this lesson as most suitable to the rational
nature that a human being should imitate God as much as may be [μιμεῖσθαι
θεὸν καθ᾽ ὅσον οἷον τε] and leave nothing undone that may promote such
assimilation as is possible [εἰς τὴν ἐνδεχομένην ἐξομοίωσιν].[20]

Two points may be made about this last text. First, the reference in it to
the "rational nature" (τῇ λογικῇ φύσει) of humanity indicates the primary

**129**

metaphysical basis upon which Philo grounds this imitation. There is nothing, he says, "more godlike" (θεοειδέστερον) in the universe than the human person, for this is shaped according to the pattern of the archetypal form of God's own reason or *logos* (*Spec. Leg.* 3.83). That is, imitation is grounded in the order established in creation. God's *logos* is made "in the image of God," and the human person—or his or her rational soul—is made "after the image" (Gen. 1:26–27).[21] Although we as humans are viewed proximately as images and copies of the *logos*, Philo also states that our minds have a direct likeness (ὁμοίωσις) to the Father.[22] But if the order of creation provides the primary ground, the order of revelation also is significant. As we saw, for example, in the passage from the life of Moses (1.158) referred to previously, Moses was able to be a copy of God because of his vision of God's "paradigmatic essence."

The second point to be made about the passage from *De virtutibus* is that this text clearly indicates that Philo equated "imitation of God" with the much better attested ethical goal of "assimilation to God" (ἐξομοίωσις or ὁμοίωσις θεῷ). This formulation directly descends from the classic statement of the ethical *telos* found in Plato's *Theatetus* (176A–B), a text which is in fact cited verbatim by Philo (*Fug.* 63):

> A man highly esteemed, one of those admired for their wisdom, says . . . in the *Theatetus*: 'Evils can never pass away, for there must always remain something which is antagonistic to God. Unable to have a place among divine beings in heaven, they must inevitably hover about mortal nature and this earthly sphere. Therefore we ought to flee from earth to heaven as quickly as we can. This flight means to become like God as far as is possible [ὁμοίωσις θεῷ κατὰ τὸ δυνατόν]. In turn this becoming like Him means with the help of insight to become just and holy' [ὁμοίωσις δὲ δίκαιον καὶ ὅσιον μετὰ φρονήσεως γενέσθαι].

Besides these references to "assimilation to God" found in *Fug.* 63 and *Virt.* 168, Philo clearly refers with approval to this Platonic formula in eight other places.[23] The assertion made by Hans Dieter Betz that "imitation of God is the great theme of Philonic ethics" therefore seems entirely correct.[24]

That Philo viewed the ethical task in this way is not surprising. In John Dillon's fundamental study of Middle Platonism, Philo is included as a representative figure, and his indebtedness especially to the Platonist Eudorus of Alexandria (flor. first century B.C.) is underscored.[25] Within Middle Platonism the formula found in the *Theatetus*, ὁμοίωσις θεῷ, achieved a kind of canonical status from the first century B.C. onward as *the* statement of the purpose of human existence.[26] It is so employed by Eudorus, Plutarch, Albinus, Apuleius, and Philo himself.[27] Philo therefore stands in this regard within a clear philosophical tradition.

Philo, to be sure, is not primarily a philosopher, as we categorize these things, but an exegete; he uses philosophical thought to unravel the various meanings of the biblical text.[28] Because Moses is viewed by him as the father of philosophy, there is a necessary congruence between Greek wisdom and the wisdom of the Scriptures. *De aeternitate mundi* 17—19 expresses the basic point of view: what Plato and the other Greeks said, Moses said long before them. The biblical texts are, therefore, philosophical wisdom "writ large," and Platonism will necessarily provide a valuable hermeneutical key to their interpretation.[29] For Philo, then, the doctrine of "assimilation to God," formulated as (ἐξ)ὁμοίωσις θεῷ or as μιμεῖσθαι θεόν / or as ἔπεσθαι θεῷ ("to follow God"), was the ethical goal or *telos* proposed by Moses himself.[30] Philo does not suppose that this "assimilation" implies an equality with God; his use of the word "god" (θεός) for humans is, as indicated previously, exceptional and is to be understood in the general framework of his archetype-copy, Platonic metaphysics. What is, however, everywhere clear is that this assimilation takes place through ethical or virtuous human activity.

## THE RELEVANCE OF PHILO FOR
## INTERPRETING EPHESIANS

If Samuel Sandmel were correct when he described Philo as a "marginal" and "unique" figure, "remote" from the mainstreams of Hellenistic Judaism, then this extended discussion of the theme of "imitation of God" in Philo, if applied to Eph. 5:1, would be a textbook case of "parallelomania."[31] To the contrary, however, recent scholarship has succeeded in demonstrating that Philo stands within Judaism in a long school tradition of biblical exegesis, a tradition that in particular made use of Platonic perspectives. That Philo relied extensively on prior exegetical traditions, a thesis originally advanced by Wilhelm Bousset at the beginning of this century, is a position now supported by such investigators as Robert Hamerton-Kelly, Burton Mack, David Hay, and Thomas Tobin.[32]

Since Tobin's recent study seems particularly relevant in the present context, let me briefly say something about the main points that it advances. In examining those passages in the Philonic corpus which deal with the account of the creation of humanity in Genesis 1—2, Tobin utilizes both external indicators of source traditions (e.g., "Some say . . . but I say") and tensions and conflicting statements within textual units to identify various levels of interpretation. On the basis of this analysis, Tobin offers what he calls a "plausible theory" for organizing these various types of interpretation into a historical sequence. First in time came isolated, antianthropomorphic interpretations of an apologetic sort, cast either in a Stoic or, especially after c. 100 B.C., in a Platonic thought pattern. Then came two different levels of definably Middle Platonic exegesis, levels classed also by Tobin as pre-Philonic. Finally, following Bousset, Tobin argues that Philo himself contributes a level of interpretation based upon the "allegory of the soul."[33]

What is important to note, Tobin stresses, is that Philo carefully retains all these various levels of interpretation without attempting to harmonize away the various tensions. While he does, for example, subordinate Stoic interpretations to principal interpretations cast in a Platonic mold, he does not eliminate them.[34] They are all treated as inspired; the biblical text, that is, is conceived of as a "multifaceted reality which yields a number of inspired interpretations."[35] Noting the presence of numerous Middle Platonic philosophers in Alexandria prior to and contemporaneous with Philo, Tobin is able to establish many links between Philo's thought and the writings of these individuals. Tobin warns, however, that he has sketched a partial history of Jewish exegetical tradition valid only for Alexandria—his results are not to be generalized without further investigation.[36]

With respect to the theme of "imitation of God," however, I will dare to draw a connecting line between the works of Philo and the Letter to the Ephesians, even though we may safely assume that the author of the latter document did not have the Philonic treatises open on his desk as he wrote. There are four reasons permitting the construction of such a link. First, the lapse of a century or more between this Platonizing exegetical activity in Alexandria and the writing of Ephesians gave ample time for the spread of such ideas through Diaspora Judaism in the eastern Mediterranean. Second, whether or not Tobin's history-of-interpretation framework has wider applicability in Greco-Roman Judaism, the sheer variety of Platonic exegetical traditions attested in Philo indicates that much work of this type was being done over a relatively long period of time by certain Greek-speaking Jews. That is, for a fairly significant segment of such Jews, to think in a biblical manner was to think in a Platonic manner. The occurrence, then, of Platonic language in a Greek text with numerous Jewish affiliations would seem traceable to circles of this sort. In this environment a reference to "imitation of God" would not seem like a foreign intrusion into the text but as much a part of traditional language as "to walk in love" (Eph. 5:2). Third, Philo's reference to predecessors who call parents "gods" (*Decal.* 120) strongly suggests that "imitation of God" language was in use in Jewish exegesis prior to the time of Philo and so is not his own idiosyncratic *theologoumenon*. Finally, if the letters of Paul constitute the most proximate source for the use of "imitation" language in Ephesians,[37] the precise reference in Eph. 5:1 to an "imitation of *God*" finds its closest verbal parallels in Alexandrian Jewish texts. While Plato occasionally employed derivatives of μιμεῖσθαι in speaking of the imitation of God, his Middle Platonic successors generally preferred the formula from the *Theatetus*, ὁμοίωσις θεῷ.[38] Philo's treatises and the *Letter of Aristeas* are different. Philo often uses μιμεῖσθαι and derivatives when speaking of the imitation of God, and the *Letter of Aristeas* does so always.[39] In calling for believers to be "imitators [μιμηταί] of God," Eph. 5:1 stands in line with these latter traditions.[40]

Some scholars have argued that the twin formulas ὁμοίωσις θεῷ and μίμησις θεοῦ cannot be traced to anything more definite than "Hellenistic popular philosophy."[41] As I have indicated above, John Dillon's work has made it clear that this sort of language characterized Middle Platonic ethical thought. From the first century B.C. onward, such modes of thought became deeply embedded in significant streams of Hellenistic Jewish exegesis. Because Eph. 5:1 appears to stand in line with such traditions, I would contend that it preserves a specific Middle Platonic statement of the purpose of human existence even though such a formulation was no doubt deemed fully consonant with biblical revelation.

## EPHESIANS 4:24 AND THE
## IMITATION OF GOD

This clarification of the conceptual background of Eph. 5:1 helps, I believe, to explain another important verse in the "ethics section" of the letter, Eph. 4:24. Like 5:1–2, Eph. 4:22–24 functions as an ethical generalization concluding a unit of more specific parenesis.[42] From a different perspective it, too, provides a statement of Christian ethical finality. The three infinitives that govern 4:22–24 are grammatically dependent on the verb ἐδιδάχθητε in 4:21 ("you were taught that you are to do these things") but possess as well a certain imperative tonality ("now do them—this is truth in Jesus" [4:21b]).[43] The imagery of "stripping off the old humanity and putting on the new" and indeed much of the other specific vocabulary of this passage are drawn from Col. 3:8–10. This fact will allow us here to pass over the source material, material which has been extensively discussed elsewhere, and to concentrate upon certain of the redactional shifts introduced by the author of Ephesians.[44]

In 4:24, the recipients of the letter are reminded that they have been taught that they are "to put on the new humanity [ἄνθρωπον] created ["by God" understood] in accord with God [ματὰ θεόν] in true justice and holiness" (literally: "in justice and holiness of the truth";[45] RSV: "the new nature, created after the likeness of God in true righteousness and holiness"). The parallel verse in Col. 3:10, reads, "And have put on the new humanity [RSV: "nature"] which is being renewed in knowledge after the image of its creator [εἰς ἐπίγνωσιν κατ' εἰκόνα τοῦ κτίσαντος αὐτόν]." The author of Ephesians has therefore introduced two important changes: he

133

has dropped the reference to Gen. 1:26–27 (κατ᾽ εἰκόνα)—the εἰκών language used in Colossians is never taken over by Ephesians—and substituted κατὰ θεόν, and he has added a description of the ethical character of the "new humanity." I will consider the second of these changes first, since I believe that this will make the substitution of the κατὰ θεόν phrase more intelligible.

The "new humanity," says the author of Ephesians, will be characterized by "justice and holiness." The specification of this as *true justice and holiness* both serves to contrast it with the *deceptive* desires" ascribed to the "old humanity" in 4:22 and suggests, in light of the overall attack in 4:17–24 on the life style of non-Christians, a definite polemical intent: "Only ours is the *true* justice and holiness."[46] When commentators deal with the pair of virtues mentioned, they are generally content to note biblical parallels (Deut. 9:5; Ps. 144:17 [LXX]; Wis. 9:3; Luke 1:75; 1 Thess. 2:10[47]) and to observe that in Plato's *Gorgias* the terms "justice" and "holiness" are referred, respectively, to ethical responsibilities to other humans and to the gods (*Gorgias* 507A–B).[48] There is more to be said than this.

The phrase δίκαιος καὶ ὅσιος ("just and holy") occurs fairly frequently in the writings of Plato, and generally in that order, as a comprehensive synonym for "living virtuously."[49] In *Theatetus* 176B, "assimilation to God" is specifically defined as "becoming with the help of insight just and holy." Only in *Gorgias* 507A–B are the two virtues assigned, respectively, to human and divine affairs. We might expect that if Plato normally understood this phrase in this manner he would have tended to mention "holiness" before "justice." While Plato's own religious sensibilities in this cannot be determined, those of Philo can be. Philo also uses either this adjective pair or the correlative noun pair δικαιοσύνη/ὁσιότης as a shorthand expression for the totality of ethical life.[50] When he refers specifically to our ethical duties toward God, he is careful to mention "holiness" first.[51] If Philo's procedure is in any way indicative of more general Hellenistic Jewish usage, it is probable that in mentioning "justice" before "holiness" the author of Ephesians intends at the end of 4:24 to refer simply to "virtuous living" as a whole.

Further affecting the interpretation of these words in Eph. 4:24 is the fact that all of the Septuagint parallels either directly or indirectly insist that it is *God* who is truly just and holy. Deuteronomy 32:4 and Ps. 144:7 expressly assert this, and Deut. 9:5 denies that human justice and holiness had anything to do with Israel's reception of its inheritance. Even Wis. 9:3, which speaks of human governance of the world "in holiness and justice," does so in the context of stressing that it was *God* who established this order (9:1–2).

When we come, then, to Eph. 4:24, we may therefore assume that the justice and holiness proper to the "new humanity" are seen as proper first and foremost to God. We may also safely assume that a Greco-Roman audience would have understood this phrase as a statement encompassing the sum of all virtue and excellence. Together, these two dimensions suggest that consciously or unconsciously the writer of Ephesians is alluding here to the definition of "assimilation to God" found in *Theatetus* 176B: "To be just and holy with the help of insight." The "new humanity" is endowed with the excellence proper first and foremost to God—therefore it is "of the truth"—and it is to live this out. That is, it is to imitate God.

This perception is strengthened by the use in 4:24 of the phrase "created κατὰ θεόν." Schnackenburg rightly notes that the passive participle alone (κτισθέντα) indicates the agent; the (new) creation was accomplished by God.[52] The prepositional phrase κατὰ θεόν designates the relationship of the "new humanity" to God; it is "in accordance with God," "similar to God," "Godlike."[53] The "new humanity" is thus contrasted with the "old humanity that is perishing" (4:22). κατὰ θεόν may also have a teleological connotation: the "new humanity" is created "Godlike," and it is therefore also to be "Godlike." This formulation of the ethical *telos*, "to live in accord with God" (τὸ ζῆν κατὰ θεόν or equivalent), is found, for example, in Josephus and in the second-century Christian wisdom text, the *Sentences of Sextus*.[54]

The source text for Eph. 4:24—Col. 3:10—describes the "new humanity" as "being renewed after the image [κατ᾽ εἰκόνα] of its creator." This gives us a metaphysical system of three levels in the manner of Philo and of Middle Platonism generally: God, Christ the image, and the "new humanity," which is made "after the image"—an allusion to Gen. 1:26–27.[55] Thus, in Platonic terms the "new humanity" is the copy or image of an image.

In Ephesians, a text which avoids speaking of Christ as "the image," the "new humanity" consists both of Christ and the community of believers, the church. The key text in Scripture that apparently led the writer of Ephesians to this conclusion was Gen. 2:24 ("the two become one"—cited in 5:31), a text which had been already employed in an ecclesial sense by Paul himself (1 Cor. 6:15–17). Ephesians is quite clear: the primary referent of this "mystery" is Christ and the church (5:32), and true Christian marriage is a copy of this reality. To be sure, Christ is head, and the church is the body, but together they form a *single* reality. That is why we encounter in 3:20–21, the closing doxology for the first half of Ephesians, language so strange to ears accustomed to conventional Christian formulas of prayer: "To him [God] be glory in the church and in Christ Jesus." Here the church and Christ are paired as apparent equals. Indeed, the church is even mentioned before Christ, a state of affairs that caused apoplexy to many later copyists.[56] For the author of Ephesians, the church and Christ are conjoined; together, they are the "new humanity," even though individual believers have to "grow into" this reality (4:15). The community of believers joined with Christ has direct access (προσαγωγή) to God (2:18, 3:12; see 2:14) and therefore the possibility of imitating God Himself directly.[57]

## THE THEME OF IMITATION OF GOD
## ELSEWHERE IN EPHESIANS

Therefore, it is not only Eph. 5:1 but also 4:24 which defines the goal of Christian discipleship in terms of "assimilation to God." Ephesians 4:24 even does this in language reminiscent of Plato's formula in the *Theatetus*. Besides these two texts, I believe that this motif makes yet a third appearance in Ephesians in the conclusion of the "ethics section," Eph. 6:10–20. I have discussed this passage extensively elsewhere and so will not repeat all those arguments here.[58] Suffice it to say that though the language is drawn directly from the Bible rather than from scholastic Platonism, the point is still the same. In Eph. 6:10–11 the believer is told to be strong in the strength of the Lord's might (see Isa. 40:26) and to put on the very armor that God himself wears as "the Divine Warrior" (see Isa. 59:15–20). This armor is described in 6:14–17 in terms of virtues and gifts (truth, justice, readiness for the gospel, faith, salvation, and the Word of God). It is God's armor; it is given to believers; and it allows believers to resist and to stand firm in the face of assaults from evil cosmic powers. Although not equal to God, believers do have the power of God. They must, however, be exhorted to "be strong" in this power, to "put it on," to "take it up."

My argument, therefore, is that the reference to "imitation of God" in Eph. 5:1 is not an isolated fragment drawn into the letter from some amorphous popular philosophical context but a fundamental statement of what the author considered the goal of discipleship to be. As has been demonstrated, this theme appears at several key points in Ephesians 4—6, and it appears that other statements of the ethical *telos* found scattered through the letter generally conform to this perspective. For example, the pronouncement in 2:10 that "we are God's workmanship [ποίημα] created in Christ Jesus for good works" is a clear reference to the "new humanity" which exists as reality and yet is to be achieved in the existential order by actual believing communities.[59]

## THE SPECIFIC CHARACTER OF IMITATION OF
## GOD AS FOUND IN EPHESIANS

There are, finally, two points that should be made about the ethical demand to "be imitators of God" as this is found in Ephesians. In Philo the possibility of this imitation is grounded primarily in the order of creation. This order, it is true, has to be known, and maximal wisdom, the wisdom of Moses, seems finally to be a matter of revelation (*Moses* 1.158). What is revealed, however, is the fundamental created order as it actually exists, the true metaphysical relationship of human beings to the universe and to God, and this order is available as possibility to all human beings; hence, the felt congruence between Greek philosophy and Moses. Ephesians, on the other hand, makes use of creation language (1:4; 2:10, 15; 3:9 and 15 are clear examples) but almost always—3:9 is an exception—in terms of the Pauline "new creation," the new soteriological community. Only those who have "heard the word of truth and who are sealed with the Holy Spirit of the promise" (1:13–14) belong to this community. To put it in the language of 5:1, insiders are "children of God."[60] All other human beings are "alienated," "strangers," "without hope," "in the universe without God" (2:12; see 2:19).[61] This soteriological order is in fact viewed as being prior to the created order.[62] Because of this it must be revealed; it is not perceived through the normal activity of the human mind. While Platonism certainly speaks of knowledge in soteriological terms—the "Myth of the Cave" in *Republic* 7 is an obvious example—the true knowledge of philosophy stands in a linear sequence with all previous knowledge as archetype to copy. It is this direct linear sequence that Ephesians ultimately rejects; the revealed knowledge possessed now by believers was simply unobtainable previously (2:1–3; 3:5).[63]

The second point I would wish to make has reference to the ethical content associated with "imitation of God." As we find it in Eph. 5:1, this theme occurs in the midst of an exhortation to kindness, love, and forgiveness (4:32 and 5:2)—believers should be forgiving, as God in Christ has been forgiving to them. Philo has a quite similar statement:

> He [Moses] adds to those already mentioned another wise precept, not to show pity to the poor man in giving judgment. And this comes from one who has filled practically his whole legislation with injunctions to show pity and kindness. . . ! For what one of the men of old aptly said is true, that human beings do nothing more akin to God than showing kindness [παρακλήσιον οὐδὲν ἄνθρωποι θεῷ δρῶσιν ἢ χαριζόμενοι].[64] For what greater good can there be than that they should imitate God [μιμεῖσθαι θεόν]. . . .[65]

Further, in *Decal.* 72–76 Philo speaks of "assimilation to God" in the context of contrasting true worship with the worship of idols, a context not unlike that found in Eph. 4:17–24. But if these fairly close parallels to the two passages of Ephesians do exist, it is nonetheless clear that Ephesians views the task of ethical endeavor in a manner quite different from the Platonic flight of the soul from earth to heaven (*Theatetus* 176A–B).[66] On the one hand, probably no New Testament writing makes the heavenly status of believers more clear and explicit: "[God] made us alive together with Christ . . . and raised us up with him and made us sit with him in the heavenly places in Christ Jesus" (2:5–6). Yet this status is existentially achieved in very "earthly" activity: speaking the truth (4:25), controlling anger (4:26), working with one's hands (4:28), loving one's wife (5:25), obeying parents (6:1), etc. These ordinary tasks are given the highest ontological significance. Human marriage, for example, serves as the best image of ultimate heavenly realities (5:22–33). For the author of Ephesians, that is, "imitation of God" is achieved and made manifest in living responsibility in this world and not by a flight from this world.[67]

To conclude, in its formulation of the goal or end of Christian discipleship, the Letter to the Ephesians stands in a clear Platonic tradition mediated through Hellenistic Judaism. The discovery of Platonic *theologoumena* in a text like Ephesians should not evoke any particular surprise. As various scholars have pointed out, Platonism was a very "religious" philosophical tradition and consequently was employed in a variety of religious contexts in this period (Isis worship, Mithraism, Judaism, Christianity) as a means to provide a better understanding of these beliefs and practices.[68] Each tradition, of course, utilized this Platonic conceptual schema in its own way—philosophy, if we may say so, stood in the service of particular theologies. The use of "imitation of God" language by the author of Ephesians therefore reveals characteristics not necessarily found elsewhere in the use of this Platonic formulation. This is because this writer is not first and foremost a member of a philosophical school tradition but a believer in the revelation of God and a disciple of Jesus Christ.[69]

## NOTES

1. For a convenient overview, see G. Delling, "Telos-Aussagen in der griechischen Philosophie," *ZNW* 55 (1964) 26–42.

2. Of the recent commentaries, those by M. Barth (*Ephesians* [2 vols.; AB 34–34A; Garden City, N.Y.: Doubleday & Co., 1974]) and by R. Schnackenburg (*Der Brief an die Epheser* [EKKNT 10; Zürich: Benziger Verlag, 1982]) in particular stress the Old Testament and Jewish roots of Ephesians.

3. K. G. Kuhn, "The Epistle to the Ephesians in the Light of the Qumran Texts," in *Paul and Qumran. Studies in New Testament Exegesis* (ed. J. Murphy-O'Connor; Chicago: Priory Press, 1968) 115–31; and F. Mussner, "Contributions Made by Qumran to the Understanding of the Epistle to the Ephesians," in ibid., 159–78. In my own view, the commonality of language is probably most often explainable on the basis of shared sources and traditions, especially the biblical text.

4. Ephesians 2:10; 4:1, 15, 22–24; 5:1–2, 7–11, 15; and 6:10–14 are also formulations of the Christian *telos*.

5. The eight uses of περιπατεῖν in Ephesians either refer positively (2:10; 4:1; 5:2, 8, 15) or negatively (2:2 and 4:17) to the authentic ethical goal for humanity.

This word is used elsewhere in the Pauline corpus but never as frequently as in Ephesians: Romans (four times), 1 Corinthians (two), 2 Corinthians (five), Galatians (one), Philippians (two), Colossians (four), 1 Thessalonians (four), and 2 Thessalonians (two).

6. Exodus 29:18, 25, 41; and Ezek. 20:41. See also Gen. 8:21; Lev. 1:9, 13, 17; 2:2, 9; and Phil. 4:18.

7. Only in Wisdom (4:2; 9:8; and 15:9) and in 4 Maccabees (9:23 and 13:9).

8. Imitation of Paul: 1 Cor. 4:16; 11:1; Phil. 3:17; and 1 Thess. 1:6. Imitation of other churches: 1 Thess. 2:14. Imitation of Christ: 1 Cor. 11:1 and 1 Thess. 1:6. Close verbal parallels to Eph. 5:1, possibly even direct citations, are found in Ignatius, *Ephesians* 1.1, *Trallians* 1.2, and in *Diognetus* 10.4–6.

9. The word μιμητής is very rare in Philo, occurring only four times in his writings.

10. See also *Abr.* 144. The translations, with occasional slight adjustments, are those of F. H. Colson et al., eds., *Philo* (12 vols.; LCL; Cambridge: Harvard Univ. Press, 1929–62).

11. *Letter of Aristeas* 210, 281; see 188. For further references in ancient literature to this theme, see W. Michaelis, "μιμέομαι, κτλ.," *TDNT* 4 (1967) 664 n. 8.

12. See also *Sacr.* 9. In *Leg. All.* 1.40, Philo applies Exod. 7:1 to the allegory of the soul: the νοῦς is as a θεός to the unreasoning part of the soul.

13. *Moses* 1.158. See also *Plant.* 23–26. For a very close parallel to the passage from *De vita Mosis*, see Josephus, *Antiquities* 1.proem.4, 19–20. See also Clement of Alexandria, *Stromateis* 6.12.104.

14. On this, see B. Mack, "Imitatio Mosis," *SP* 1 (1972) 27–55.

15. See also *Decal.* 107 and *Spec. Leg.* 2.2. *Decal.* 107 speaks of an "assimilation of parents to God [πρὸς θεὸν . . . ἐξομοίωσιν]."

16. Dicaeogenes (fifth or fourth century B.C.), frag. 5 (ed. A. Nauck and B. Snell, *Tragicorum graecorum fragmenta* [3d ed.; Hildesheim: Georg Olms, 1964] 776): "For those with perception parents are the greatest god"; Hierocles of Alexandria (early second century A.D.) (cited in Stobaeus, *Eclogai* 3.96 [ed. A. Meineke]): "One would not err, if it is right to speak thus, in calling parents, on account of their nearness, secondary and earthly gods as it were and more precious to us than gods"; Nilus (cited in J. F. Boissonade, *Anecdota graeca* 4.438): "Consider parents to be gods for yourself." The sentiments of Hierocles, a Stoic philosopher, are close to those ascribed to Zeno in *Diogenes Laertius* 7.120: "It is fitting to reverence parents and brothers in the second place just after the gods."

17. Contra Michaelis, "μιμέομαι," 665.

18. *Spec. Leg.* 2.225. In several places Philo is also willing to say that the human mind is "in some manner" a "god" (*Op.* 69, *Leg. All.* 1.40).

19. This despite Philo's understandably negative stricture against the "crafting" of a μίμημα of God (*Spec. Leg.* 2.224). See also *Leg. All.* 2.1: οὐδὲν δὲ ὅμοιον θεῷ. Philo makes this observation in the course of arguing that God is "sole and alone" (μονος καὶ εἷς). In following this line of argumentation elsewhere (*Op.* 151; see also *Abr.* 87) Philo says that Adam was "assimilated to God" when he was alone prior to the creation of Eve. "Adam" here stands for the rational part of the soul.

20. On this, see also *Op.* 79 and *Plant.* 73 and 94. *Leg. Gai.* 87, 88, and 110 refer to the imitation of Greek gods.

21. *Op.* 24–25; *Leg. All.* 3.95–96; *Spec. Leg.* 1.80–81, 3.83, and 207; *Q. Gen.*

2.62; etc. For an extensive discussion of this aspect of Philo's thought, see T. Tobin, *The Creation of Man: Philo and the History of Interpretation* (CBQMS 14; Washington, D.C.: Catholic Biblical Association, 1983).

22. *Her.* 236. See also *Det.* 83.

23. *Op.* 144, 151; *Abr.* 87; *Decal.* 73; *Spec. Leg.* 4.188; *Virt.* 8 and *Q. Gen.* 4.147 and 188. *Leg. Gai.* 78, 111, and 114 apply this maxim to the Emperor Gaius's supposed kinship with Hellenic gods. *Cher.* 31, which speaks of Abraham's flight to God from the created realm, may also allude to *Theatetus* 176B.

24. H. D. Betz, *Nachfolge und Nachahmung Jesu Christi im Neuen Testament* (BHT 37; Tübingen: Mohr/Siebeck, 1967) 132. See also J. Dillon, *The Middle Platonists* (London: Duckworth, 1977) 145–46. In twelve or fourteen places (*Op.* 144; *Sacr.* 2; *Mig.* 128, 131, 146, 173; *Mut.* 46; *Abr.* 60; *Decal.* 98, 100; *Spec. Leg.* 4.187; *Praem.* 98; and possibly also *Fug.* 165 and *Decal.* 81), Philo defines the ethical task in terms of "following God" (ἕπεσθαι θεῷ), a Pythagorean formulation adopted with enthusiasm by Platonism. In *Op.* 144 and *Spec. Leg.* 4.187–88, Philo makes it clear that he equates this formulation with "assimilation to God." In this he is in agreement with Eudorus (cited in Stobaeus, *Eclogai* 2.49.8–16 [ed. K. Wachsmuth and O. Hensel]).

25. Dillon, *Middle Platonists*, 139–83. See also Tobin, *Creation of Man*, 9–19. Dillon (ibid., 145–48; see 44) argues that Philo followed Eudorus in adopting "likeness to God" as his basic statement of the purpose of life, even though in other aspects of his ethics Philo often employs formulations drawn from Stoic tradition. A similar pattern is found in Clement of Alexandria—see J. Zandee, *"The Teachings of Silvanus" and Clement of Alexandria* (Leiden: Ex Oriente Lux, 1977) 1 and 104–11.

26. See Dillon, *Middle Platonists*, 44 and 306; Delling, "Telos-Aussagen," 30; and M. Pohlenz, *Die Stoa* (2 vols.; Göttingen: Vandenhoeck & Ruprecht, 1948–49) 1:357–58 and 2:174. For a discussion of this theme in Plato, see A. Schulz, *Nachfolgen und Nachahmen. Studien über das Verhältnis der neutestamentlichen Jüngerschaft zur urchristlichen Vorbildethik* (SANT 6; Munich: Kösel-Verlag, 1962) 207–9; and H. D. Betz, *Nachfolge und Nachahmung Jesu Christi*, 111–17.

27. Eudorus (cited in Stobaeus, *Eclogai* 2.49.8–12 [ed. Wachsmuth and Hensel]); Plutarch, *De sera numinis vindicta* 550D; *De tranquillitate*, frag. 143 (ed. F. H. Sandbach); Albinus, *Didascalia* 28; Apuleius, *De dogmate Platonis* 2.23. For the use of this formula by the later Stoics, see H. Merki, ΟΜΟΙΩΣΙΣ ΘΕΩ *von der platonischen Angleichung an Gott zur Gottähnlichkeit bei Gregor von Nyssa* (Fribourg, Switz.: Paulusverlag, 1952) 8–17.

28. This point is stressed by Dillon (*Middle Platonists*, 144).

29. Tobin, *Creation of Man*, 130–31. See also Dillon, *Middle Platonists*, 119 and 143. Dillon (ibid., 117–21 and 143) notes the assimilation of Moses in Philo's *De vita Mosis* to Pythagoras. Within large segments of Middle Platonism, the latter was viewed as the source of many Platonic doctrines.

30. See n. 24 above.

31. S. Sandmel, *Philo of Alexandria: An Introduction* (New York and London: Oxford Univ. Press, 1979) 147. See also B. Lindars, "Imitation of God and Imitation of Christ," *Theology* 76 (1973) 401. This point of view goes back particularly to H. A. Wolfson (*Philo. Foundations of Religious Philosophy in Judaism, Christianity, and*

*Islam* [2 vols.; Cambridge: Harvard Univ. Press, 1948]), who stressed the originality of Philo.

32. W. Bousset, *Jüdisch-christlicher Schulbetrieb in Alexandria und Rom: Literarische Untersuchungen zu Philo und Clemens von Alexandria, Justin und Irenäus* (FRLANT 6; Göttingen: Vandenhoeck & Ruprecht, 1915) 8–154; R. G. Hamerton-Kelly, "Sources and Traditions in Philo Judaeus: Prolegomena to an Analysis of His Writings," *SP* 1 (1972) 3–26; B. L. Mack, "Exegetical Traditions in Alexandrian Judaism: A Program for the Analysis of the Philonic Corpus," *SP* 3 (1974–75) 71–115; D. M. Hay, "Philo's References to Other Allegorists," *SP* 6 (1979–80) 41–75; and Tobin, *Creation of Man*.

33. Hay ("Philo's References," 60) has criticized Bousset's view—Tobin's work was not then available—that Philo was exclusively interested in psychological allegory and that other types of allegory therefore derive from sources. I myself believe that Tobin has met the challenge posed by Hay for establishing such sources, but this will be a matter for future Philonic scholarship to decide.

34. Tobin, *Creation of Man*, 164–65.

35. Ibid., 166.

36. Ibid., 179–80.

37. 1 Thess. 1:6; 2:14; 1 Cor. 4:16; 11:1; Phil. 3:17.

38. Plato also can speak of "imitating" (μιμούμενος) a god (*Phaedo* 252D) and can equate this with "assimilation to God" (εἰς ὁμοιότητα . . . τῷ θεῷ—*Phaedo* 253B), but it is this latter formulation that is normative in later Platonism.

39. See also *Testament of Asher* 4.3. On the *Letter of Aristeas* as deriving from Alexandria, see G. W. E. Nickelsburg, *Jewish Literature Between the Bible and the Mishnah* (Philadelphia: Fortress Press, 1981) 168. On linguistic and conceptual similarities between the *Letter of Aristeas* and Philo, see R. Hecht, "Patterns of Exegesis in Philo's Interpretation of Leviticus," *SP* 6 (1979–80) 112–14 and 149 n. 51.

40. Just as C. Colpe in an important study ("Zur Leib-Christi-Vorstellung im Epheserbrief," *Judentum-Urchristentum-Kirche* [ed. A. Eltester; BZNW 26; Berlin: Alfred Töpelmann, 1960] 172–87) found in the writings of Philo the clearest parallels with the concept in Ephesians of "the body of Christ," so here I find Philo's thought and traditions to be very akin to the statements in Ephesians on the *telos*.

41. Schulz, *Nachfolgen und Nachahmen*, 213; H. D. Betz, *Nachfolge und Nachahmung Jesu Christi*, 93 (see 135); and K. M. Fischer, *Tendenz und Absicht des Epheserbriefes* (FRLANT 111; Göttingen: Vandenhoeck & Ruprecht, 1973) 140.

42. Following H. Schlier (*Der Brief an die Epheser* [3d ed.; Düsseldorf: Patmos-Verlag, 1962]) and Schnackenburg (*Der Brief an die Epheser*), I take the divisions in Ephesians at this point to be 4:17–24, 4:25—5:2, 5:3–14. Others, e.g., Barth (*Ephesians*, vol. 2), J. Gnilka (*Der Epheserbrief* [HTKNT 10.2; Freiburg: Herder Verlag, 1971]), and C. L. Mitton (*Ephesians* [NCB; Grand Rapids: Wm. B. Eerdmans, 1973])—treat 4:17–32 as a unit with 5:1–14 or 20 as a following unit.

43. So, in general, Schnackenburg, *Der Brief an die Epheser*, 203; see also Mitton, *Ephesians*, 164. Gnilka (*Der Epheserbrief*, 229) and Barth (*Ephesians*, 2:506) consider the infinitives to be dependent on the καθώς phrase in 4:21.

44. For bibliography on this imagery of "stripping off the old humanity and putting on the new," see, e.g., E. Lohse, *Colossians and Philemon: A Commentary on the*

*Epistles to the Colossians and to Philemon* (trans. W. R. Poehlman and R. S. Karris; Hermeneia; Philadelphia: Fortress Press, 1971) 140–43, and Fischer, *Tendenz und Absicht*, 152–61. Such imagery probably originally had its place in a baptismal context (see Gal. 3:2), but in the New Testament it most often appears in a parenetic environment (as in Rom. 13:14, Col. 3:9–10, and here). P. W. van der Horst ("Observations on a Pauline Expression," *NTS* 19 [1973] 181–87) has found an exact verbal parallel for the phrase "putting off the man" in a story about Pyrrho of Elis reported in Antigonus of Carystus's popular and much-utilized handbook of philosophy (third century B.C.): "Pyrrho [who was renowned for teaching that we should ignore sense impressions] when attacked by a dog climbed up a tree. When he was spotted by those passing by, he said, 'It is difficult to put off the man [τὸν ἄνθρωπον ἐκδῦναι]' " (cited in Eusebius, *Praeparatio evangelica* 14.18.26 and in *Diogenes Laertius* 9.66).

45. For the grammatical understanding that allows for this translation of the genitive τῆς ἀληθείας, see C. F. D. Moule, *An Idiom-Book of New Testament Greek* (2d ed.; Cambridge: Cambridge Univ. Press, 1959) 38 and 174–76.

46. See M. Barth, *Ephesians*, 2:510; Schlier, *Der Brief an die Epheser*, 222; Schnackenburg, *Der Brief an die Epheser*, 205.

47. 1 Thessalonians 2:10 lists a triplet of virtues and so turns out to be a false parallel.

48. T. K. Abbott, *A Critical and Exegetical Commentary on the Epistles to the Ephesians and to the Colossians* (ICC; New York: Charles Scribner's Sons, 1916) 138–39; M. Barth, *Ephesians*, 2:510; Gnilka, *Der Epheserbrief*, 233; Schlier, *Der Brief an die Epheser*, 221–22; Schnackenburg, *Der Brief an die Epheser*, 205.

49. *Apology* 35D; *Crito* 54B; *Theatetus* 172B, 176B; *Gorgias* 507A–B; *Republic* 10.615B; *Laws* 2.661B, 2.663D; see also *Apology* 32D. The reverse order, ὅσιος καὶ δίκαιος, is found in *Republic* 5.461A and 463D and in *Laws* 2.663B and 8.840D.

50. The noun pair is found in *Sacr.* 57 (citing Deut. 9:5), *Spec. Leg.* 1.304; see *Virt.* 47. The triplet φρόνησις /δικαιοσύνη /ὁσιότης seen in *Spec. Leg.* 2.12 and *Praem.* 66 is a possible allusion to *Theatetus* 176B. The adjective pair appears in *Sobr.* 10 (citing Deut. 32:4), *Fug.* 63, *Spec. Leg.* 2.180, *Virt.* 50.

51. *Abr.* 208, *Moses* 2.108 (in speaking of sacrifices), *Spec. Leg.* 2.63.

52. Schnackenburg, *Der Brief an die Epheser*, 205. See Eph. 2:10: "For we are his [God's] workmanship, created in Christ Jesus."

53. This is certainly the meaning of the phrase in 2 Cor. 7:9–11 where "grieving κατὰ θεόν" is contrasted with "the world's grieving," and is probably also the sense in Rom. 8:27. The translation of this phrase as "according to God's will" seems misleading—more is involved than a voluntaristic relationship.

54. Josephus, *Antiquities* 4.6.10,143: τὸ κατὰ θεὸν βιοῦν; *Sentences* of Sextus Empiricus 201, 216, 399: ζῆν κατὰ θεόν. These formulations are unquestionably related to the Stoic ζῆν κατὰ φύσιν. A Stoic could accept either formula; a Platonist might assimilate such statements with the help of *Laws* 682A.

55. On a mediator figure as a characteristic feature of Middle Platonism, see Dillon, *Middle Platonists*, 45–46. That Christ is here the "image" is made clear by Col. 1:15. For the interpretation of κατ᾽εἰκόνα as "in accord with" or "after the image," see the references to Philo given in n. 21 above and Tobin, *Creation of Man*.

56. Numerous efforts were made to "correct" this text. D*, F, G, Ambrosiaster,

Victorinus place the reference to Christ before the reference to the Church. D[2], ψ, Majority Text, vg[ms], sy, sa[mss], bo[ms], Cassiodorus omit the καί.

57. Contra M. Barth, *Ephesians*, 2:591.

58. R. A. Wild, "The Warrior and the Prisoner: Some Reflections on Ephesians 6:10–20," *CBQ* 46 (1984) 284–98.

59. See also the reference in 4:13 to attaining to the "perfect man."

60. The description of believers as "children of God" provides the basis upon which the demand is made to imitate God. So also Mitton, *Ephesians*, 175; Schlier, *Der Brief an die Epheser*, 230; and C. Spicq, *Théologie morale du Nouveau Testament* (2 vols.; EBib; Paris: J. Gabalda et C[ie], 1965) 2:702.

61. Schnackenburg (*Der Brief an die Epheser*, 197) particularly stresses this differentiation.

62. See also the predestination language of 1:5, 11, 12.

63. Relevant to this matter is the splendid article by N. Dahl: "Cosmic Dimensions and Religious Knowledge (Eph. 3:18)," in *Jesus und Paulus* (ed. E. E. Ellis and E. Grässer; Göttingen: Vandenhoeck & Ruprecht, 1975) 57–75.

64. This sort of language is found in the traditions surrounding Pythagoras: "Pythagoras said that the two best gifts of the gods to human beings were speaking the truth and showing kindness, and he added that both resembled the works of the gods" (Aelian, *Varia historia* 12.59). In the sixteenth-century collection of ancient Greek sayings and maxims put together by Arsenius, Demosthenes is reported as saying something similar: "Being asked what man has like God, Demosthenes said, 'Showing kindness and speaking the truth'" (*Violarium*, 189 [ed. E. L. von Leutsch]).

65. *Spec. Leg.* 4.72–73; see also *Virt.* 165–70.

66. J. Dillon ("Self-Definition in Later Platonism," in *Jewish and Christian Self-Definition*, vol. 3: *Self-Definition in the Greco-Roman World* [ed. B. F. Meyer and E. P. Sanders; Philadelphia: Fortress Press, 1982] 66) associates the Middle Platonic *telos* of "likeness to God" with an overall "ascetic, world-negating tendency."

67. I have not tried here to evaluate Philo himself in this respect. His preference for the "allegory of the soul" is more in keeping with a Platonic return of the soul from earth to heaven. Yet it is equally clear that Philo also values traditional halachic observance.

68. This point is made by Tobin, *Creation of Man*, 19.

69. The present essay clearly takes a quite different stance than the viewpoint enunciated by Lindars ("Imitation of God," 395): "Imitation of God . . . is neither biblical nor true to the ethical position of Jesus and the early Church."

# 7

# The Followers of the Lamb: Visionary Rhetoric and Social-Political Situation*

## ELISABETH SCHÜSSLER FIORENZA

> Our visions, stories and utopias
> are not only aesthetic:
> they engage us.
>
> Amos Wilder

In his summary of the overall outline and analysis of the Apocalypse, W. Bousset stresses that Rev. 14:1–5 was not taken over from a source but that it is formulated as "contrast-image" by the author. But he concludes: "It is not quite clear what the author means by this scene."[1] This exegetical helplessness before the passage is confirmed by I. T. Beckwith (1919) and repeated by R. H. Mounce (1977): "Verses 1–5 are often referred to as in some respects the most enigmatic in the book."[2] Such an exegetical conundrum is surprising because this passage (14:1–5) has a clearly marked composition and structure: it consists of

1. *Vision:* 14:1 describes the 144,000 with the Lamb on Mount Zion,
2. *Audition:* 14:2–3 announce the voice from heaven and the choral song before the throne of God which none could learn except the 144,000 and
3. *Explanation:* 14:4–5 identify the 144,000 with a four-fold characterization: they are virgins, followers of the Lamb, a first fruit, and blameless.

The literary context of this segment is also clear: the 144,000 around the

---

*This chapter also appears as chapter 7, "Visionary Rhetoric and Social-Political Situation," in *The Book of Revelation—Justice and Judgment* (Philadelphia: Fortress Press, 1985).

Lamb on Mount Zion are the anti-image of the beast and its followers which were depicted in the preceding chapter (Revelation 13). The tableau is followed by three angelic proclamations to the whole world; the first angel proclaims the gospel of God's judgment and justice to all the world. These "glad tidings" consist especially in the "fall of Babylon," as the second angel underlines (14:8). The third angel threatens those who worship the beast with eternal punishment (14:9–11). The whole section of proclamation is concluded with two sayings addressed to Christians: 14:12 is a comment of the seer with respect to the *hypomonē* ("consistent resistance") of the saints while the blessing (*makarismos*) in 14:13 is pronounced by a voice from heaven. It refers to those who "die in the Lord," a traditional Christian expression.

While one might quibble over the translation of certain expressions in the angelic warnings or in the description of the two beasts and their mark or stamp (*charagma*), the overall interpretation of the context is not contested. The *zeitgeschichtlich* interpretation (history contemporary to the author) of the beast and its cult agent as referring to Rome is widely accepted, although exegetes might differ on whether the "beast" refers to Nero or Domitian. Although today we have widespread agreement on the 144,000 as the anti-image to the followers of the beast, commentators do not come to the same conclusions as to their identity. Some of the following identifications are suggested. The 144,000 are understood as Jewish Christians, elect and "saved" Christians, Christian ascetic males, the eschatologically saved and protected "holy rest" of Israel, the "perfect" victims and sacrifice, the high priestly followers of the Lamb, the military army of the Lamb gathering on Zion for the messianic battle, those who have followed the Lamb into death, or those who follow the Lamb in heaven.[3]

For each of these interpretations (and others could probably be added) some contextual or tradition-historical argument can be adduced. The possibility of interpretational variance would increase even more if we would hold a church- or world-historical rather than an eschatological *zeitgeschichtlich* interpretation, or if we would see the visions of the book as predictions of events in our times and as promises to readers of today rather than to those in the first century. Finally, a "timeless" interpretation would add a different kind of variance insofar as it sees in the 144,000 symbols of "timeless truth" about discipleship, victory, or sacrifice; structuralist charting of opposites or types in turn could endow such a synchronic interpretation with apparent scientific exactitude. No wonder many exegetes and Christians throughout the centuries have relinquished an understanding of the book in despair while others have found it to be a source not only of spiritual but also artistic inspiration.

Rather than add one more "definite" interpretation of the 144,000 followers of the Lamb on Mount Zion, I would like to explore some of the conditions and possibilities for interpreting the language of Revelation in general and of this passage in particular. I will do so in order to complement my analysis of the composition, form, and macro-structure,[4] as well as the prophetic-apocalyptic setting of Revelation,[5] with an analysis of its rhetorical language and symbolic universe. I have selected Rev. 14:1–5 as an example to show how the rhetorical language of a text must be explored so that its symbolic-poetic images make "sense" within its overall context and it has "meaning" and the power of "persuasion" in its own particular historical-social situation.

I will therefore argue that Revelation must be understood as a poetic-rhetorical construction of an alternative symbolic universe that "fits" its historical-rhetorical situation. An adequate interpretation of Revelation 14:1–5, therefore, must first explore the poetic-evocative character of its language and symbols; second assess its rhetorical dynamics in a "proportional" reading of its symbols to elucidate their particular interrelations and the author's persuasive goals; and third show why the construction of the symbolic universe of Revelation is a "fitting" response to its historical-rhetorical situation. It has become clear by now that I understand symbolic actions not to be just linguistic-semantic but also always social-communicative. They need to be analyzed as text as well as subtext in terms of their historical-social "world": as subtext insofar as history is not accessible to us except in textual reconstructions although history itself is not a text. In other words, we are never able to read a text without explicitly or implicitly reconstructing its historical subtext within the process of our reading.[6]

## THE MYTHOPOEIC LANGUAGE OF REVELATION

In 1972 N. Perrin insisted that literary criticism "has to include consideration of the ways in which literary types and forms of language function, and a consideration of the response they evoke from the reader or hearer."[7] He argues that Jesus' preaching of the kingdom of God (*basileia tou theou*) has been misunderstood as apocalyptic conception because its symbolic language character has been overlooked. In his understanding of symbol N. Perrin follows P. Wheelwright's distinction between steno- and tensive symbol.[8] Whereas a steno-symbol always bears only a one-to-one relationship and is mostly used in scientific discourse, the tensive symbol can evoke a whole range of meanings and can never be exhausted or adequately expressed by one referent.

According to N. Perrin, Jewish as well as early Christian apocalyptic symbols are generally steno-symbols whereby each symbol has a one-to-one meaning relationship with the persons and events depicted or predicted.

This is also the case when authors no longer refer to persons or events of the past but express their hope and vision for the future. Apocalyptic language is a secret code or sign-system depicting events that can be equated with historical persons or theological themes. Insofar as Perrin classifies apocalyptic symbols as steno-symbols or "signs" which must be decoded into a one-to-one meaning, he perpetuates the dichotomy between apocalyptic language and eschatological content or essence that has plagued scholarship in the past two hundred years.

The notion that the "essence" of theological meaning can be distilled from apocalyptic language reflects two rather prevalent but nevertheless inadequate assumptions in biblical interpretation: on the one hand the assumption that we are able to separate linguistic form and theological content and on the other hand the claim that imaginative symbolic language can be reduced to abstract philosophical language and conceptuality.[9] As early as 1779 J. G. Herder had poked fun at such an attempt:

> It [Revelation] carries, like everything else, its destiny along with itself. . . .
> The book consists of symbols; and philosophers cannot endure symbols. The truth must exhibit itself pure, naked, abstract, in a philosophical way. . . . No question is asked whether the symbols are pregnant with meaning, true, clear, efficient, intelligible, or whether there is in the whole book nothing but symbols. It is enough that there are symbols. We can make nothing out of symbols. At the best they are mere descriptions of the truth and we wish for demonstrations. Deductions, theorems, syllogisms we love. . . . Nature herself attempers different minds in various ways. She gives to one more of the power of abstraction, to another more of the power of synthesis; seldom are both found in company. In our academic education, there are unspeakably more teachers of that than of this. One is formed more for abstraction than for inspection; more for analysis than for pure comprehension, experience, and action. . . . Full of his systems of learning, of prejudices, and polemic hypotheses, let him indeed read anything in it, but let him not venture to condemn. . . . To the dumb one does not speak. The painter does not perform his work for the blind.[10]

The American scholar M. Stuart, who in 1845 published an excerpt from Herder's book *Maran Atha* as an appendix to his two-volume commentary on the Apocalypse, also underlined the aesthetic character of the work. He develops the following three hermeneutical principles: (1) The Apocalypse is a book of poetry; (2) it has to be understood in terms of Oriental poetry and therefore requires the same principles of interpretation as the parables of Jesus; and (3) generic and not specific and individual representations are to be sought in the book before us. Therefore in discussing Rev. 14:1–5 he points to the "episode" character of this passage but insists that "all which is intended by the symbols there exhibited, is merely to indicate the certainty of victory."[11]

This tendency to reduce the particular historical symbolic universe and literary expression of Revelation to the "generic" has prevailed among scholars who have advocated a literary analysis of Revelation in the most recent past. P. Minear has most consistently pursued a literary-critical analysis of its mythopoeic language and symbols. He objects to an understanding of Revelation as a system of signs in need of decoding, of symbols as equations with historical events and persons, and of images forecasting definite incidents and happenings.

He argues, for instance, against an interpretation of Revelation 17—18 that understands these chapters as anti-Roman polemics. To "equate Babylon with Rome would be literalism and historicism of the worst sort. The figure Babylon can convey the prophetic message and mentality without such an explicit association. We do not first require an exact knowledge of his immediate circumstances to grasp his message."[12] According to Minear the symbol Babylon as well as "the prophetic master-image of warfare between the rival kings points to realities of a primordial and eschatological order";[13] it points to the archetypal conflict of the demonic and the divine. "The invisible struggle among transcendent powers is for the prophet himself a fully contemporaneous reality, yet the struggle itself could not be compressed within the bounds of specific circumstances."[14]

In a similar fashion J. Ellul asserts that those exegetes who understand Babylon as the symbol of Rome and the "seven kings" as Roman emperors confuse the symbolic language of Revelation with a secret code. According to him, "Babylon is not the symbol of Rome, it is Rome, a historical reality which is transformed into a more polymorphous reality of which Babylon traditionally has been the expression. Rome is an actualized symbol, the historical presence of a permanent complex and multiple phenomenon . . . it is the historical actualization of the Power."[15] According to him Rome is the historical representation not just of ultimate Power but also of "the City" as the construction of all human culture and all civilization. It stands for all cities, those of the past and of the present. E. Lohmeyer and H. Schlier had already argued in a similar fashion.[16]

While Minear stresses that the historical references to Rome enhance our understanding of the underlying mythological, archetypal reality Babylon, Ellul maintains that the historical reality Rome is the representation of *the* ultimate Power and City. It seems that for both scholars the concrete historical reality and conditions of Roman power and rule along with its oppressive consequences for Christians in Asia Minor have become the symbolic manifestations of ultimate, transhistorical reality and archetypes. This interpretation, however, overlooks the fact that not Rome but the image of Babylon is the symbolic representation in Revelation. To understand the symbolic representation not in historical but in archetypal or philosophical terms does not avoid its interpretation as "representation" of something which the interpreter is able to name. Archetypal, ontological interpretation reduces symbolic language to essential substance but does not explore its evocative powers in a given historical situation.

Rather than explore and highlight "the disposition of the work for openness," essentialist interpreters assume it is like "an apricot with a hard and definite meaning at its core."[17] To understand Revelation as a poetic work and its symbolic universe and language as an asset rather than as a "scholarly confusion," it becomes necessary for interpreters to acknowledge the ambiguity, openness, and indeterminacy of all literature. Nevertheless, an intellectually rigorous and historically careful reading of Revelation can show that

> this indeterminacy of meaning has nothing in common with the conception that poetic language has no *particular* meaning, but is valuable only as a stimulus of feeling. Indeterminacy sees the language of poetry and fiction as at least as precise as ordinary language, but as having a different function— that of opening up rather than limiting meanings. The indeterminacy is not on the surface; we know exactly what (the writer) did and even why he [sic] did it. What is open are the full implications, the values, and the various incidents. The 'confusion' . . . is at 'the deep level where it is required' . . . because a literary experience is by nature open [emphasis and parentheses added].[18]

In order to explore the whole range of the symbols in Rev. 14:1–5— take, for instance, the symbol of Mount Zion, which in N. Perrin's terms is a symbol of ancestral vitality—it would be necessary to develop a lexicon of the imagery in Revelation with respect to its sources and its idioms together with a history of its traditions and interpretations as well as their influence or effective history. Although G. Herder had already demanded such a lexicon, it is still a desideratum of scholarship today.

The "range" of meaning that the symbol of "Mount Zion" evokes becomes obvious in the commentaries. Reference is made to the historical Mount Zion, its use as a short form for Jerusalem, to the heavenly Jerusalem, to eschatological expectations that the Messiah will appear on Mount Zion for eschatological warfare, as well as to the promise that the "holy rest" of the people of God will be gathered and protected there. But attempts to show that the author means the heavenly and not the historical or the eschatological and not the heavenly temple-berg are inconclusive.[19] Moreover, attempts to show that the seer is influenced here by a definite prophetic[20] or apocalyptic text expectation[21] are also inconclusive. Yet this indeterminacy could become a plus if we would understand apocalyptic language as poetic language, that is, as opening up rather than limiting, as evoking rather than defining meanings. Only then would we be able to perceive the strength of the image with all its possible overtones of meanings for the writer as well as for the audience.

## THE RHETORICAL STRATEGY OF REVELATION

If Revelation is not to be likened to an "apricot with a hard core" but more to an "onion" consisting of layers and layers of meaning, then the question arises, how are we able to say that it is an "onion" and not a heap of apple peels? In other words, how can we delineate the "particular" meaning of Revelation without ending up in total confusion and without accepting every abstruse interpretation that is proposed for the book's often bizarre symbols? Is the book "open" to any interpretation, or does its "particularity" require that a proposed "meaning" must make "sense" with regard to the overall structure of the book as well as with respect to its "function" within a particular historical situation?

These questions can be further explored if we consider Revelation not just as a symbolic-poetic work but also as a work of visionary rhetoric. While the poetic work seeks to create or organize imaginative experience, the rhetorical seeks to "persuade" or "motivate" people "to act right."[22] Poetry works by representation and is fulfilled in creation while rhetoric seeks to teach and instigate; poetry invites imaginative participation while rhetoric instigates a change of attitudes and motivations. Or in the words of A. Wilder: "Our visions, stories, and utopias are not only aesthetic: they engage us."[23]

Since participation and persuasion, imagination and change are not exclusive of each other, poetic and rhetorical elements can be successfully intertwined in a single work. Speaker, audience, subject matter, and "rhetorical situation" are constitutive for any rhetorical utterance. In these terms Revelation is a poetic-rhetorical work. It seeks to persuade and motivate by constructing a "symbolic universe" that invites imaginative participation. The strength of its persuasion for action lies not in the theological reasoning or historical argument of Revelation but in the "evocative" power of its symbols as well as in its hortatory, imaginative, emotional language, and dramatic movement, which engage the hearer (reader) by eliciting reactions, emotions, convictions, and identifications.

In writing down "the words of prophecy" to be read in the worship assembly of the community, John seeks to motivate and encourage Christians in Asia Minor who have experienced harassment and persecution. John does not do so simply by writing a letter of exhortation but by creating a new "plausibility structure" and "symbolic universe" within the framework of a prophetic pastoral letter. Apocalyptic vision and explicit parenesis have the same function. They provide the vision of an "alternative world" in order to encourage Christians and to enhance their staying power in the face of persecution and possible execution.

Rather than "essentialize" the individual image, therefore, we must trace its position within the overall form-content configuration (*Gestalt*) of Revelation and see its relationships to other images and within the "strategic" positions of the composition. Images are not simply patterns or ornaments but they are "about something." Only a "proportional" analysis of its images can determine what they are about within the structure of the work by determining the phase of action in which they are invoked. Such an analysis of symbolic relations must highlight the hortatory or persuasive functions of the multivalent images and symbols in producing cooperative or noncooperative attitudes and actions.

Whereas the poetic image can employ a full range of meaning and often contains a complex bundle of meanings which can be contradictory if they are reduced to their ideational equivalents, rhetorical symbols are related to each other within the structure of a work in terms of the ideas, values, or goals of the author, which must be at least partially shared with the audience.[24] In interpretating Revelation as a rhetorical work we must therefore look first for the strategic position and textual relations of the symbols and images within the overall dramatic movement of the book. Second, we must pay attention to the explicit rhetorical "markers" that seek to "channel" the audience's understandings, emotions, and identifications in such a way that it is persuaded and moved to the desired action.

First, since I have elsewhere analyzed the overall compositional movement of Revelation, I will presuppose this analysis here in order to indicate how Rev. 14:1–5 makes "sense" within the overall dramatic action. According to my interpretation, this segment belongs to the central section of Rev. 10:1—15:5, which, in ever-new episodal images interprets the present situation of the community on earth in its confrontation with Rome's power and cult.[25] An "episode" is thereby understood as a "brief unit of action" that is integral but distinguishable from the continuous narrative. If we assume that the "narrative" line of Revelation is indicated by the four septets then this segment is similar in function to the first septet of the messages and it is the center around which the septet of plagues is grouped.

The vision of the 144,000 with the divine name on their foreheads is clearly an antithetical vision to those of the dragon and the two beasts. It continues the motif of the measuring of the temple, the two witnesses, and the woman with the child, while anticipating the vision of the victors who sing the song of Moses and the Lamb (15:2–4). It is also interlinked with other heavenly-earthly-eschatological visions of redemption and salvation: on the one hand, it recalls the exaltation and enthronement of the Lamb in chap. 5, the "sealing" of the 144,000 elect of the tribes of Israel as well

151

as the eschatological great multitudinous company of the Lamb in chap. 7; on the other hand it points forward to the victory of the Lamb and those with him in 17:14, to the vision and audition of the "sacred marriage of the Lamb" in 19:10, to the Messianic millennial reign in 20:4–6, and to the "liturgical" service of those with the divine name on their heads in the New Jerusalem (22:3–5). It also alludes to the promise to the victor in 3:12 and the new "Zion"/Jerusalem in 21:1—22:5.

At the same time the vision of the 144,000 followers of the Lamb is the anti-vision of the "Lamb-like" beast and its followers who have taken the beast's name on their right hands and foreheads (chap. 13), as well as the antipode to the gathering of the anti-divine forces at Har Magedon (16:17). It is a "warning" to those who are in the process of losing their share in the New Jerusalem. Similarly the audition refers the audience back to the heavenly liturgies of 5:11–12; 7:11–12; 11:15–19; 12:10–12 and points forward to the song of the eschatological victors in 15:2–4 and 19:1–5. Its antidotes are the worship of the dragon and the blasphemies of the beast from the sea (13:4–6; 16:11, 21) as well as the lament of the kings, merchants, and seafarers over Babylon (18:9–20).

These auditions have the same function of commenting on the dramatic action and of guiding the perception of the audience which the choir had in the classical drama. By juxtaposing visions and auditions of salvation with those of the anti-divine powers, the seer seeks to persuade and motivate his audience to make their decision for salvation and for the world of God in the face of the destructive power represented by the beasts and Babylon as the symbols of Rome. This function is underlined by the explanatory remark that closes the vision and audition in v. 3: it underlines this eschatological tension of decision by stressing that only the 144,000 are able to "learn" the "new song" which the heavenly choir sings. They are those who are bought free, "separated out," or liberated from the earth (*apo* implies their separation from the earth).[26]

Second, the strategic function of the vision and audition of 14:1–3 is underlined by its explicit interpretation in vv. 4–5, by the following section with three angelic proclamations to all of humanity of vv. 6–11, and by the special words of blessing to the Christians in vv. 12–13. They function as rhetorical markers that appeal to the active decision of the audience and make sure that the multivalent images and symbols are understood in a certain way. They must be understood in the context of the explanatory remarks of chap. 13 and the proclamation of 14:6–13.

This interpretation of Rev. 14:1–5 understands those who are bought free from the earth as *parthenoi* (male virgins), as the followers of the Lamb, and as spotless first fruits. The present status of the eschatologically redeemed is a consequence and outcome of their behavior in the past. The first and last part of the interpretation stress the cultic purity of the 144,000 who are characterized in this vision as high priests, because they have the name of God and the Lamb on their foreheads. The middle section of the interpretation elaborates their "being with the Lamb" as following the Lamb.

This interpretation given by the author is grammatically difficult because the text leaves open whether they were or are followers of the Lamb. If the statement is parallel to the other two in structure, then the verb *ēsan* (they were) should be inserted. This, however, makes the grammatical reading of the sentence difficult. As the sentence stands now the reader can add the past and the present tense simultaneously: they have been and still are followers of the Lamb.[27] Whereas the beast from the abyss will "go" (*hypagei*) to destruction (17:18), the Lamb leads to eschatological salvation (cf. 7:17). Yet we are also reminded of the oracular pronouncement in 13:10: if anyone is to be taken captive, into captivity she or he goes (*hypagei*). Following the Lamb in the past included going to captivity, while now on the eschatological Zion it means salvation and fullness of life.

Whereas the statement that the 144,000 are first fruits and spotless because in their mouth was found no lie, is clear in the context of the book, the explanation that they are *parthenoi* (for they have not soiled or defiled themselves with women) is most difficult. Part of the difficulty, however, results from the mistaken assumption of exegetes that they must take this statement literally,[28] when they usually do not take either *agorazein* (to purchase), Mount Zion, *hypagein* (to go), *aparchē* (first fruits), or *amōmoi* (spotless) in a literalist sense but interpret them within the language context of the book. To assume that either the heavenly or the eschatological followers of the Lamb are a class of exclusively male ascetics[29] seems to be unfounded in the overall context of the book.

The expression *parthenoi* probably points, within the present scene, to the cultic purity of the Lamb's followers as well as to their representation of the "bride of the Lamb," the New Jerusalem, which is qualified as "holy" in 21:9–11. The anti-image to the holiness of the bride arrayed in white linen is that of Babylon who corrupts the nations with oppressive power.[30] The mention of "women" could also allude to the prophetess in Thyatira called Jezebel, who in John's view "seduces" Christians to idolatry and accommodation to pagan society. This possibility is enhanced but not proven if we consider that the expression "in their mouth was found no lie" not only refers to the list of vices which excludes people from the New Jerusalem (21:7; 22:15) but also to those people who claim to be Jews but lie (3:9) and to the second beast, the false prophet (16:13; 19:20; 20:10).

Thus, the interpretation of the vision and audition is not given in less symbolic language and cannot be reduced to a one-to-one meaning. Its function is to underline the agency of the 144,000. While the vision and audition highlight the election of those who are with the Lamb on Mount Zion, an accurate interpretation stresses that their actions and lives are the preconditions for such eschatological salvation. It thus has the same rhetorical function as the angelic proclamation, which calls all of humanity—of which the 144,000 are the first fruits—to the worship of God, announces the fall of Babylon in whose abominations the 144,000 *parthenoi* did not share, and threatens with eternal punishment the worshipers of the beast who take its sign, while those who have the name of God on their foreheads are promised participation in the liturgy of heaven in the future.

Here, at this opposition between the worship of God and that of the beasts, the *hypomonē*, that is, the "consistent resistance" or "staying power" of the saints, who keep the word of God and the faith of Jesus, come to the fore. The macarism at the end of this section sums up its overall rhetorical message and thus forms a transition to the judgment visions in 14:14–20. "Blessed [*makarismos*] are the dead," according to a word of the Spirit, who have died "in the Lord," that is, as Christians. Like the souls under the heavenly altar in 6:9–11 they can rest from their labors because their deeds or what they have become in their actions follow them.

In conclusion, the vision and audition of Rev. 14:1–3 function within the context of the book to highlight the election as well as the eschatological salvation of the 144,000, while the attached interpretation (vv. 4–5) underlines that their life-practice is the condition for eschatological salvation. The tableau functions at the same time as anti-image to that of the beast and its followers as well as to the glory of Babylon. Thus the whole section 14:1–5 in its wider context underlines the fundamental decision that the audience faces: either to worship the anti-divine powers embodied by Rome and to become "followers" of the beast (cf. 13:2–4) or to worship God and to become "companions" of the Lamb on Mount Zion. This decision jeopardizes either their lives and fortunes here and now or their future lives and share in the New Jerusalem, Mount Zion.

The images of eschatological salvation and the heavenly world of God seek to mobilize the readers' emotions, to attract and persuade them to make the right decision here and now and to live accordingly in this life. At the same time these passages seek to alienate their allegiances and affects from the present symbols of Roman power by ascribing to it images of degradation, ugliness, ultimate failure, and defeat. With ever new images and symbols of redemption and salvation the visionary rhetoric of Rev. 10:1—15:4 seeks to persuade the audience to decide for the worship of God and against that of the beast, which is shown as doomed to failure and destruction. The book of Revelation not only seeks to convince Christians that this is the right decision but also seeks to provoke them to stake their lives on it.

## THE RHETORICAL SITUATION OF REVELATION

My elaboration of the rhetorical strategy of Revelation has already indicated the kind of rhetorical situation which has generated it. It now remains to elaborate why its particular rhetorical response to the social-political and religious situation of the churches in Asia Minor is a "fitting" response. In other words, the social-historical-political parameters which are the ultimate horizon of Revelation as of any other cultural artifact must be (re)constructed, in the words of F. R. Jameson, so

> as to constitute not merely a scene or background, not an inert context alone but rather a structured and determinate situation, such that the text can be grasped as an active response to it. . . . The text's meaning then, in the larger sense of *Bedeutung* will be the meaningfulness of a gesture that we read back from the situation to which it is precisely a response.[31]

What is the rhetorical situation to which the particular world of vision of Revelation can be perceived as an active response? In addressing this question it must be kept in mind that it is the rhetorical situation that calls forth a particular rhetorical response and not vice versa.

A rhetorical situation is characterized by exigency and urgency. An exigency which cannot be modified through the rhetorical act is not rhetorical. Thus the controlling exigency of the situation specifies the mode of discourse to be chosen and the change to be effected. In other words, any rhetorical discourse obtains its rhetorical character from the exigency and urgency of the situation that generates it. And yet the rhetorical situation is not only marked by urgency but also constituted by two types of constraints: those which affect the audience's decision or action and those which are limitations imposed on the author.[32]

The exigency of the rhetorical situation of Revelation is best characterized by the letter of Pliny to the emperor Trajan:

> In the meanwhile the method I have observed towards those who have been denounced to me as Christians is this: I interrogated them whether they were Christians; if they confessed it I repeated the question twice again adding the threat of capital punishment; if they still persevered, I ordered them to be executed. . . . Those who denied they were, or had ever been Christians, who repeated after me an invocation to the Gods, and offered adoration with wine and frankincense to your image, which I had ordered to be brought for that purpose, together with those of the Gods, and who finally cursed Christ— none of which acts it is said, those who are really Christians can be forced into performing—these I thought it proper to discharge. Others who were named by that informer, at first confessed themselves Christian and then denied it. . . . They all worshipped your statue and the images of the Gods and cursed Christ.[33]

Pliny states here in plain words what Revelation tells us in images and symbols, especially in chap. 13. Yet Revelation adds another aspect when it stresses that those who do not have the mark of the beast are not able to buy or to sell.[34] Not only threat to life, imprisonment, and execution but also economic deprivation and destitution are to be suffered by those who refuse to take the mark of the beast, that is, to be identified as its followers. Although exegetes are not quite able to explain the mark of the beast and its number,[35] its economic significance is plain. In other words the beast not only threatens the followers of the Lamb with death, but also makes it impossible for them to have enough to live.

Under the Flavians, especially Domitian, the imperial cult was strongly promoted in the Roman provinces. Domitian demanded that the populace acclaim him as "Lord and God" and participate in his worship. The majority of the cities[36] to which the prophetic messages of Revelation are addressed were dedicated to the promotion of the emperor cult. Ephesus was the seat of the proconsul and competed with Pergamum for primacy. Like Smyrna it was a center of the emperor cult, had a great theater, and was famous for its gladiatorial games. Pergamum was the official center of the imperial cult. Already in 29 B.C.E. the city had received permission to build a temple to the "divine Augustus and the goddess Roma," which is probably referred to in Rev. 3:13 by the expression "the throne of Satan." In Thyatira the emperor was worshipped as Apollo incarnate and as the son of Zeus. In 26 C.E. Sardis competed with ten other Asian cities for the right of building a temple in honor of the emperor but lost out to Smyrna. Laodicea was the wealthiest city of Phrygia and had especially prospered under the Flavians.

The Asiarchs, the high priests of the Asian Koinon (assembly), presided over the imperial cult. One high priest was probably elected annually from one of the Asian cities to the most prestigious office a wealthy citizen could aspire to. "These priests wore unusually ornate crowns adorned with miniature busts of the imperial family."[37] In such an environment Christians were bound to experience increasing conflicts with the imperial cult, especially since they claimed Jesus Christ and not the Roman emperor as "their Lord and God." Revelation knows of harassment and persecutions of individual Christians in various localities. It anticipates an increase of persecutions and sufferings for the near future, not least because of the increasing totalitarianism of the reign of Domitian.

This experience or harassment, persecution, and hostility challenged Christians' faith in Christ as Lord. Their experience of hunger, deprivation, pestilence, and war undermined their belief in God's good creation and providence. Christians experienced painfully that their situation in no way substantiated their faith conviction that they already participated in Christ's kingship and power.[38] This tension between theological conviction and experienced reality must have provoked difficult theological questions that seemed to have been addressed differently by leading prophets in the churches of Asia Minor. The Book of Revelation implicitly informs us of such a theological dilemma by arguing against rival Christian apostles and prophets and by indicting the Jewish community as a "synagogue of Satan." In a situation where the leader does not control the production of symbols or where there are competing voices, she or he must defend their message over and against heresies and extend its range of consensual validations.[39] These are the rhetorical constraints on the audience that intensify the exigency of the political situation of Revelation.

First, the political situation was aggravated and the necessity to make a decision became more pressing because Jewish Christians like John could less and less claim Jewish political privileges for themselves. Jews had the privilege of practicing their religion in any part of the empire and were exempted from military service and the imperial cult. Under the Flavians, however, their situation had become more precarious. Vespasian ordered that all Jews and proselytes had to pay a special tax to the Romans in place of the tax formerly paid to the Jerusalem temple. Domitian[40] enforced the tax and singled out for payment especially the proselytes and God-fearers who were not Jews by birth. Moreover, Judaism was regarded with suspicion because of its strange customs and refusal to participate in the civil religion of its political environment. After the destruction of Jerusalem and the temple the self-interest of Jewish communities in Asia Minor demanded that they get rid of any potential political "trouble-makers" and "messianic elements" in their midst, and Christians certainly seemed to be among them.[41]

The messages to the churches of Smyrna and Philadelphia reflect this conflict. John's identification of the synagogue as a congregation of Satan should not be misread as anti-Judaism since he has great appreciation for the faith and the symbols of "true Judaism." But apparently true Judaism for him is messianic apocalypticism. As a Jewish Christian John is well aware that the established Jewish communities of Asia Minor could not tolerate the deviance of Christians who seem also to have been poor and powerless in Smyrna and Philadelphia and to have experienced slander from their Jewish communities.[42]

Second, not only among Jews but also among Christians there was a tendency to adapt and acquiesce to the political powers. John bitterly polemicizes against rival Christian prophets in Ephesus, Pergamum, and Thyatira. Ephesus is praised for rejecting "the false apostles" and for its hatred of the works of the Nicolaitans, whereas Pergamum is severely criticized for tolerating those who hold the teachings of Balaam. The community in Thyatira in turn is censured for accepting the influence and teaching of a woman prophet and her school.[43] It is likely that all three code names

"Nicolaitans, Balaam, and Jezebel" characterize the same group of Christian prophets who allowed eating food sacrificed to idols and accepted compromise with the emperor cult. This theological stance had great political, economic, and professional advantages for Christians in Asia Minor, for the meat sacrificed to idols was served at meetings of trade guilds and business associations as well as private receptions.[44]

This alternative prophetic position thus proposed a theological compromise that allowed Christian citizens to participate actively in the commercial, political, and social life of their cities. They probably justified their stance with reference to Paul (Rom. 13:1–7). Like Timothy, they might have urged their congregations to make supplications, prayers and intercessions for kings and those in "high places" in order to be able to lead a "quiet and peaceable life, godly and respectful in every way" (1 Tim. 2:2–3). Like 1 Peter[45] they could have admonished: "Fear God. Honor the emperor" (2:17). Since "honoring the image of the emperor" did not demand credal adherence but was a civil-political gesture, some might have argued it was possible to do so without compromising one's faith.

Moreover, to oppose the imperial cult and to refuse participation in socio-religious affairs would mean to take the religious claims of the imperial religion at face value. The religious claims of the emperor and state, on the one hand and the claims of God and Christ on the other hand are not in conflict because both claims belong to a radically different order as is maintained, for example, in John 18:36–38. Jesus Christ's claim to kingship and power is not of a political nature but pertains to the spiritual-religious life of the church, since Christians are taken out of this world and by virtue of their baptism already share in the kingly power of their Lord. No one, not even Satan, can harm the elect for they have insight into the very depth and mystery of the demonic and divine.[46]

In responding to this theological challenge John, like Paul before him, stresses that behind idols stands the demonic power of Satan, the ultimate adversary. No compromise with the imperial cult is possible because God and Christ are the true rulers of the world. John's theological response is rooted in a different social-political experience. He himself seems to have experienced suffering and exile,[47] while the two communities that deserve Christ's praise and receive no censure are obviously poor and without power. Those communities that receive censure are rich, complacent, and do not experience any harassment.[48]

It seems, therefore, that John advocates an uncompromising theological stance toward the imperial religion because, for him and his followers, the dehumanizing powers of Rome and its vassals have become so destructive and oppressive that a compromise with them would mean an affirmation of "those who destroy the earth" (11:18). Therefore Revelation stresses

"Christ is alive, although he was killed." Those who will resist the powers of death determining their life will share in the power and glory of Christ. To those who are poor, harassed, and persecuted the promises to the "victor" pledge the essentials of life for the eschatological future: food, clothing, home, citizenship, security, honor, power, glory.[49]

To achieve acceptance for his alternative prophetic stance, however, John did not claim exceptional personal status and authority. He consistently calls himself *doulos* (slave) rather than *prophētēs* (prophet) and places himself emphatically on the same level with the audience (1:9). He also does not write a pseudonymous book appropriating the authority of one of the great prophets or apostles of the past for his message. Neither does he appeal to any church leaders or offices known in the communities of Asia Minor.[50] He does rely on legitimization, but it derives not from human authority but from Christ himself. Like the prophets of old he proclaims: "Thus says the Lord" (as in *tade legei*). Like the apocalyptic seers he creates a symbolic universe that is mythological insofar as it represents a conception of reality that points to the ongoing determination of the world by sacred forces.

A strategic legitimating function of symbolic universe for individual as well as communal life according to P. Berger and T. Luckmann is the "location" of death. It enables individuals to go on living and to anticipate their own deaths with the terror of death sufficiently mitigated. "Symbolic universe shelters the individual from ultimate terror."[51] The same is true for its social significance: it is a sheltering canopy over institutions and legitimates the political order by reference to a cosmic order of justice and power. With respect to the future it establishes a "common frame of reference" bestowing meaning on the suffering of the community and on individual death. The empirical community is transported to a cosmic plane and made majestically independent of the vicissitudes of individual existence.

Such world construction in myth is primarily occasioned by conflicting definitions of reality which are aggravated if only one party has the power to enforce its own interpretation of reality. This was the case as we have seen in the rhetorical situation of Revelation. In constructing a symbolic universe John attempts to maintain the superiority of his prophetic view of reality and of God as well as to help individual Christians face the terror of death. Since the exigency of the situation is defined not just in terms of Roman power but represents political power in cultic terms, the symbolic universe of Revelation needed to appeal to common traditional cultic symbols in order to be competitive. Yet such an appeal was not possible since Christians had no cult, no temples, no priests, no sacrifices.[52] Since John rejects all pagan cultic activity as idolatry and seeks to alienate his audience from the magnificent symbols and cultic drama of the emperor cult, he could not, as Ignatius did, appeal to the symbols and images of the mystery cults. "You are all taking part in a religious procession carrying along with you your God, shrine, Christ, and your holy objects, and decked out from tip to toes in the commandments of Jesus Christ" (Ignatius, *Eph.* 9:2).

Although the open and multivalent images of Revelation have many overtones derived from Greco-Roman society and religion, the dominant tenor of its symbolic language is the cult of Israel. The symbols of temple, priest, sacrifice, garments, headdress, hymns, altar, incense and cultic purity are all derived from Jewish religion. In taking over these traditional Jewish symbols John makes a plea to Jews and Jewish Christians who "own" the tradition to accept him and his vision. At the same time it must be observed that Revelation never uses cultic symbolic language to describe Christian worship and communities. The cultic-religious symbolic language of Israel serves as a "language" to construct the heavenly world and the future where no cultic mediation is necessary anymore.[53] By employing traditional Jewish cultic symbols John seeks not only to alienate his audience from pagan mysteries and the emperor cult, but also to project essential stability, collective coherence, and eternal bliss in order to overcome their experienced alienation.[54]

I have argued that the symbolic universe and action of Revelation is a "fitting" response to its rhetorical situation. It remains to show how the dramatic action of the overall composition fulfills this rhetorical function. According to K. Burke[55] the mythic or ritual structure which follows the form of a cathartic journey moves the audience from alienation through purification to redemption. The first part, which is considered a *viaticum*, is "the way in." It states the primary conditions in terms of which the journey is to be localized or specified in time. This function is fulfilled by the first section, the seven messages of Revelation (1:9—3:21).

The next part within the journey metaphor is the definite "pushing off from shore" and the certainty "of being underway." On a particular journey one can be underway for varying periods of time. Chapters 4—9 culminating in the seventh trumpet take the audience "on the way" of the journey which opened up with the death, resurrection, and exaltation of Christ.

Eventually, according to Burke, one has to arrive at the "withinness of withinness." Here one arrives at knowledge and perception of the tensions (e.g., pollution, psychosis, civil disorder, class conflicts), that is, at the exigency of the rhetorical situation that is symbolized and explored. Chapters 10—14 and 15:2-4 represent structurally this "withinness of withinness" of the symbolic drama of Revelation.

From this point on "we are returning" and shall go back to the starting point, but with a "difference" which is constituted by an emotional or intellectual "splitting," a "separating out" which happens in Rev. 15:1—

19:10. The last part of the dramatic action completes the journey and the separating-out process. The journey is complete "when the passion (persecution and suffering) has been transformed into an assertion." The book closes with such a "final separating out" and an assertion in 19:11—22:5. Language cannot remove or correct "the brute realities" of the social-political exigency and of religious "tensions," but it can help us to control their destructive effects. In taking his audience on the dramatic-cathartic journey of Revelation, John seeks to "move" them to control their fear and to sustain their vision.

Finally, a theological interpretation of the NT has to assess the impact of John's world of vision and dramatic symbolic action on the contemporary reader and audience. W. C. Booth has argued for a revived ethical and political criticism that would "appraise the quality of the response invited by the whole work. What will it do with or to us if we surrender our imaginations to its path?"[56] Critics of Revelation have pointed out that the book preaches vengeance and revenge but not the love of the Sermon on the Mount.[57] It is therefore sub-Christian, the Judas of the NT. I myself in turn have argued that the book is written "with a jail-house" perspective, asking for the realization of God's justice and power. It therefore can only be understood by those "who hunger and thirst for justice."[58]

This dispute can be clarified through the concept of "rhetorical situation" that I have tried to develop here. If the "rhetorical situation" generates a "fitting" response, then Revelation cannot be understood when its "rhetorical situation" no longer "persists." Wherever it persists, however, the book will continue to evoke the same response sought by its author. In other words, wherever a social-political-religious "tension" generated by oppression and persecution persists or re-occurs, the dramatic action of Revelation will have the same cathartic effects it had in its original situation.[59]

Wherever a totally different "rhetorical situation" exists, however, the book no longer elicits a "fitting" response. What I am arguing here is that we should not reduce "the reader" to a timeless, ideal reader because in so doing we essentialize and dehistoricize the book. Rather than pose an abstract reader, we must detect and articulate our own presuppositions, emotions, and reaction to the work in an explicit way, as well as sort out what kind of quality of response becomes dominant in our own reading.

What will Revelation do to us if we surrender our imagination to its dramatic action? For example, the symbols for Revelation for both the oppressive and eschatologically redemptive communities are female because cities were personified as women. Moreover, Revelation symbolizes idolatry in the prophetic and cultic language of Israel as "whoring" or as "defilement with women." In our present rhetorical situation where we have become conscious of androcentric language and its socializing function we can detect a quite different rhetorical function and impact of these symbols. They no longer seek to persuade all Christians to persistent resistance and loyal faithfulness unto death, but they appeal to quite different emotions. Revelation engages the imagination of the contemporary reader to perceive women in terms of good or evil, pure or impure, heavenly or destructive, helpless or powerful, bride or temptress, wife or whore. Rather than instill "hunger and thirst for justice," the symbolic action of Revelation therefore can perpetuate prejudice and injustice if it is not "translated" into a contemporary "rhetorical situation" to which it can be a "fitting" rhetorical response.

## NOTES

1. W. Bousset, *Die Offenbarung Johannes* (MeyerK 16; 6th ed.; Göttingen: Vandenhoeck & Ruprecht, 1906) 146.

2. R. H. Mounce, *The Book of Revelation* (Grand Rapids: Wm. B. Eerdmans, 1977) 266; see also I. T. Beckwith, *The Apocalypse of John* (1919; Grand Rapids: Baker Book House, 1967) 653.

3. For a recent review of literature, cf. O. Böcher, *Die Johannesapokalypse* (Erträge der Forschung 41; Darmstadt: Wissenschaftliche Buchgesellschaft, 1975) 56–63. W. Weicht's "Die dem Lamm folgen: Eine Untersuchung der Auslegungen von Offb. 14, 1–5 in den letzten 80 Jahren" (Diss.: Pont. Univ. Gregorianae, Rome, 1969) was not available to me.

4. See Schüssler Fiorenza, *The Book of Revelation—Justice and Judgment* (Philadelphia: Fortress Press,, 1985), chap. 1 on "History and Eschatology in Revelation," and chap. 6 on "Composition and Structure of Revelation."

5. See Schüssler Fiorenza, *Book of Revelation*, chap. 3 on "The Quest for the Johannine School," and chap. 5 on "Apokalypsis and Propheteia."

6. For the distinction between text and subtext, cf. F. R. Jameson, "The Symbolic Inference; or Kenneth Burke and Ideological Analysis," in *Representing Kenneth Burke* (ed. H. White and M. Brose; Baltimore: Johns Hopkins Univ. Press, 1982) 68–91.

7. N. Perrin, "Eschatology and Hermeneutics," *JBL* 93 (1974) 1–15, esp. 10.

8. Cf. P. Wheelwright, *Metaphor and Reality* (6th ed.; Bloomington, Ind.: Univ. of Indiana Press, 1975). See also N. Perrin, *Jesus and the Language of the Kingdom* (Philadelphia: Fortress Press, 1976) 21–32.

9. See Elisabeth Schüssler Fiorenza, "The Phenomenon of Early Christian Apocalyptic: Some Reflections on Method," in *Apocalypticism in the Mediterranean World and the Near East* (ed. D. Hellholm; Tübingen: Mohr/Siebeck, 1983) 295–316, for a discussion of this problem.

10. M. Stuart, *Commentary on the Apocalypse* (2 vols.; New York: Van Nostrand & Terrett, 1845) 2: 502–3.

11. Ibid., 1: 202.

12. P. S. Minear, *I Saw a New Earth. A Complete New Study and Translation of the Book of Revelation* (Washington, D.C.: Corpus Books, 1968) 246.

13. Ibid., 233.

14. Ibid., 246.

15. J. Ellul, *Apocalypse. The Book of Revelation* (New York: Seabury Press, 1977) 189.

16. E. Lohmeyer, *Die Offenbarung des Johannes* (2d ed.; Tübingen: Mohr/Siebeck, 1953); H. Schlier, "Zum Verständnis der Geschichte nach der Offenbarung des Johannes," in *Die Zeit der Kirche* (Freiburg: Herder, 1958) 265–74; "Jesus Christus und die Geschichte nach der Offenbarung des Johannes," in *Besinnung auf das Neue Testament* (Freiburg: Herder, 1964) 358–75.

17. Cf. R. Barthes, *Critique et Vérité* (Paris: Éditions de Seuil, 1966), 50, and P. Rosenthal, "Deciphering S/Z," *College English* 37 (1965) 133.

18. W. Heyman, "Indeterminacy in Literary Criticism," *Soundings* 59 (1976) 352.

19. The "indeterminacy" of meaning is given in the text: On the one hand Mount Zion is clearly distinguished from "heaven," for while the voice comes "from heaven" the 144,000 stand on Mount Zion. Nevertheless, the issue is not clear-cut, since the 144,000 are also characterized as "following the Lamb" who stands before the throne of God in "heaven" (cf. Rev. 5) or shares God's throne in the New Jerusalem.

20. Cf. 2 Kings 19:20–34; Isa. 11:9–12; 24:23; 25:7–10; Zeph. 3:13; Mic. 4:6–8; or Joel 2:32.

21. Cf., e.g., *4 Esdras* 13:25–50; *2 Apoc. Bar.* 40:1–2 or *4 Esdras* 2:42–47.

22. See K. Burke, *The Philosophy of Literary Form: Studies in Symbolic Action* (New York: Vintage Books, 1956); idem, *A Grammar of Motives and a Rhetoric of Motives* (Cleveland: Meridian Books, 1962). For an elaboration and discussion of Burke's work, see esp. W. H. Rueckert, *Kenneth Burke and the Drama of Human Relations* (Berkeley and Los Angeles: Univ. of California Press, 1982) and H. D. Duncan, *Communication and Social Order* (New York: Bedminster Press, 1962).

23. A. Wilder, *Theopoetic: Theology and Religious Imagination* (Philadelphia: Fortress Press, 1976) 79. I presented this paper in a much shorter and less developed form at the SBL annual meeting in 1980, and I would like to thank Professor A. Wilder for his very helpful response to the earlier form.

24. See H. D. Duncan, *Language and Literature in Society* (Chicago: Univ. of Chicago Press, 1953) 109–10.

25. See Elisabeth Schüssler Fiorenza, *Invitation to the Book of Revelation* (Garden City, N.Y.: Doubleday & Co., 1981) 107–50. For different understandings of this section, see the review of J. Lambrecht, "A Structuration of Revelation 4, 1—22, 5," in *L'Apocalypse johannique et l'Apocalyptique dans le Nouveau Testament* (BETL 53; Louvain: The Univ. Press, 1980) 77–104.

26. Rev. 5:9 which speaks about the redemption of Christians uses *agorazein* with *ek*. See Schüssler Fiorenza, *Book of Revelation*, chap. 2 on "Redemption as Liberation."

27. D. Guthrie, "The Lamb in the Structure of the Book of Revelation," *Vox Evangelica* 12 (1981) 64–71.

28. For a review of interpretations given to this difficult passage, see C. H. Lindijer, "Die Jungfrauen in der Offenbarung des Johannes XIV 4," in *Studies in John: Festschrift J. N. Sevenster* (NovTSup 24; Leiden: E. J. Brill, 1970) 124–42.

29. A. Yarbro Collins (*The Apocalypse* [NTM 22; Wilmington, Del.: Michael Glazier, 1979] 100) suggests that the approval of celibacy in Rev. might have been inspired by the Israelite traditions of holy war and priesthood. John's exclusively

male terminology is therefore explainable since only men were warriors and priests in Israel.

30. Rather than to see *parthenoi* in the context of the symbolic action in Rev., Lindijer seeks to connect the word with all the other passages in the NT, contemporary Jewish, and early Christian writings which speak about virgins/virginity/ celibacy.

31. Jameson, "The Symbolic Inference," 83.

32. See esp. L. F. Bitzer, "The Rhetorical Situation," in *Rhetoric: A Tradition in Transition* (ed. W. R. Fisher; East Lansing, Mich.: Michigan State Univ. Press, 1974) 247–60.

33. *Letters* X.96. Pliny the Younger, *Letters* (Loeb Classical Library; Cambridge: Harvard Univ. Press, 1969) 2:401–2.

34. Cf. also A. Yarbro Collins, "The Political Perspective of the Revelation to John," *JBL* 96 (1966) 252–54.

35. For a review, see Böcher, *Die Johannesapokalypse*, 84–87; B. Reicke, "Die jüdische Apokalyptik und die johanneische Tiervision," *RechSR* 60 (1972) 189–91; W. G. Baines, "The Number of the Beast in Revelation 13:18," *HeyJ* 16 (1975) 195–96.

36. See W. M. Ramsay, *The Letters to the Seven Churches of Asia* (New York: A. C. Armstrong & Son, 1904); E. Yamauchi, *The Archeology of New Testament Cities in Western Asia Minor* (Grand Rapids: Baker Book House, 1980); C. J. Hemer, "Unto the Angels of the Churches," *BH* 11 (1975) 4–27, 56–83, 110–35, 164– 90.

37. Yamauchi, *The Archeology*, 110.

38. For the elaboration of this traditional Christian self-understanding, see my work in *Priester für Gott. Studien zum Herrschafts- und Priestmotiv in der Apokalypse* (NTAbh 7; Münster: Aschendorff, 1972) 168–290.

39. Cf. Duncan (*Language and Literature*, 87) who stresses the "persuasive functions of symbols in the production of cooperative and non-cooperative attitudes."

40. E. M. Smallwood, "Domitian's Attitude Towards the Jews and Judaism," *Classical Philology* 51 (1956) 1–13; P. Keresztes, "The Jews, the Christians, and Emperor Domitian," *VC* 27 (1973) 1–28.

41. See M. Hengel, "Messianische Hoffnung and politischer 'Radikalismus' in der 'jüdisch-hellenistischen Diaspora,' " in *Apocalypticism in the Mediterranean World*, 655–86. For the "muted and fragmentary form" of apocalyptic elements in rabbinic literature, cf. A. J. Saldarini, "The Uses of Apocalyptic in the Mishna and Tosepta," *CBQ* 39 (1977) 396–409.

42. It is debated whether the author has Jewish or Jewish-Christian communities in mind. H. Kraft (*Die Offenbarung des Johannes* [HNT 16a; Tübingen: Mohr/Siebeck, 1974] 61) thinks of a Jewish-Christian group which seeks to avoid persecution by calling themselves "Jews." This is not stated in the text, however.

43. For a discussion of Jezebel and the Nicolaitans, see Schüssler Fiorenza, *Book of Revelation*, chap. 4, "Apocalyptic and Gnosis." Today, however, I would be more hesitant to characterize this group as "gnosticizing."

44. See also Mounce, *The Book of Revelation*, 102–4.

45. See, however, N. Brox, *Der erste Petrusbrief* (EKKNT 21; Neukirchen-Vluyn: Neukirchener Verlag, 1979) 116–17. He argues that v. 17 is traditional and not formulated by the author of 1 Peter. Yet the statement fits well in the overall

context of the household-code (*Haustafel*) admonitions as D. Balch (*Let Wives Be Submissive: The Domestic Code in 1 Peter* [SBLMS 26; Chico, Calif.: Scholars Press, 1981]) has elaborated.

46. See Schüssler Fiorenza, *Book of Revelation*, chap. 4 on "Apocalyptic and Gnosis."

47. For such an understanding, see Ramsay, *The Letters to the Seven Churches*, 82–92. Kraft argues, however, that John went to Patmos in order to have a revelatory experience (*Die Offenbarung des Johannes*, 40–41). His argument is not convincing.

48. The communities in Smyrna and Philadelphia were powerless and poor. These two communities receive only praise.

49. See also D. Georgi, "Die Visionen vom himmlischen Jerusalem," in *Kirche: Festschrift für G. Bornkamm zum 75, Geburtstag* (ed. D. Lührmann and G. Strecker; Tübingen: Mohr/Siebeck, 1980) 351–72.

50. See Schüssler Fiorenza, *Book of Revelation*, chap. 5 on "Apokalypsis and Propheteia." See also D. E. Aune, "The Social Matrix of the Apocalypse of John," *BR* 36 (1981) 16–32. Aune, however, misrepresents my proposal.

51. P. L. Berger and T. Luckmann, *The Social Construction of Reality: A Treatise in the Sociology of Knowledge* (Garden City, N.Y.: Doubleday & Co., Anchor Books, 1967) 102.

52. See E. Schüssler Fiorenza, "Cultic Language in Qumran and in the New Testament," *CBQ* 38 (1976) 159–77.

53. See Schüssler Fiorenza, *Priester für Gott. Studien zum Herrschafts- und Priestermotiv in der Apokalypse* (NTAbh 7; Münster: Aschendorff, 1972), 397–416.

54. For the stabilizing effect of ritual and cult, see M. Douglas, *Natural Symbols* (New York: Vintage Books, 1973) and the review of her work by R. Isenberg and D. E. Owen, "Bodies, Natural and Contrived: The Work of Mary Douglas," *RSR* 3 (1977) 1–16.

55. K. Burke, "Othello: An Essay to Illustrate a Method," *Hudson Review* 4 (1951) 165–203; cf. Rueckert, *Kenneth Burke*, 208–26.

56. W. C. Booth, "Freedom of Interpretation: Bakhtin and the Challenge of Feminist Criticism," *Critical Inquiry* 9 (1982) 45–76, esp. 59.

57. See esp. A. Yarbro Collins, "Revelation 18: Taunt-Song or Dirge," in *L'Apocalypse johannique et l'Apocalyptic dans le Nouveau Testament*, 204.

58. See esp. Schüssler Fiorenza, *Invitation to the Book of Revelation* for her perspective on interpretation.

59. This explains why the political left as well as the political right can appeal to the book. It is therefore important in preaching and teaching to elaborate the original "rhetorical situation" of Rev. Since it does not address a democratic and highly technologized society, the book would be misunderstood if it were seen, e.g., as advocating political quietism and resignation in the face of the possible nuclear devastation of the world.

# 8

## Friendship with the World/
## Friendship with God:
## A Study of Discipleship in James

### LUKE T. JOHNSON

A discussion of discipleship in the Letter of James must begin with some adjustments in perspective. We must first ask of James a different sort of question. To ask about discipleship in James is really to ask about the shape of Christian existence,[1] for in spite of the definite connections between James and the gospel tradition,[2] the distinctive synoptic way of defining Christian life is not found in James.[3] If our question, therefore, is, What does James tell us about the nature of Christian existence, we find ourselves looking not merely for specific observations or commands but for an overall sense of Christian identity.

The second adjustment required of us is to read James on its own terms. This adjustment demands three separate shifts from ways in which this often unread letter is too often read. When James is noticed at all, it is usually as a foil to Paul, even in those studies which seek to rehabilitate James from its stepchild status in the New Testament canon. The rather minor semantic differences between James and Paul on the matter of faith and works is treated obsessively as though it were all in James that is worth studying.[4] To treat James on its own terms means first, then, reading it neither as Pauline nor as anti-Pauline but simply as an extra-Pauline witness to Christian existence.

When a historical fixation is not operative, a literary one frequently is. I refer to the pervasive impact of Martin Dibelius's magisterial commentary on all subsequent study of James.[5] Building on the work of J. B. Mayor[6] and J. H. Ropes,[7] among others, and using his own extensive knowledge of Hellenistic literature, Dibelius stated that the key to understanding James was its genre (*Gattung*), and that its genre was, simply, parenesis.[8] This was a great half-truth. Dibelius was correct in seeing James not as a systematic theology or innovative argument but, rather, as an exhortation which employs traditional ethical teaching, parallels to which can be found in many other Greek and Jewish writings.[9] Unfortunately, Dibelius's knowledge did have limits. He wrongly identified parenesis as a genre. It is better described as a mode of ethical teaching which can be fitted to many different literary genres. He was mistaken as well in his insistence that parenesis was totally without structure. Sometimes, parenetic materials do appear in loosely arranged aphorisms. But other times, they are found in rather impressively articulated structures.[10] On the basis of this somewhat partial view of parenesis, Dibelius made rather sweeping judgments regarding James. He refused it any possibility of literary unity: James would be regarded only as a kind of storehouse of traditional lore. And if that was the case, then it was out of the question to find in James any theology, or even the basis for deriving a theology.[11] In both these assertions, Dibelius was wrong. It would be inappropriate to deny that part of Dibelius's great achievement which was correct, but it is important to recognize that wisdom writings, too, have their own inner coherence and that it is hazardous to move rapidly from general characterization to exegetical fiat.[12]

Finally, taking James on its own terms means not assuming ahead of time that we know what it means, whether because of its supposed genre, its putative historical setting, or its possible social functions.[13] It means being willing to expend the same exegetical patience on James that we do with Paul. This is all the more necessary because of the deceptive simplicity of wisdom writings. They often lack the punch of parables or the bite of argument, sometimes seducing us into a presumption that we grasp their message.[14] In the matter of trying to discover James's teaching on Christian existence (discipleship), this attitude implies a readiness to follow the contours of particular texts in their particularity, not seeking too quickly to fit them to molds, exercising instead the classical rules of our discipline. These insist we attend carefully both to the content and context of statements, both to their form and function. We allow them to become very strange before our eyes and ears, so that we can be sure it is the text and not our own presuppositions to which we hearken.

## THE IMMEDIATE CONTEXT

My proposal here is a simple one: to pay close attention to a single verse in James, to see where it will lead. The text is James 4:4: "Unfaithful creatures! Do you not know that friendship with the world is enmity with God? Therefore whoever wishes to be a friend of the world makes himself an enemy of God." At first glance, this does not appear to be either a pleasant or promising statement. But it may open for us some of the distinctive richness of James's understanding of Christian existence.

What first drew me to this verse was its appearance of sane clarity in an otherwise hopelessly confused section of James. This first impression quickly changed as the verse began to look stranger and increasingly difficult to swallow. But first, the reason for that first impression: the mess surrounding the verse on either side. James 3:13—4:10 is notorious for its exegetical problems. Questions concerning the proper text,[15] the meaning of words,[16] and the way to punctuate[17] abound. Some time spent hacking through this tangle, however, convinced me that the problems were connected to the habit Dibelius had instilled in us of reading James as a set of disconnected sayings. As an experiment, I pulled 3:13—4:10 out as a unit for closer inspection. What did I find? In broadest terms, I discovered a coherent literary structure: as a whole, it appears as a call to conversion from one way of life to another. James 3:13—4:6 sets up an indictment, to which 4:7–10 responds.[18] The connective "therefore" (οὖν) in 4:7 indicates that the series of imperatives following it is based on the indictment. The conclusion, "Humble yourselves before the Lord and he will exalt you," (4:10) clearly picks up from 4:6, "God . . . gives grace to the humble." The section containing the indictment (3:13—4:6) is even more refined in its rhetoric, moving forward by a series of antithetical contrasts and rhetorical questions. Far from a congeries of aphorisms, then, this part of James appears as a coherent rhetorical unit.

My next step was to read the passage against the broad background of Hellenistic moral philosophy. When I did this, I found that James was using a *topos* on envy to give substance to his conversion call.[19] To know how the vice of envy is typically discussed by moralists is to understand not only the repeated presence of "bitter jealousy" in 3:14, and "jealousy" in 4:2, and the climatic "envy" in 4:5, but also to see why many other terms denoting social unrest (ἀκαταστασία, 3:16), warfare (πόλεμοι, μάχαι, 4:1), and even murder (φόνος, 4:2) are found here, for they are commonplace associations in discussions of envy.[20] Greek moralists, however, would not have put quite the emphasis James has on murder, nor on those cosmic forces, the spirit (πνεῦμα, 4:5) and the devil (διάβολος, 4:7). These symbols are due to the development of the theme of envy in Hellenistic Jewish texts, beginning in the Septuagintal Book of Wisdom (2:24) and elaborated most extensively in the Greek *Testament of Simeon*.[21]

As a call to conversion employing the *topos* on envy, we see that James 3:13—4:10 is organized according to sharp contrasts. The most obvious is that between the attack and the command, between the indictment and the exhortation. The reader is told to replace one way of life with another.[22] Corresponding to this contrast is another between two measures of reality, which derive from different sources and lead to different actions. The wisdom from above which leads to goodness and peace (3:17) derives, we gather, from the spirit which God made to dwell in humans (4:5). In contrast, there is a wisdom from below, which is characterized by bitter envy and which comes from another force, the devil (4:7). It is demoniacal, psychic (that is, without spirit), and "earthly" (3:15–16). Those addressed by James are told to shift allegiance from one power to another and from one measure of reality to another. They do this by "turning," here expressed in terms of "resisting" the devil and "drawing near" to God (4:7–8). This means, in effect, submitting to the power of God (4:7, 10). What is most striking in all of this is that the only part of this section of James that cannot be paralleled in Hellenistic or Jewish texts is 4:3–4, to which we must now turn. What does it say, and how does it fit into the context I have described?

## THE TEXT: JAMES 4:4

I will now examine this single text carefully in each of its parts, and from several points of view. Such a procedure seems particularly appropriate in this case. Despite a superficial air of clarity, James 4:4 makes a fairly outrageous and not-at-all-clear claim.

### "Unfaithful Creatures!"

The Greek μοιχαλίδες is both more specific and harsher: "You adultresses!" Now, it is characteristic of diatribal material to have sudden expostulations.[23] But what has motivated such an unprecedented outbreak in James? And why adultresses? He has not been accusing them of adultery in the literal sense but of envy and violence. Some early scribes apparently thought that it was a matter of sexual sin and wanted to be fair, so they made it "you adulterers and adultresses!"[24] We can ask, further, whether it is self-aggrandizing attitudes and antisocial jealousies in general which have so exercised James, or whether it is, in particular, a way of praying.

He has just mentioned in 4:3 that they ask for what they desire (ask God, we presume), but they do not receive because they ask "wrongly." They turn to prayer, we notice, only as a last expedient, and then they ask wrongly. But is the Greek word κακῶς adequately translated by "wrongly"? Better would be "wickedly." Why is this important? For one thing, the term "wrongly" could be taken to mean that they did not follow the right method of prayer, whereas it is really a question of praying wickedly, in a perverted way. How is this? They are trying to use God as one more means of gratifying their desires: "[You ask] to spend it on you passions." They see God as part of a closed system with themselves. This is, of course, the attitude characteristic of idolatry: to regard God solely as the fulfiller of our desires.[25] This reminds us, in turn, that the language of adultery is used frequently by the prophets in their accusations against Israel of covenantal infidelity, an infidelity which almost always was associated with idolatry.[26] The first part of this verse places us rather squarely, therefore, in the context of idolatry and covenant fidelity. But let us go further.

## "Do You Not Know?"

οὐκ οἴδατε is a stock phrase in parenesis, in which the point is remembering traditional ethical standards, not learning new ones.[27] This is the only time it occurs in James,[28] though it is an expression familiar to us from Paul's letters, where it introduces elements of traditional Christian understanding,[29] or even proverbial sayings.[30] The phrase not only reminds the readers of what they already know; its negative phrasing suggests a rebuke as well— they should not need reminding. It also serves to establish a ground of shared understanding: if they agree to this, then they can follow the conclusion built on it as well.

## "Friendship with the World Is Enmity with God"

This is the content of what they know. No problem with the Greek: the genitive constructions are plainly objective; that is, the friendship is one directed toward, not received from, the world.[31] A bigger problem has to do with the supposedly traditional nature of this statement. Why should they know this? We know of no such proverb in all the Hellenistic literature, nor is it found in Old Testament wisdom texts or in the Hellenistic Jewish literature.[32]

Critical editions and commentaries point us to another Christian text, 1 John 2:15–17, and it is, without question, the closest parallel to what we find in James 4:4:[33]

> Do not love the world or the things in the world. If any one loves the world, love for the Father is not in him. For all that is in the world, the lust of the flesh and the lust of the eyes and the pride of life, is not of the Father but is of the world. And the world passes away, and the lust of it; but he who does the will of God abides for ever.

There are some obvious similarities between the two passages. They have a similar structure. 1 John 2:15–17 makes a statement on the division between the world and God and follows it with a conditional sentence— "whoever loves the world"—just as James does in 4:4. In addition, the notion of "desires" is in each case associated with the world. The language of 1 John, though, is one of love, not of friendship; it lacks the note of enmity toward God; and the essential contrast is between the permanence of God and the transitoriness of the world. Still, it is the most helpful analogy to the passage in James.[34] But what is the connection between them? Few would want to argue for a literary relationship between John and James, so it may be that both were independently working out of a shared tradition (whose origin we no longer know), each shaping it to his own perceptions. John does not much help us, then, except to make even clearer the distinctly Christian sentiment here being expressed,[35] and to suggest that the dualism here is less cosmological than religious or ethical. It is not, in either text, the "world," as the place of trees and cities, which is the problem but "the world" as a system of untrameled desire and arrogance. We have yet to discover the exact shape of James's perception, though, and will have to delay that until we look a bit at the last part of 4:4.

### "Therefore, Whoever Wishes to Be a Friend of the World Makes Himself an Enemy of God"

The Greek here is, again, clear enough. It is a question of friendship toward the world and enmity toward God. But notice how the "therefore" (οὖν) creates a small argument. The truth of the first statement ("Do you not know?") permits a conclusion, "Therefore." We note in passing that the conclusion leads to one direction for life. Another "therefore" in 4:7 points out the other direction. Although the sentence seems almost tautologous, two small features deserve attention. First, the "wishing" (βούλομαι) indicates an effective choice, as it does also in James 1:8. Wanting to be a friend already has another consequence. That consequence is expressed in especially harsh terms: "makes himself" is too weak for the Greek verb καθίστημι, which in the New Testament and elsewhere has almost an official tone.[36] Better would be "is established as"—the desire itself has the effect of placing one in a state of enmity with God! Only in one other place do we find a similarly harsh characterization: in Rom. 8:7, Paul says, "The desire of the flesh is enmity toward God."

We have now disassembled the verse and have found it to be as threatening as we first suspected. The only parallel passage we could find was just as harsh. But we have not yet made much progress in understanding it, for we do not yet know how to evaluate the two key terms in the verse: "friendship" and "world." How is James using these terms? Is he establishing a metaphysical dualism, whereby material reality must be shed if one is to find God? Or is he presenting an ethical dualism? If so, how precisely are we to understand it? Where is this "world?" Is it outside us or also within us? Does James define it cosmologically or axiologically? We cannot affirm or reject this fundamental assertion by James—an assertion which clearly anchors this whole section—unless we grasp securely what he means by "world" and "friendship."

## THE TERMS "WORLD" AND "FRIENDSHIP"

### "World" (κόσμος)

James uses the term "world" (κόσμος) three times outside this passage, and each time it means something more than the merely material world or even the structures of human society. It points to a kind of measure or system of meaning.

1. The occurrence in 3:6 is the most difficult and elusive. James calls the tongue a κόσμος τῆς ἀδικίας, a "world of wickedness," or if we take the genitive adjectivally, "a wicked world," among the members of the body. It is an ambiguous expression,[37] but it is clearly metaphorical, and it moves in the direction of understanding "world" as a category of value. Notice that James says it "stains the whole body"—we meet this idea of "staining" again shortly.

2. The use of "world" in 2:5 is somewhat clearer. There, James says that God chose τοὺς πτωχοὺς τῷ κόσμῳ to be rich in faith and heirs of the kingdom promised to those who love God. The question is how to put together the words "world" and "poor." It could be read simply as "the poor," but then "the world" would be redundant. Or it could mean "poor people *in* the world," as one textual variant has it.[38] But the best text uses what we can loosely call a dative of reference,[39] which enables us to read "poor from the world's point of view," or "according to the world's measure, poor." That this is at least generally correct is shown by the way in which the expression is contrasted to the measure of God's kingdom, the measure of faith. In this passage, therefore, "world" is a measure distinguishable from God's.

3. The usage in 1:27 is decisive. James characterizes "pure and unstained religion before God and the Father" as one expressed by the visiting of orphans and widows in their distress and by "keeping oneself unstained from the world" (ἀπὸ τοῦ κόσμου). What exactly does this mean? First, there is absolutely no indication in James that Christians are to observe ritual separation from other people or from any class of objects which are regarded as "impure." Nor does James ever suggest that Christians flee the customary social structures and seek or establish alternative life styles. On the contrary, as we shall see, he envisages Christians taking full part in the affairs of the world: commerce, landowning, judging, owning and distributing possessions, having houses for hospitality.

Being "unstained from the world," then,[40] does not mean physical or ritual separation. Instead, "world" here stands as a measure or standard, which is distinguishable from that of "God and the Father." "World" and "God" are opposed as measures of valuation. We notice as well that meeting God's measure is done not just by control of speech (the subject of the context, 1:26) but, above all else, by "visiting orphans and widows in their affliction."[41] These actions show one to be unstained by the world's view of things. But as we can see everywhere in the Law and Prophets, effective care for orphans, widows, and sojourners is shorthand language for meeting covenantal obligations.[42] It is also a sign of conversion to the covenant after apostasy.[43]

These three uses of "world" confirm what we saw in James 4:4. In James, "the world" does not refer positively to God's creation. Nor is it used neutrally to mean the arena of human endeavor. Rather, it represents a measure of reality, or a system of meaning, which can be contrasted to that of God. Indeed, these passages virtually suggest that "the world" is a measure that does not take God's existence, and therefore his claims, into account. But this may be anticipating. We need now to look at the other key word, "friendship."

## "Friendship" (φιλία)

What does James mean by this term? We shall not get far if we view friendship in contemporary terms, as a sort of affection, benevolence, or positive attitude toward another. In the Greek world, friendship was among the most discussed, analyzed, and highly esteemed relationships. Epicurus included it among the highest of goods available to humans.[44] The Pythagoreans founded a way of life on its basis.[45] For Plato, it was the ideal paradigm for the city-state.[46] Even the more pragmatic Aristotle considered friendship the prime metaphor and motive for society.[47]

The word "friend" was not used lightly in these circles, nor was friendship considered simply a casual affection. On the contrary, it was regarded as a particularly intense and inclusive kind of intimacy, not only at the physical level but, above all, at the spiritual. Already in the *Orestes* friends are called "one soul" (μία ψυχή),[48] and Aristotle quotes this among other proverbial expressions of the sort by means of which the Greeks typically expressed their deepest perceptions.[49] To be "one soul" with another meant, at the least, to share the same attitudes and values and perceptions, to see things the same way. Indeed, the friend was, in another phrase frequently repeated, "another self."[50] Still another proverb had it that "friends hold all things in common." So seriously was this taken that communities of shared possessions were founded on that ideal.[51] The sharing of material possessions symbolized a sharing in spiritual values. Fellowship (κοινωνία) *was* friendship, because "friendship is equality."[52]

The ideal of friendship moved in the direction of equality, or even identity. And if James understands by "the world" a system of values distinct from God's, how would the phrase "friendship with the world" be heard by ears of that age? It would be heard not as a statement of positive regard for God's creation but, rather, as a statement of profound agreement with a measure opposed to God's. One would see things exactly the way "the world" does.[53]

## Friend of God

This understanding is given further support by James's only other use of friendship language. James 2:23 states that Abraham was called "friend of God."[54] James says this was so because he "believed God" (Gen. 15:6) and because, when he was tested in the matter of sacrificing his son Isaac, he allowed faith to find its perfection in his faithful actions (2:22).[55] We should note exactly what is being said. Once more, the genitive is objective: Abraham shows himself to be "friend toward God." But why did faith make him so? For James, it is because Abraham accepted God's way of seeing the situation and acted on it. According to the measure of "the world," the sacrifice of his own beloved son would have been senseless, and doubly so since Isaac was a gift from God himself (Gen. 18:9; 21:1–2). If Abraham had seen things the way "the world" did—a measure of reality, we remember, which excludes God's claim—he would have rejected God's call to obedience. He would have striven "according to the flesh" to create a blessing for himself with this possibility of biological descent.[56] But he did not. He showed himself friend toward God. His faith made him act according to a measure that made the world not a closed system of meaning, but a system open to the meaning given by God's word.

## Conclusions

By studying James 4:4 in the light of his other language about the world and friendship, therefore, we can reach the following conclusions:

1. The world can be regarded as a system of meaning and values which excludes God from consideration and is hostile to God's claim.

2. Friendship with the world means accepting that system as one's own, identifying oneself with it, measuring oneself by that measure.

3. Doing so makes one an enemy toward God. Indeed, simply *willing* to be friend to this closed system establishes one in a state of enmity, which means, of course, alienation and estrangement.[57]

4. This "friendship" language, therefore, makes a statement about human freedom, values, and ways of acting. One can choose the system of values by which one will live. One can lead one's life as though God had no claim

on it—be a friend to the world—or one can acknowledge that claim in faith and action as did Abraham and be a friend toward God.

The question immediately arises: Am I over-reading this small verse? Is there evidence elsewhere in James that this interpretation accurately represents his view? Yes, it is everywhere.

## LIVING BY OPPOSING MEASURES

### Living According to the Measure of the World

1. We find this in the immediate context of James 4:4. James is attacking actions that flow from envy: social unrest, divisiveness, hostility, murder. Why does envy lead to such behavior? The ancients defined envy as a kind of sorrow that is experienced simply because another has something.[58] If I see the world as a closed system, if I forget that everything comes as a gift from God (1:17), then I identify what I have with who I am. And I can be more only if I have more. If another has more, then the other is a threat to me, makes me less. Envy, then, moves inexorably toward hostility and murder: I can be more only if I eliminate the other. Among the pious, this logic might work itself out in manipulating God in prayer, so that I can gain something and "spend it on my drives" (4:3). If the world is a closed system (one unmeasured by the transcendence of God), then self-aggrandizement has a certain implacable logic.[59]

2. In James 3:6–8 we hear of the vicious use of speech—the tongue as instrument of destruction. James points out the conflict between perspectives: we curse people with the same tongue with which we praise God. But the one we curse is made in God's image (3:9).

3. James 4:13–16 gives us another sharp vignette: this time, of people carrying out grand business projects as though the future were secured by the plans they make, as though the world were a closed and utterly predictable system. They forget their own utter contingency—they are like mist that passes away (4:14). They forget that only God's will determines all futures (4:15). They act as though God had no power over or claim on the world. They boast in their arrogance (4:16).

4. In 2:1–7 we find Christians discriminating between wealthy and poor in their assemblies—showing themselves to be corrupt judges by allowing themselves to be bribed by the powerful impression made by the wealthy.[60] They forget that God has chosen the poor for the kingdom (2:5), that the rich will pass away like the flower of the field (1:10), and that God will judge those who judge by the standard they have used (2:12–13).

5. In 5:1–6 wealthy landowners defraud workers of their wages and

ignore their cries of suffering. They trust in their storehouses of gold and silver (5:3). They kill innocent people (5:6). They forget that the Lord is judge and that judgment is certain (5:7–8).

So do people act who live according to the measure of the world, who are "friends of the world."[61] And because they ignore God's claim, they establish themselves thereby as his enemies.

## God's Measure

We are able to see the measure of the world as inadequate precisely because we have been given another measure by which to view it. For James, this measure is a gift which is given humans by God. The ultimate dependence of all on God is fundamental for James: "Every good endowment and every perfect gift is from above" (1:17). And James 1:18 adds, "Of his own will he brought us forth by the word of truth that we should be a kind of first fruits of his creatures." James is speaking not only of "creation" here but of the re-creation of humans by that faithful utterance which is God's Word, most specifically, the Gospel (as in Col. 1:5, Eph. 1:13).[62] This makes those who receive it a sign and promise of what all "creatures" can be.

In 1:21 we find this: "Receive with meekness the implanted word, which is able to save your souls." What is symbolized by the "implanted word" here is exactly what is signaled by the "wisdom from above" in 3:15, the "spirit God made to dwell" in 4:5, and "grace" in 4:6.[63] God has made available to humans another way of viewing and measuring reality: not as a closed system but as an open one. God's word has given us birth, has been implanted in us; we can receive it, and we can become "doers of the word" (1:22). What this means specifically is living out the demands of the law of the kingdom, "Love your neighbor as yourself" (2:8), as this is explicated by the words of Scripture and as understood in the light of Jesus the Messiah.[64] But a "law of God's kingdom" which is a law of love— therefore, of self-disposing concern—makes sense only if the world is not closed in on itself, only if we dwell in a fundamentally open system (one in which God is judge), not a closed one which destroys those who give it their friendship.

## The Double-Minded

It is, finally, in this connection that we meet the one James is specifically addressing with this call to conversion, the "double-minded" person (δίψυχος).[65] What makes someone double-minded is precisely the desire to live by both measures at once, to be friends with everyone. In James 1:8 we meet him as the man who wants to pray, but he does so without really being convinced that this is an open system. He doubts and therefore never breaks out of his idolatrous circle. And in this call to conversion, we read, "Cleanse your hands, you sinners, and purify your hearts, you men of double mind" (4:8). Purity of heart, of course, is simplicity: not that of compulsion but that of choice. For James, one must choose one's friends; one cannot have it both ways. Even to "wish" to live by the world's standard is already to live by its measure.

This whole call to conversion in James 3:13—4:10, then, reminds those Christians who would like to hedge their bets that the process of turning from one measure to another is never over, that it must continually be renewed. Although that word which shapes their Christian identity has been "implanted" in them, they must still "accept it with meekness," they must continually become "doers" of it; therefore, even for those already converted, the prophetic call to conversion is appropriate.[66] So soon as they even wish to compete enviously with one another (3:14—4:2); so often as they rely on a merely formal profession of God's existence (2:14–19) without translating that into effective care for others and obedience as did Abraham (2:20–26); so much as they would wish to manipulate the divine power in prayer (4:3), not praying in the simplicity of faith as did Elijah, who also was only a man (5:15–18); so frequently as they would wheel and deal and cheat and hold violent grudges against each other (4:13—5:9), rather than wait patiently for the judgment of the Lord, as did the patient Job (5:10–11); then they are not really "doers" of God's word (1:22) but double-minded, and must be called back, as James now calls them, to that other measure, knowing that for those who do submit themselves to the measure of God's power even greater gifts will be given, and they will be raised up (4:6, 10; cf. 5:15).

## CONCLUSION

This short analysis cannot pretend to exhaust the meaning of discipleship, or of Christian existence, in the Letter of James. I hope that it has shown something of the distinctive way James employs the language and perceptions of Hellenistic culture and of the Scripture and of faith in the Lord Jesus Christ, as well as the way theological warrants like that in James 4:4 function within his work as a whole. Most of all, by trying to respect the way in which James gives expression to his Christian witness, I hope I have shown he deserves such respect.

## NOTES

1. That James is in fact a thoroughly Christian writing and not a lightly reworked Jewish document should no longer be doubted. Although Jesus is only mentioned twice (1:1; 2:1), the specifically Christian connections are pervasive. Some of them will emerge in this study.

2. Among others, see P. Minear, "Yes or No: The Demand for Honesty in the Early Church," *NovT* 13 (1971) 1–13; M. H. Shepherd, "The Epistle of James and the Gospel of Matthew," *JBL* 75 (1956) 40–51; L. T. Johnson, "The Use of Leviticus 19 in the Letter of James," *JBL* 101 (1982) 391–401.

3. The terms characteristic of the Synoptics are either missing or used differently: "teacher" (διδάσκαλος) is used in 3:1 of community teachers; "to follow" (ἀκολουθέω) and "disciple" (μαθητής) are absent.

4. For example, J. Jeremias, "Paul and James," *ExpTim* 66 (1965) 368–71; D. O. Via, "The Right Strawy Epistle Reconsidered: A Study in Biblical Ethics and Hermeneutics," *JR* 49 (1969) 253–67; J. G. Lodge, "James and Paul at Cross-purposes? James 2,22," *Bib* 62 (1981) 195–213.

5. First published in 1921 as part of the Meyer commentary series, its latest apparition is M. Dibelius, *James: A Commentary on the Epistle of James* (rev. H. Greeven; trans. M. Williams; Hermeneia; Philadelphia: Fortress Press, 1976). In subsequent commentaries which deal with the question of genre at all, the influence of Dibelius can be seen clearly in O. Bardenhewer, *Der Brief des Heiligen Jacobus* (Freiburg: Herder Verlag, 1928); T. García, *Epistola Sancti Jacobi* (Rome: Lateranum, 1954); J. Catinat, *Les Épîtres de Saint Jacques et de Saint Jude* (SB; Paris: J. Gabalda, 1973); H. Windisch, *Die Katholischen Briefe* (2d ed.; HNT 15; Tübingen: Mohr/Siebeck, 1951); F. Mussner, *Der Jacobusbrief* (3d ed.; HTKNT 13; Freiburg: Herder Verlag, 1975). The most explicit rejection of Dibelius is found in J. B. Adamson, *The Epistle of James* (NICNT; Grand Rapids: Wm. B. Eerdmans, 1976).

6. A great deal of comparative material had already been gathered by J. B. Mayor, *The Epistle of St. James* (3d ed.; London: Macmillan & Co., 1910), cf. esp. cx–cxxvii.

7. J. H. Ropes (*A Critical and Exegetical Commentary on the Epistle of St. James* [ICC; Edinburgh: T. & T. Clark, 1916]) saw the particular pertinence of the *Testaments of the Twelve Patriarchs* for understanding James (20–21) and emphasized the diatribal character of the writing (10–18).

8. Dibelius, *James*, 1–3.

9. In addition to the parallels collected by Mayor and Ropes, Dibelius made extensive use of lexical materials from the Greco-Roman moralists, Hellenistic Jewish writings such as *The Sentences of Pseudo-Phocylides*, and Christian parenetic writings like *The Shepherd of Hermas*.

10. See the observations of A. J. Malherbe, "Hellenistic Moralists and the New Testament," in *Aufstieg und Niedergang der Römischen Welt* (ed. H. Temporini; 3, 26 [forthcoming]), and the application of these to a particular personal parenetic letter in L. T. Johnson, "II Timothy and the Polemic Against False Teachers: A Reexamination," *JRelS* 6/7 (1978–79) 1–26.

11. Dibelius, *James*, 11. Dibelius's influence is seen in a recent attempt at describing the theological outlook of James in R. Hoppe, *Der theologische Hintergrund des Jacobusbriefe* (FzB; Würzburg: Echter-Seelsorge, 1977). As I do in this essay, Hoppe regards James 3:13–18 as part of James's own theology. But following Dibelius's literary norms (1), he separates 3:13–18 from 3:1–12 and 4:1–10 (9, 44), a procedure opposite the one followed here.

12. Dibelius does recognize some "treatises" in James (such as 2:1—3:12) but resists all further attempts at finding structure (*James*, 22). Certainly, overly clever schemes should be avoided. But one can note simply that statements of theme made by way of aphorism in chap. 1 have a rather consistent way of being developed by

way of essay in the other chapters, so that the opening set of verses functions as a sort of "table of contents" of the book: see, e.g., 1:2–4, 12–15 (trials), in 5:7–11; 1:9–11 (rich and poor), in 4:13—5:6; 1:19–21, 26 (speech), in 3:1–18; 1:22–26 (doing the word), in 2:14–26; 1:5–8, 16–18 (true wisdom), in 3:13—4:10.

13. See the unfortunate examples of M. T. Townsend, "James 4:1–14: A Warning Against Zealotry?" *ExpTim* 87 (1975) 211–13; and L. G. Perdue, "Paraenesis and the Letter of James," *ZNW* 72 (1981) 241–56.

14. Wisdom literature may be general in intention, but it is particular in expression. Even minimal arrangement of materials represents an interpretation and point of view. Furthermore, aphorisms may be worn to cliches, but they do claim to make statements about reality—not only to say something well but to say *something.* Testing such statements may require very special tools, but they should be no less sharp than those laid to argument and narrative. The characterizations of James found in J. T. Sanders (*The Ethics of the New Testament* [Philadelphia: Fortress Press, 1975] 115–28) show no such acuity.

15. Should we read φονεύετε ("you murder") in 4:2, or φθονεύετε ("you are envious")? Erasmus thought the context demanded the latter, so he emended it to that. But the harder reading is "you murder," and it is supported by the connection between killing and envy in the moralists' discussions.

16. The δαιμονιώδης ("devilish") of 3:15 and the ἀδιάκριτος ("without uncertainty") of 3:17 are *hapax legomena* and difficult until they are linked to the διάβολος ("the devil") of 4:7 and the δίψυχος ("double-minded man") of 4:9, although commentators never make this linkage.

17. The punctuation of 4:2 and 4:5–6 are complex and much discussed by commentators. For 4:2, the best solution is that of Mayor (*Epistle of St. James,* 136); for 4:5–6, see S. Laws, "Does the Scripture Speak in Vain? A Reconsideration of James 4:5," *NTS* 20 (1973–74) 210–15.

18. The vocabulary of 4:8–10 recalls the threat/repentance language of the Prophets in the Septuagint: ταπεινόω ("to humble"), Hosea 5:5; 7:10; καθαρίζω ("to cleanse"), Ezek. 36:25; πένθος ("mourning"), Amos 8:10; Lam. 5:15; πενθέω ("to mourn"), Amos 9:5; Joel 1:9, 10; Isa. 24:4; 33:9; Jer. 4:28; 14:2; κλαίω ("to weep"), Joel 1:5; 2:17; Isa. 22:4; 30:19; 38:3; Jer. 9:1; 22:10.

19. See L. T. Johnson, "James 3:13—4:10 and the *Topos* περὶ φθόνου," *NovT* 25 (1983) 327–47.

20. For a thorough review of the *topos* in Greek writers, see E. Milobenski, *Der Neid in der griechischen Philosophie* (Klassisch-Philologische Studien 29; Wiesbaden: Otto Harrassowitz, 1964).

21. The *Testament of Simeon* is entitled in Greek περὶ φθόνου and places the *topos* within the context of "two spirits" language and a call to conversion, as in James. See esp. *Testament of Simeon* 2:13; 4:4; and Johnson, "James 3:13—4:10."

22. The descriptive terms of the exhortation mirror the terms of the indictment: the "lowering" of 4:7 and 10 corresponds to the "from above" in 3:15; the "cleansing of heart" in 4:8 picks up the "selfish ambition in your heart" in 3:14; the κατήφεια ("dejection") of 4:9 opposes the ὑπερηφανία ("pride") of 4:6; the δίψυχοι ("double-minded men") of 4:8 matches the ἀδιάκριτος ("without uncertainty") of 3:17; the cleansing and purifying of 4:8 corresponds to the "pure" of 3:17.

23. See Ropes (*James*, 10–15) who isolates many dialogical-diatribal features in James. The best treatment of the diatribe is now S. K. Stowers, *The Diatribe and*

*Paul's Letter to the Romans* (SBLDS 57; Chico, Calif.: Scholars Press, 1981) esp. 85–100.

24. μοιχοὶ καὶ μοιχαλίδες is found in ℵ², P, Ψ and the mss of the *koine* tradition. The shorter and better reading is held by ℵ*, A, B, and others.

25. We are not surprised, then, that one of the few occurrences of "wicked prayer" in the Septuagint is in a characterization of idolators (Wis. 14:30).

26. Cf. e.g., Hosea 3:1; Ezek. 16:38; 23:45; Isa. 57:3; Jer. 3:9; 13:27.

27. See Malherbe, "Hellenistic Moralists," and idem, "Exhortation in First Thessalonians" (a paper delivered to the Society of Biblical Literature Seminar on the Thessalonian Correspondence, 1981) 2.

28. Similar expressions, indicating recollections of previous knowledge, are found at 1:3 (γινώσκοντες); 1:19 (ἴστε); the series of negative rhetorical questions following ἀκούσατε in 2:5–7; 3:1 (εἰδότες); 5:11 (ἠκούσατε, εἴδετε); and the alternative reading at 5:20 (γινώσκετε).

29. "Do you not know that you are God's Temple?" (1 Cor. 3:16); "Do you not know that the saints will judge the world?" (1 Cor. 6:2).

30. "Do you not know that a little yeast leavens the whole lump?" (1 Cor. 5:6). Cf. also Rom. 6:16; 11:2; 1 Cor. 9:14.

31. Dibelius, *James,* 220; Ropes, *James,* 260.

32. Mayor's suggestion—"The reference is to our Lord's words, Mt 6:24"—is surely wrong, for though the substance of the statement is similar, the phrasing, and even the sense, are different. The commentators are not able to adduce any parallels from the Hellenistic or Jewish materials. In the *Testaments,* which otherwise parallel James on so many points, there is only the expression "from the desire of the world" (ἀπὸ τῆς πλάνης τοῦ κόσμου), *Testament of Issachar* 4:6. For many expressions in the apocrypha of *hostility* to the world as an evil place, see Dibelius, *James,* 194. None of them really correspond to James's usage.

33. It is far closer than another New Testament text sometimes cited, 2 Tim. 3:4, which says of false teachers that they are "lovers of pleasure rather than lovers of God" (φιλήδοναι μᾶλλον ἢ φιλόθεοι).

34. For a discussion of 1 John 2:15–17, see R. E. Brown, *The Epistles of John* (AB 30; New York: Doubleday & Co., 1982) 306–28. The fact that the Johannine writings generally are comfortable with "friendship" language makes the differences here the more striking. In John 15:19, e.g., we find: "If you were of the world, the world would love its own" (εἰ ἐκ τοῦ κόσμου ἦτε, ὁ κόσμος ἂν τὸ ἴδιον ἐφίλει). See also John 15:13–15; 16:27; 20:2; 21:15–17; 3 John 15.

35. See the discussion by H. Sasse, "κοσμέω, κτλ.," *TDNT* 3 (1965) 894–95.

36. Cf. LSJ, s.v., καθίστημι, and the use in (LXX) Exod. 2:14 and Ps. 8:7, picked up by Acts 7:10 and Heb. 2:7, respectively, as well as Matt. 24:47, Luke 12:42, Rom. 5:19.

37. We notice that καθίστημι appears here as well, so that the Dibelius-Greeven-Williams translation seem apt: "And the tongue is a member [the tongue presents itself among our members as the evil world] staining the whole body" (Dibelius, *James,* 181). See his discussion, 194–95, as well as that of Sasse, "κοσμέω," 883–84.

38. Both ἐν τῷ κόσμῳ and τοῦ κόσμου have poorer attestation, are longer, and are more easily explained as clarifications of τῷ κόσμῳ, which is shorter, harder, and better.

39. See the discussion of ambiguous datives by C. F. D. Moule, *An Idiom-Book of New Testament Greek* (2d ed.; Cambridge: Cambridge Univ. Press, 1959) 45–46, and his second thoughts concerning James 2:5 (204). See also J. H. Moulton, *A Grammar of New Testament Greek* (vol. III: N. Turner, *Syntax* [Edinburgh: T. & T. Clark, 1963]) 238.

40. We have seen how that "world of wickedness," the tongue, "stains" the whole body (3:6). "Pure religion" is here called ἀμίαντος. We notice as well that the call to conversion demands "cleansing" the hands and "purifying" the heart (4:8).

41. The obvious salvific implications of ἐπισκέπτομαι ("to visit") as it is used in the Septuagint (cf. Gen. 21:1; Exod. 3:16; 4:31; and many more times) is picked up in the New Testament mainly by Luke-Acts (cf. Luke 1:68, 78; 7:16; Acts 7:23; 15:14).

42. Cf. Exod. 23:10–11; Lev. 19:9–10; 23:22; Deut. 14:28–29; 26:12–15; Amos 2:6–8; 3:2; Hosea 12:7–9; Micah 3:1–3; Zeph. 1:9; 3:1–3; Mal. 3:5; Isa. 3:5, 14–15; 5:7–10; 30:12; 58:3; Jer. 5:25–29.

43. Cf. Zech. 7:8; Jer. 21:12; 22:3; Hosea 12:6; Isa. 33:15–16; 56:1–6; Jer. 7:5–7; Ezek. 18:7–9.

44. Among Epicurus's *Sovereign Maxims* is the following (number 27): "Of all the means which are given by wisdom to ensure happiness throughout the whole of life, by far the most important is the acquisition of friends." For other notes on friendship among the Epicureans, cf. Diogenes Laertius 10.10, 11, 120.

45. Cf. Diogenes Laertius 8.10; Iamblichus, *VP* 5.26–27, 18.81; Porphyry, *VP* 5.29, 6.30–32.

46. Plato, *Republic* 24A, 449C–D, 462A–C; cf. *Laws* 708D, 742E.

47. Aristotle, *Politics* 1287B, 1280B.

48. Euripides, *Orestes* 1046.

49. Aristotle, *Nichomachean Ethics* 9.8.2, where he also quotes κοινὰ τὰ φιλῶν ("friends hold all things in common") and ἰσότης φιλότης ("friendship is equality"). For μία ψυχή, cf. also Plutarch, *Am. Mult.* 96F.

50. Aristotle, *Nichomachean Ethics* 9.4.5, 9.1, 9.10. Cf. Cicero, *De amicitia* 21.80; Plutarch, *Am. Mult.* 93E.

51. See L. T. Johnson, *Sharing Possessions: Mandate and Symbol of Faith* (OBT; Philadelphia: Fortress Press, 1981) 117–48.

52. Plato, *Laws* 757A, 744B; Aristotle, *Nichomachean Ethics* 8.5.5, 6.7, 8.5; Iamblichus, *VP* 29.162, 30.167; Plutarch, *Frat. Am.* 484B–C. For the role of "likeness" in friendship, cf. Plato, *Lysis* 214B; Cicero, *De amicitia* 14.50; 19.69; Plutarch, *Am. Mult.* 96D. For a general guide to the *topos*, see the references in G. Stählin, "φίλος, κτλ.," *TDNT* 9 (1974) 147–57; G. Bohnenblust, *Beiträge zum Topos περὶ φιλίας* (Berlin: Universitäts-buchdruckerei von Gustav Schade, 1905); and L. Dugas, *L'Amitié antique* (Paris: Felix Alcan, 1914).

53. That friendship involved such a sharing of values can be seen in Iamblichus, *VP* 17.75, 33.240; Cicero, *De amicitia* 4.15, 6.20; Plutarch, *Am. Mult.* 96F; Plato, *Laws* 693C, 694B, 697C. That both Luke and Paul use such friendship language in connection with the sharing of possessions has been noted often before; see L. T. Johnson, *The Function of Possessions in Luke-Acts* (SBLDS 39; Missoula, Mont.: Scholars Press, 1977) 2–5, 32–36. Paul can also use the language effectively apart from considerations of monetary sharing: Phil. 2:1–2 stresses the sharing of outlook in spiritual fellowship.

181

54. The roots of James's expression here remain obscure and cannot be clarified satisfactorily in this paper. The following points are intended only as a guide. (1) The "friendship" language of the Septuagint is restrained. There are discussions of friendship in the wisdom writings (cf., e.g., Sir. 6:1–17; 37:1–6), but without the distinctive Hellenistic coloration. In Wis. 1:16 we find people who are friends with death, and in Deut. 13:7 there is a warning against ὁ φίλος ὁ ἴσος τῆς ψυχῆς σου, leading one astray into idolatry. (2) The possibility of friendship with God is found explicitly only in the Book of Wisdom: the gift of wisdom (7:7) enabled "friendship with God" (φιλία πρὸς θεόν, 7:14), and it is said that wisdom enters souls and makes "friends of God and prophets" (φίλους θεοῦ καὶ προφήτας, 7:27). (3) The only individual explicitly called a friend of God is Moses. God spoke to him face to face as if he had been speaking to his own friend, φίλον (Exod. 33:11)—translating the Hebrew r'hw. Abraham is not called "friend." In 2 Chr. 20:7 and Isa. 41:8, the Septuagint translates the Hebrew 'hb with forms of "to love" (ἀγαπάω). (4) The passage concerning Abraham that gave rise to calling him a friend of God seems, above all, to be Gen. 18:7: "Shall I hide from Abraham what I am about to do. . . ?" Philo rendered this: μὴ ἐπι καλύψω ἐγὼ ἀπὸ Ἀβραὰμ τοῦ φίλου μου, Sobr. 56. Note that friends share spiritual goods. (5) A full discussion of the usage in Jewish texts is found in M. Dibelius (*James,* 172–74). A more convenient listing of Philo's references to the patriarchs as friends can be found in Stählin, "φίλος," 158. (6) In contrast to the treatment of Dibelius, I am less concerned with the general under-standing of the term in James's environment—a concern made critical, given his methodology—or with fitting it to a Pauline understanding of faith than I am with connecting it to James's own perceptions.

55. It is *faith* which is brought to completion: deeds (not works of the law) bring faith itself to expression (cf. 1:3–4). Faith co-works the works. The distinctive emphasis of James here should not be missed. For a fine treatment of Abraham in James, see R. Ward, "The Works of Abraham: James 2:14–26," *HTR* 61 (1968) 283–90.

56. I am aware of the Pauline tone of this characterization (cf. Rom. 4:1–2). James would have referred to an "earthly wisdom" (3:15). I am suggesting, of course, that at a deep level Paul and James see the choice before humans in a remarkably similar fashion.

57. Cf. the use of ἔχθρος ("enemy") in Rom. 5:10 and 11:28; Gal. 4:16; Col. 1:21; and ἔχθρα in Eph. 2:14–16. Cf. also LSJ, s.v., ἔχθρος, III.

58. Aristotle, *Rhetoric* 1387B.

59. I have developed this line of thought in *Sharing Possessions,* 80–88.

60. For the setting here, cf. R. Ward, "Partiality in the Assembly," *HTR* 62 (1969) 87–97.

61. James puts a definite and sardonic twist on the "friendship" language. The Hellenistic *topos* constantly asserts that true friendship is possible only between the virtuous and is incompatible with *envy.* Here, "friendship with the world" is illus-trated precisely by envy. Cf., e.g., Iamblichus, *VP* 17.75, 22.101–2, 31.198; Plato, *Lysis* 214D; Cicero, *De amicitia* 5.18, 7.23–24, 18.65, 22.83; Plutarch, *Frat. Am.* 484B, 485B; Aristotle, *Nichomachean Ethics* 8.12.6, 9.3.2, 12.3; Plato, *Laws* 837A–B; Pseudo-Phocylides, *Sentences* 71–75.

62. 1:18 is undeniably difficult. Despite the dissenting voice of L. E. Elliott-Binns ("James 1:18: Creation or Redemption?" *NTS* 3 [1957] 148–61), I think the views

of Ropes (*James*, 166), Dibelius (*James*, 105), and Mayor (*Epistle of St. James*, 63), to be correct. It should be noted, though, that it is still a measure from God in either case—the world is to be regarded as answerable to God. In this light, see how James calls the envious attitude one which "boasts and is false to the truth" (3:14, cf. also 4:16).

63. More work is still required on the sort of psychology presupposed by the language of James. As in the Rabbinic talk of the *yetzerim* or the loose characterizations of the spirits (πνεύματα) in the *Testaments of the Twelve Patriarchs*, there do not seem to be hard and fast distinctions drawn between "created" and "uncreated" factors. For James, *all* comes from God, both the gift and the possibility of receiving it (cf. 1:21). The connection between spirit and wisdom in James 3:13 and 4:5 seems clear enough. See J. A. Kirk, "The Meaning of Wisdom in James: Examination of a Hypothesis," *NTS* 16 (1969) 24–38.

64. This positive side of James's teaching is developed in Johnson, "Use of Leviticus 19," 400–401.

65. For the term, see O. J. F. Seitz, "Antecedents and Significance of the Term 'Dipsychos,'" *JBL* 66 (1947) 211–19; idem, "Afterthoughts on the Term, 'Dipsychos,'" *NTS* 4 (1957) 327–34; and W. Wolverton, "The Double-minded Man in the light of Essene Psychology," *ATR* 38 (1956) 166–75.

66. Is it by accident that 3:13—"By his good life let him show his *works* in the meekness of wisdom" is the last appearance of ἔργον in James? Up to this point, he has used it some fourteen times. The point is always the contrast between verbal or ideal assent to truth and the living out of it. This is a contrast typical of Hellenistic moralists. Among countless examples, cf. Lucian of Samosata, *Hermotimus* 79; *Timon* 54; *Runaways* 19; Epictetus, *Dissertations* 2.1.31, 2.9.21, 3.22.9; Julian the Apostate, *Oration* 7:225a; Dio Chrysostom, *Oration* 35.2, 3, 11.

# 9

# Backward and Forward "In His Steps": Following Jesus from Rome to Raymond and Beyond. The Tradition, Redaction, and Reception of 1 Peter 2:18–25*

## JOHN H. ELLIOTT

In 1896, Charles Monroe Sheldon published one of the most successful religious best sellers of all time: *In His Steps*.[1] Since its first printing, more than thirty million copies have been sold. Although its setting is typical Americana at the turn of the century, the book has been translated into more than twenty languages. According to a publisher's introductory comment in its most recent reprint of May 1973, this book "deserves a place among great religious books not because it represents impeccable literary craftsmanship, but because it clings to the idea and the ideal that captured the imagination of millions—[that] the teaching of Jesus Christ is indeed practical and workable if fearlessly put to the test." That simple test is for a follower of Jesus to ask before every undertaking of life: What would Jesus do? *In His Steps* is a novelistic essay on modern Christian discipleship. Set in the fictitious town of Raymond, U.S.A., it relates the story of how the complacency of a respectable congregation and its pastor, Dr. Henry Maxwell, was shattered by the tragic death of an unemployed printer seeking help and how this experience transformed the lives of pastor, parish, and community. The book takes its title from the biblical text upon which the parson was preaching when this death took place: "For to this you have been called, because Christ also suffered for you, leaving you an example, that you should follow in his steps." That text is 1 Peter 2:21.

---

*Presidential address delivered at the annual meeting of the Society of Biblical Literature, Pacific Coast Region, held at California State University, Fullerton, Calif., 8 April 1983.

184

## THE PROBLEM

In modern theological or exegetical treatments of discipleship, on the other hand, such as Dietrich Bonhoeffer's *The Cost of Discipleship*[2] or Eduard Schweizer's *Lordship and Discipleship*,[3] reference is made at best in passing to 1 Peter, and this Petrine text receives little if any attention. The reason is not difficult to surmise: "Discipleship", as conventionally perceived, is not a dominant theme in 1 Peter. It is, rather, in the Gospels and Acts that this concept receives its detailed and predominant articulation. It is these latter documents that employ the specific terms μαθητής and ἀκολουθέω; that develop the semantic fields of related terms and concepts such as disciple-teacher, "following" (both in literal and metaphorical sense), on the "way" or "journey"; that emphasize the radical demands of following Jesus (namely, separation from home, family, shelter, and possessions); and that present a portrait of disciples called to share in the itinerant ministry and ultimate destiny of the Son of man.

In 1 Peter, on the other hand, the explicit terminology of discipleship as found in the Gospels and Acts fails to appear. The same is true of the rest of the New Testament, with the sole exception of Rev. 14:4. It is thus understandable that exegetical studies of discipleship in the New Testament focus almost exclusively on the Gospels and Acts. There would be no point to faulting Sheldon on this score, since his book is a novel using 1 Peter as a pretext. It would be more to the point to ask whether there is any valid, exegetical reason for including 1 Peter in a study of discipleship in the New Testament. There is, of course, a certain traditional, religious aura about the term "discipleship" and no small degree of emotional attachment to the term in Christian circles. Like many theological concepts, such as eschatology, christology, soteriology, or ecclesiology, we can shape and define the category "discipleship" as inclusively or narrowly as we choose. Such conceptual constructs play a valid and necessary role in the organization and interpretation of exegetical data. But in the use of such time-honored and ecclesiastically cherished categories, how do we avoid forcing biblical texts and their specific frame of discourse onto prefabricated and preconceived procrustean beds? One way to avoid such radical surgery of textual implanting is, as the majority of exegetical studies of discipleship have done, to restrict attention to those biblical texts where the precise terminology is employed—namely, the Gospels and Acts. There is a point in asking, however, whether 1 Peter does not deserve closer exegetical attention after all; for in the Petrine text which gave Sheldon the title for his book are several indications of a fusion of concepts and traditions which place 1 Peter closer to the subject of discipleship than is generally recog-

185

nized. In what follows, then, I shall attempt to track some of the traces of this Petrine text; its place, significance, and function in 1 Peter; its affinity with broader currents of early Christian teaching, particularly those familiar to the Christians at Rome; and finally, its significance for contemporary ethical reflection.

## 1 PETER 2:21 IN CONTEXT

1 Peter 2:21 belongs to a larger textual unit of thought comprising an exhortation of Christian household servants (2:18–20), followed and supported by an extensive christological rationale (2:21–25). This unit, in turn, continues part of a line of thought, beginning at 2:11, which introduces a second major section of the letter (2:11—4:11). In the first major section of the letter (1:1—2:10), stress is laid on the distinctive communal identity and the divinely conferred dignity of Christian believers who live within a hostile society as "strangers and resident aliens" (1:1, 17: cf. 2:11). Through the mercy of God (1:3; 2:10) and faithful response to the gospel (1:12, 25), the "reborn" (1:3, 22) addressees have become "obedient children" (1:14; cf. 2:2) incorporated into the household or family of God (2:4–10). Sanctified by the call of the holy God (1:14–16), and united in faith with "the elect and holy one," Jesus Christ, they constitute an elect and holy community called to live a distinctly obedient and holy way of life within an unholy and hostile environment.

Following this affirmation of the distinctive communal identity of those who have been elected, sanctified and united with Jesus Christ, attention is turned next to the conduct of the household of God within the structures of society (2:11—3:12). While distancing themselves from the ways of the nonbelieving Gentiles (2:11), and though slandered as evildoers, believers are nevertheless to lead such an attractive way of life that even their detractors "may see your good deeds and glorify God on the day of visitation" (2:12). To illustrate social conduct which is appropriate to the household of God, civic and domestic duties are then discussed, the latter according to a modified schema of a traditional household code (2:13—3:7). "Doing what is right" (2:14, 15, 20; 3:6, 17; 4:19) in "subordination" (2:13, 18; 3:1, 5; cf. 5:5) to the "will of God" (2:15; cf. 3:17; 4:2, 19) "for the Lord's sake" (2:13), in contrast to "doing wrong" (2:14, 19; 3:9, 10, 11, 12, 13; 4:15)—all function as thematic terms for describing and integrating various sectors of Christian responsibility. In 3:8–12 this enumeration of domestic duties is brought to a preliminary close (cf. 5:1–5a) with an appeal for mutual humility and internal cohesion (3:8–9) addressed to *all* the readers (cf. 5:5b–7). In 3:10–12 a concluding quotation from Ps. 33(34):12–16

186

underlines the thought that the righteous who innocently suffer nevertheless have been called by God to avoid evil and do what is right.

These concluding verses draw our attention back to 2:21 and its immediate context; for a clause contained in 2:21 is repeated in 3:9—namely, "to this you have been called." This clause serves as a frame integrating the section 2:18—3:9 (12). Thus, the quotation of Psalm 33 in 1 Peter 3:10—12 provides a final scriptural substantiation for the exhortation beginning at 2:18 concerning doing what is right in the face of innocent suffering.

With this context in mind, we can now turn to a closer examination of 1 Peter 2:18–25 and the issue of discipleship. Here, the general themes of subordination and doing what is right (2:13–17) are applied specifically to the behavior of household servants; the focus moves from the wider public scene (2:14–17) to that of duties within the household; and the letter's key term for suffering, πάσχω,[4] makes its first appearance. In accord with the general principle that all believers are to be subordinate to every human institution for the Lord's sake (2:13), household servants are enjoined to be subordinate to their masters and do what is right even in the face of innocent suffering; for they have been called to follow in the steps of their innocent, suffering Lord. In Jesus Christ, the obedient, suffering servant of God, obedient, suffering servants have both an enabler and an exemplar.

The emphatic location of this slave exhortation, the nature and extent of its supporting theological rationale, its unusual terminology and fusion of traditions, and its paradigmatic function are all features which highlight the significance of this passage within the general strategy of 1 Peter.

In commenting on the significance of the passage as a whole, I draw on some observations presented in a previous work, A Home for the Homeless.[5] First, the design and function of 1 Peter 2:18–25 are indicated by certain modifications made here in the use of a traditional household code underlying the material in 2:18—3:7. Second, in contrast to other New Testament domestic codes where an exhortation of slaves (and masters) follows that of husbands/wives and parents/children (Col. 3:18—4:1; Eph. 5:22—6:9; 1 Tim. 2:8—6:2; Titus 2:1–10), thereby reflecting the inferior rank of slaves on the social ladder, here slaves are addressed first and are given striking pride of place. Furthermore, the conventional term for "slaves" (δοῦλοι) in the domestic codes has been replaced here with the term οἰκέται, "household servants." The substitution calls explicit attention to the exhortation's household (οἶκος) sphere of reference. Third, though "masters" (δεσπόται) are mentioned, nothing is said of their reciprocal responsibility. All attention is focused on the condition and conduct of the household servants. Fourth, and finally, various household members are addressed in 1 Peter (slaves, wives, husbands; see also elders and novices in 5:1–5); only the exhortation of household slaves, however, is given an extensive christological foundation.

Taken together, these factors indicate that what is stated here concerning the οἰκέται is fundamental and paradigmatic for the entire οἶκος τοῦ θεοῦ. Their social condition and divine vocation are typical of the condition and vocation of the entire Christian brotherhood. Their exposure to harsh as well as kind masters (2:18) typifies the vulnerability of all the πάροικοι to the pressures of their Gentile neighbors (2:11–12, 15; 3:13–17; 4:4, 12–19; 5:9–10). Servants, like other believers, are to be subordinate (2:18; 2:13; 3:1; 5:5) and to do what is right (2:20; 2:12, 14, 15; 3:6, 17; 4:19) with a clear conscience (2:19; 3:6, 17; 4:19). The criterion of their behavior is the same standard for all the believers: reverence (φόβος) for God alone (2:18; 1:17; 2:17; 3:2) and obedience to his will (2:18; 1:17; 2:15, 17; 3:2, 17; 4:2, 19). Their experience of suffering, despite such obedience and doing what is right, is shared by all the faithful (2:19–20; 1:6; 3:13–17; 4:1–6, 12–19; 5:9–10), just as it is the bond which unites *all* believers with their obedient, suffering Lord (2:21, 23; 4:1, 12–19). The calling of the οἰκέται (2:21) is the calling of all (3:9).

Through its emphatic location and stress on themes which pervade the letter, this exhortation of household servants thus provides a model and basis for the conduct and confidence of the entire household. Accordingly, the christological rationale which it includes provides an indicative basis for the imperatives which follow as well as precede it. At the same time, the passage serves as a concrete illustration of the general principle initially expressed in 2:13. As the subordination of slaves (2:18–20) illustrates the subordination of all (2:13), so the christological statement in 1 Peter 2:21–25 relates to and expands upon the briefer christological formula in 2:13, "for the Lord's sake" (διὰ τὸν κύριον). (In 1 Peter, κύριος designates Jesus Christ [1:3, 25; 2:3; 3:15] except where the Old Testament/Septuagint is alluded to [3:6] or quoted [3:12].) The innocent suffering of righteous servants, like that of all the righteous believers (3:12; 4:18), derives its power and motivation from the vicarious suffering of the Righteous One (3:18), the Servant of God, Jesus Christ (2:21–25).

As 2:18–25 serves an illustrative and paradigmatic function within 1 Peter, so do the servants in particular. Their designation as οἰκέται rather than δοῦλοι belongs to a larger strategy in which the οἶκος or household is accentuated as the primary ecclesial metaphor of the letter.[6] The vulnerable condition of these slaves vis-à-vis their master-owners resembles closely the vulnerable condition of the entire Christian community within society, just as their innocent suffering is consistent with the suffering of all the faithful. On the other hand, within the Christian brotherhood their humble status illustrates the mutual humility which is required of all believers (3:8, 5:5–6). Similarly, the pride of place which they are given in the general scheme of household instruction underlies the new status and respect which such lowly persons enjoy in the assembly of the reborn. And finally, when we recall the role which servants play in the dominical logia concerning the reversal of status and values in the kingdom of God (Mark 10:42–45 par.; 9:33–35 par.), it comes as no surprise that in 1 Peter also it is precisely with servants that the kerygma concerning Jesus as servant is most directly associated.

## 1 PETER 2:21–25

Before we consider the verses (2:21–25) which explicate that link between servants and servant and describe the nature of this calling, we should note one feature which sets off vv. 18–20 from their broader literary context. This feature is important because it illustrates the affinity between 1 Peter and the gospel traditions, an affinity which is also important for unraveling the origin and implications of v. 21. This unusual feature concerns the meaning of the term χάρις, which forms a chiastic inclusion around vv. 19–20.[7]

### Grace

Aside from these two verses, χάρις appears eight times in 1 Peter, always with the meaning "grace" (of God). At the conclusion of the letter, the term figures prominently in an explicit statement of the letter's purpose: "By Silvanus, a faithful brother as I regard him, I have written briefly to you, exhorting and declaring that this is the true grace of God; stand fast in it" (5:12). In 2:19–20, however, χάρις appears to be used in another sense. The RSV, for instance, prefers the translation "approval": "For one is approved if, mindful of God, he endures pain while suffering unjustly. For what credit is it, if when you do wrong and are beaten for it you take it patiently? But if when you do right and suffer for it you take it patiently, you have God's approval." Commentators either concur with this RSV rendition (e.g., E. Best)[8] or compromise, as L. Goppelt[9] does, translating χάρις once with "Ruhm" as in the classical sense and then subsequently with "Gnade" in a theological sense.

E. G. Selwyn, who notes that the usage here is classical, naive, and untechnical, comes closest, I think, in detecting the term's sense and likely origin. He points to a similar sense of the term in the *verbum Christi* of Luke 6:32–34 and suggests that here 1 Peter is dependent upon a dominical logion contained in "a summary of Christian teaching intended for catechetical instruction, current in oral tradition in more than one form."[10] Further similarities between these Petrine verses and Luke 6:32–35[11] strengthen the likelihood of at least the common use of oral sayings tradition. And the synonymous use of χάρις and μισθός in the Lukan passage[12] suggests that both Luke and 1 Peter knew of this tradition in a more expanded, Hellenized form in which χάρις, like the earlier μισθός, denoted "divine approval or reward."[13] The Petrine use of presynoptic tradition has long been noted by commentators.[14] Detection of the use of influence of such tradition is not only helpful here in discerning the sense of the term χάρις, it is also useful in ascertaining the meaning and origin of the verses which follow. We turn then to the second segment of our passage, vv. 21–25.

These verses (vv. 21–25) provide a double theological substantiation (εἰς τοῦτο, γάρ, ὅτι) for the foregoing servant exhortation through reference both to the call and the saving action of God (ἐκλήθητε, v. 21; ἐπεστράφητε, v. 25; both divine passives), and to the similar innocent suffering of the Christ (καὶ χριστὸς ἔπαθεν ὑπὲρ ὑμῶν, v. 21b) which establishes an example for the servants to follow (v. 21c, d). The verb πάσχω (vv. 20, 21, 23) serves as the chief thematic linkword uniting vv. 18–20 and 21–25, just as it is the experience of innocent suffering which is stressed throughout the letter as an essential bond uniting believers with their Lord.[15] Verses 22–24 describe in further detail the innocent suffering of the obedient Christ (vv. 22–23) and its salvific effect (v. 24). Verse 25 concludes the unit with a pastoral metaphor depicting the reunion of believers and Lord: those who were once scattered have now been gathered and returned (by God) to their shepherd and guardian.

Like vv. 18–20, so this following unit contains terminology and themes which integrate it with the content and accents of the letter as a whole.[16] On the other hand, there are a number of peculiarities here which indicate the use and fusion of some pre-Petrine sources and traditions.

## A Christ Hymn

Let us look first at vv. 22–25, reserving our main verse, v. 21, for final consideration. There is a general consensus among commentators that use has been made here of early Christian liturgical tradition in the form of a "Christ hymn" or "Passion hymn" ("*Passionslied*").[17] This is indicated by the formal and material features which relate these verses to similar kerygmatic, liturgical, and creedal material both in 1 Peter[18] and other New Testament documents. The hymn has aptly been so called ("das erste uns überlieferte Passionslied der Kirche").[19]

Here in 1 Peter, elements of this christological passion hymn, together with interspersed redactional additions (in vv. 24 and 25), have been employed to elaborate on the initial statement of v. 21 that "Christ also suffered for you," and to affirm the vicarious nature and salvific consequences of this suffering which unites Lord and believers. Although Hellenistic in formulation, the hymn belongs to a broader current of tradition upon which the Synoptics also drew. Goppelt, in fact, sees the hymn as a subsequent elaboration on a primitive ὑπέρ formula whose conceptual origin he traces to words of Jesus concerning his imminent passion (Mark 10:45; 14:24 par.).[20] In the Gospels it is primarily the Psalms which are used to elaborate on the suffering of Jesus, the righteous one. In the hymn of 1 Peter, on the other hand, we have the sole New Testament instance where this suffering of the righteous one is extensively developed through the use of motifs derived from the suffering servant song of Isaiah 53. A synoptic comparison of the Greek texts of 1 Peter and Isaiah 52—53[21] makes this affinity sufficiently clear.

## A Servant Song

These traces of the Isaianic servant song in the hymn of 1 Peter touch on the fascinating issue of the role of this Old Testament passage in the formation of early christological tradition, a question far too complex and contested for discussion in this paper. Instead, let me call attention to two related observations concerning the role of this servant song and passion hymn in 1 Peter and some implications it may have for a broader tradition concerning suffering linking 1 Peter with the Gospels.

First, within the household instruction of 1 Peter 2:18—3:12 we have now noted two biblical sources which have been employed to encourage doing what is right in the face of unjust suffering. As mentioned earlier, in 3:10–12 a psalm concerning the suffering of the righteous community (Psalm 33 [34]) is cited to conclude this section and provide biblical substantiation for the imperative to "avoid evil and do what is right" (Ps. 33:13–17a). This psalm, echoed elsewhere in 1 Peter,[22] sings of the *passio iustorum*, the suffering of the *righteous community*. In 1 Peter 2:22–25, on the other hand, another source, a Christian hymn employing elements of Isaiah 53, is used to describe the innocent suffering of a righteous individual, the Lord Jesus Christ, who through his vicarious suffering has made possible the new life and righteous behavior of the believing community. In 1 Peter these sources are used in tandem to affirm the bond which unites righteous servants with their righteous servant-Lord. The *passio iustorum* is linked to and grounded in the *passio iusti*.

## Relation to the Gospels (Mark)

Second, this raises an interesting question concerning evidence in 1 Peter of a so-called *passio iusti/iustorum* tradition by which 1 Peter may be related to the Gospels and the Gospel of Mark in particular.

In Mark, as well as in 1 Peter, the suffering of the righteous community

191

is inseparably linked with and based upon the suffering of Jesus, the right-eous one. Could this conception of solidarity in suffering have belonged to a tradition underlying various compositions of the New Testament? Could Isaiah 53 together with several of the Psalms have provided the motifs for such a primitive Christian tradition?[23] What suggests this possibility is the combined material on suffering in 1 Peter, on the one hand, and a recently advanced hypothesis concerning the sources of Mark, on the other. Rudolph Pesch, in his impressive commentary on Mark, has advanced the thesis that the entire second half of this Gospel (8:27 — 16:8) incorporates, with only minor modifications, a pre-Markan passion narrative. Basic to this narrative, according to Pesch, is the theme of the suffering righteous one, the *passio iusti*, as he calls it.[24]

Pesch, of course, is concerned primarily with determining the scope of Mark's sources and the evangelist's own redactional activity. While, in my opinion, he exaggerates the extent of the former and the limited, conserv-ative nature of the latter,[25] his thesis has the merit of calling attention to an influential motif pervading the pre-Markan passion tradition. When the similarities between Mark and 1 Peter, particularly their theologies of suf-fering,[26] are also brought to bear on this question of presynoptic tradition, a broader data base is provided for the examination of his thesis.

The affinities between Mark and 1 Peter cannot be shown to be the result of direct literary dependence of either composition upon the other. Could these similarities, however, be traced to commonly used tradition? There is still no consensus regarding the influence of Isaiah 53 on Mark or on his sources. Could, however, its evident influence on the Christian *Passionslied* in 1 Peter indicate its place and role in a body of tradition concerning the suffering of the righteous, an oral tradition upon which various authors drew in various ways?[27] I have no answer to offer at this point. But I do suggest that in the light of our observations concerning the sources of 1 Peter this question deserves further scrutiny. If the use of common tradition is to provide a reasonable explanation of such affinities, then an adequate demonstration must be given of the existence, provenance, and tradents of such tradition. If and when this should ever be attempted, Pesch's theory deserves serious attention.

As we shall soon note, another passage of 1 Peter, 2:21, also has affinities with Mark. Thus, the more we probe, the more interesting becomes this issue of the Markan— 1 Peter relationship. In the case of Mark and 1 Peter, I believe a case can be made for their common origin in the city of Rome. In a recent study[28] I have presented some of the evidence supporting this theory. If there is merit to this proposal, then local oral tradition shared by various groups in Rome, together with their common social situation and socioreligious perspectives, would account for numerous points of contact between both documents, including their interpretations of solidarity in suffering and its link with the calling to follow Jesus. This leads us to the final section of this study.

## DISCIPLESHIP IN 1 PETER

1 Peter 2:21, as already noted, forms the literary and conceptual link which joins vv. 18–20 and vv. 22–25. It is a noteworthy formulation in several ways. First, this verse introduces the four verses which follow as a double theological, christological substantiation for the preceding servant exhortation. The verse literarily unites two theologically related rationales. Servants are to do what is right even though suffering unjustly, first, because this is their divine calling and second, "because Christ also suffered for you, leaving you an example, that you should follow in his steps."[29]

A second striking feature of this verse is its apparent composite character. The first two units of the verse contain terminology and ideas which recur throughout the letter. The clause "for to this you have been called" (εἰς τοῦτο γὰρ ἐκλήθητε, 2:21a) is repeated in 3:9. Thus, the exhortation of 2:18—3:9 is framed and supported by the notion of the Christians' divine calling. As further instances of καλέω in 1 Peter indicate, this calling originates with God the Father, who calls the believers to holiness (1:15), from darkness to light (2:9), and to his eternal glory in Christ (5:10).[30]

This calling, however, is linked with and mediated through the vicarious suffering of the Christ (2:21b). Thus, the next clause, "because Christ also suffered for you," further strengthens the unity of vv. 18–20 and 22–25. It explicitly introduces the christological tradition which follows and further explicates the sense of διὰ κυρίου in the general statement of 2:13.[31]

While its first half (21a, b) is thus related to the rest of the letter, the remainder of the verse is unique. The unique terms employed and the thought expressed seem to involve an abrupt interjection of something foreign into the language and logic of the letter. There is nothing else in the letter which prepares for or develops the words, "leaving you an example, in order that you should follow in his steps" (21c, d). These are the words which gave Sheldon the title for his book. It is these words which have suggested to others as well a link between 1 Peter and the theme of discipleship. On the other hand, still others detect in these words not echoes of discipleship but traces of an *imitatio Christi* piety which supposedly associates 1 Peter with a moralizing trend characteristic of later Christian writings classified as examples of "early Catholicism."

Together with their immediate context, these final elements of 1 Peter

2:21 thus raise several interesting questions, not the least of which concerns aspects of tradition and redaction common to 1 Peter and other New Testament writings.

## Terminology

The Greek terms ὑπολιμπάνων, meaning "leaving behind (for someone)," and ὑπογραμμός, meaning "example" or "pattern," occur nowhere else in the New Testament.[32] The former is also not found in the Septuagint and the latter only once (2 Macc. 2:28). The accompanying terms ἐπακολουθέω ("follow [closely]") and τὰ ἴχνη ("footprint" or "footsteps") are likewise rare New Testament vocables. The verb occurs elsewhere only twice in 1 Timothy (5:10, 24) and once in the longer ending of Mark (16:20); and the noun occurs elsewhere only twice in Paul (Rom. 4:12; 2 Cor. 12:18). The usage of all four terms outside the New Testament indicates their Hellenistic provenance; within the New Testament their combined use here is unique.[33]

However, in two later Christian letters influenced by 1 Peter—those of Clement of Rome and Polycarp to the Philippians—one of these New Testament *hapax legomena*, ὑπογραμμός, reappears in contexts quite similar to that of 1 Peter 2:21. In *1 Clement* 16 an extensive quotation from Isaiah 53 (53:1–12 in *1 Clement* 16:3–14) is used to illustrate the humility of Jesus Christ, which the readers are encouraged to emulate.[34] The passage concludes with the words: "You see, beloved, what is the example [ὑπογραμμός] which is given us; for if the Lord was thus humble-minded, what shall we do, who through him have come under the yoke of his grace?" (16:17). Here, as in 1 Peter 2, the Lord Jesus Christ is declared to be an "example" for the believers, and the continued association of this concept with Isaiah 53 is made explicitly clear.[35]

Polycarp comes even closer to the text of 1 Peter in brevity, form, content, and implicit rather than explicit reference to Isaiah 53 in *Phila.* 8:1–2:

> Let us then persevere unceasingly in our hope and in the pledge of our righteousness who is Jesus Christ, who bore our sins in his own body on the tree; who did no sin, neither was guile found in his mouth; but for our sakes, that we might live in him, he endured all things (v. 1).[36]

In the following verse the μιμητής concept of Paul is merged with the Petrine combination of "example" and "suffering": "Let us then be imitators [μιμηταί] of his endurance, and if we suffer [πάσχωμεν] for his name's sake let us glorify him [cf. 1 Peter 4:14–16]. For this is the example [ὑπογραμμόν] which he gave us in himself, and this is what we have believed" (8:2). For *1 Clement*, Christ is pre-eminently an example of humility (Clement's hortatory theme, chap. 13), and for Polycarp, of endurance (ὑπέμεινεν, 8:1; ὑπομονή, 8:2). Neither Clement nor Polycarp, however, associates "example," "humility," and "suffering" with the idea of following in Christ's steps. The constellation of concepts is still flexible rather than fixed, and the entire complex of motifs and terms found in 1 Peter is unique to this early composition.

## Relation to the Gospels (Mark)

While the specific *terms* found in 1 Peter 2:21 are unique or rare in comparison with the rest of the New Testament literature, the *concepts* of "following Jesus" and of Jesus as "example" certainly are not. Here again, the chief points of contact are with the Gospels, and with Mark in particular.[37]

First, while the expression "that you should follow in his steps" is unique to 1 Peter, Mark and the gospel tradition certainly know and indeed accentuate the theme of following Jesus as an apt expression of association, allegiance, and solidarity between Jesus and those whom he has called to join him in his ministry. The operative terms for "following," ἐπακολουθέω in 1 Peter and ἀκολουθέω in Mark, while not identical, are nevertheless paronyms; and the Petrine expression ἐπακολουθήσητε τοῖς ἴχνεσιν αὐτοῦ, while unique in the New Testament, is nevertheless synonymous in *sense* to the related expressions in Mark, δεῦτε ὀπίσω μου . . . ἠκολούθησαν αὐτῷ . . . ἀπῆλθον ὀπίσω αὐτοῦ (Mark 1:16–20; 2:14).

Second, the Petrine term ὑπογραμμός, as G. Schrenk has noted, often denoted an "example" used in a *pedagogical* sense and setting.[38] "For purposes of instruction, a word is proposed which contains all the letters of the alphabet in a form in which children can remember them, so that a model is given which is called ὑπογραμμὸς παιδικός."[39] While the "example" to which 1 Peter refers is Jesus' innocent suffering, the pedagogical connotations of the term relate it in an interesting way to the teacher-disciple relationship of Jesus and his followers as depicted in the Gospels. Although nothing certain can be deduced from the term itself in 1 Peter, its immediate context at least allows the possibility that ὑπογραμμός, together with the rest of v. 21, forms a Petrine version of and allusion to the Jesus tradition underlying Mark and the other Gospels.

A third factor indicating an affinity between 1 Peter and Mark is that both documents associate following Jesus with a *call* or summons. 1 Peter traces this call to its ultimate origin—namely, God; Mark, on the other hand, associates the call more directly with Jesus, through whom the summons to follow is issued.

Fourth, and finally, in both 1 Peter and Mark (8:27–37) the call to follow Jesus is inseparably linked to the experience of suffering shared by Jesus and his followers. The differences in terminology and formulation disallow any possibility of direct literary dependency between 1 Peter and Mark.

195

But these four instances of material similarity between epistle and Gospel do suggest the varied use of development of common pre-Petrine and presynoptic tradition to express the solidarity in suffering which unites the Lord and his followers.[40]

## THE LITERARY RELATIONSHIP OF 1 PETER

Before drawing some conclusions regarding the Petrine use of this tradition and the question of a discipleship theme in 1 Peter, I wish to touch on two broader issues involving the literary relationship of 1 Peter. The preceding analysis has detected several points of contact between 1 Peter and the Gospel of Mark. As already indicated, neither literary dependency nor use of fixed tradition can account for these various affinities. A preferable explanation, however, which takes into account both the peculiarities as well as similarities of both documents, is that both the Letter (1 Peter) and Gospel (Mark) originated in Rome and reflect, each in its own way, the fluid oral traditions, similar social conditions, and common theological perspectives of the Roman Christian community. In support of this theory, consider the following.[41]

1. Both 1 Peter and Mark are products of a marginal, sectarian community intent upon affirming and legitimating its identity over against both Judaism and Greco-Roman society. Both distinguish those who heed the call of Jesus in faith and follow him from those who reject him, the righteous elect from the unrighteous sinners, those who live by the will of God from those who follow human ordinances and conventions, insiders from outsiders.

2. Both documents, however, reveal a conservative Christian stance vis-à-vis civil government. As Mark's account of the passion seeks to exonerate the Romans in the case of Jesus' execution and highlights the confession of a Roman soldier (15:39), so in 1 Peter, Christians are encouraged to be subordinate to civil authority and to regard the emperor and his governors as those charged with maintaining justice (2:13–17).

3. Both writings reflect and support a universal mission of the faithful, a propagation of the gospel to all humanity in all corners of the earth. They are both products of a community with ecumenical, rather than only local, interests.

4. Accordingly, both documents rely upon and combine various streams of Palestinian and Diaspora Christian tradition in order to express and affirm the various bonds which unite the brotherhood from east to west.

5. Both documents reflect an eschatological interest in Jesus' imminent revelation and return.

6. According to both documents, the relation of the elect believers to nonbelieving outsiders is one of tension and conflict, resulting in the innocent suffering of both Jesus and believers.

7. Both Mark and 1 Peter describe faith, allegiance, and solidarity in terms of response to the call to follow Jesus, the essence of which for both is sharing in his innocent suffering and ultimate divine vindication.

8. Accordingly, both 1 Peter and Mark employ the kerygma of Jesus' passion, death, and resurrection (in the form of hymnic material as in 1 Peter, or in the form of a passion narrative as in Mark) to explain and justify the suffering of his followers.

9. In presenting this bond which suffering forges between the Lord and his followers, both documents stress a mutual obedience to God's will and cite the status and behavior of the servant as illustrative of a proper Christian stance. And in this connection, both depict Jesus as an innocent, suffering servant who provides the example for his followers to emulate. In 1 Peter and the tradition upon which 2:22-25 depends, this portrait has been developed through the use of the suffering servant motif of Isaiah 53. In Mark the influence of this text is less obvious but still possible. Two later documents acquainted with 1 Peter—namely, the Letters of Clement of Rome and Polycarp to the Philippians—further illustrate the course of this christological tradition and its association with the Isaianic text. As a textual comparison reveals, Polycarp's *Letter to the Philippians* is closer in its brevity and formulation to 1 Peter and involves no explicit citation of Isaiah 53. *1 Clement*, on the other hand, goes beyond 1 Peter in offering an extensive quotation of Isaiah 53 in explication of Christ's humility. If Mark shares the Roman provenance of 1 Peter and *1 Clement*, then it is possible that a substratum of local christological tradition associating the Christ and the suffering servant of Isaiah best explains many of the features common to, but differently employed by and formulated in, all three Roman writings. In this case, the influence of Isaiah 53 which remains at best implicit in Mark becomes clearer in 1 Peter and more explicit in *1 Clement*.

10. Finally, one last affinity between 1 Peter and Mark concerns the letters of Clement and Polycarp as well. Both 1 Peter and Mark employ similar ecclesial, as well as christological, motifs and images to depict the community of the faithful. Believers are the "elect" of God, sheep once scattered but eventually gathered, and those who are called to follow the Lord. Chief among such communal metaphors, however, in both 1 Peter and Mark, is the portrayal of the believing community as the new family or household of God.

In my study, *A Home for the Homeless*, I have discussed the dimensions, significance, and function of this metaphor in 1 Peter. In both documents, οἶκος and οἰκία play a major role in locating and identifying the true family of God. In both, the audiences are addressed as children or favorably compared with children and household servants. In both writings, believers are encouraged to see themselves as obedient and humble household servants, called to follow the example of their obedient and suffering Servant-Lord. Moreover, it is important to note that in 1 Peter, Mark, *1 Clement*, and Polycarp, it is the household code which provides all four documents with a framework for integrating much of their common material (see Appendix). In the case of 1 Peter and Mark in particular, it is in conjunction with internal household instruction that both documents elaborate on following Jesus or discipleship in terms of sharing in the service and suffering of their Servant-Lord.

All these points of contact deserve a closer examination. My broad sketch here is intended mainly to stimulate further research along such wider lines. When an analysis of a text such as 1 Peter 2:18–25 is approached with preconceived notions regarding the theological category of discipleship, it is inevitable that certain broader issues and lines of convergence are bound to be overlooked. The unusual components of this Petrine text have forced us to look beyond the text itself for clues as to the meaning and origin of certain terms and concepts. In the process we have come upon evidence which not only clarifies this particular text of 1 Peter but also helps determine the letter's place within, and link with, the broader stream of early Christian life and proclamation.

## CONCLUSION

What are we to say, then, about 1 Peter and the theme of discipleship? In conclusion, let me summarize the somewhat circuitous route I have taken in tracking the traces of an important early Christian topic and its Petrine treatment.

1. Technically speaking, 1 Peter never mentions the term "disciple." To ignore this letter in a discussion of discipleship, however, is to overlook a significant variation on this important New Testament theme. Indeed, the letter never uses the term μαθητής; nor is any interest shown in the role of Jesus as teacher, or in the teacher-student relationship as an illustration of the bond between the exalted Christ and the believing brotherhood. To express this bond, a wide variety of other means is employed.[42] Nevertheless, the letter does encourage its readers to "follow in the steps" of Jesus, and the tradition from which this notion derives clearly demonstrates that 1 Peter is closer to the subject of discipleship than a superficial reading might suggest.

2. To determine the significance and function of this expression within the letter as a whole, we first examined its wider and narrower contexts, and in particular, the servant exhortation of 2:18–25. An investigation of the peculiarities of v. 21 in particular led to the conclusion that in this verse, as in 2:18–25, there is a fusion of parenetic and kerygmatic, christological,

soteriological, and ecclesial motifs and traditions. We have here another example of what one scholar, Albert Vanhoye,[43] has noted as typical for the letter as a whole: namely, the intersection ("carrefour") of diverse traditions and theological perspectives. Use of these traditions links 1 Peter with the evangelists, especially Mark, as well as with *1 Clement* and Polycarp. The likely Roman origin of 1 Peter, Mark, and *1 Clement* points to the city of Rome and the Christian community there as the place where such traditions were gathered and circulated and developed. 1 Peter, exhibiting the worldwide contacts and ecumenical vision of this Roman community, combines various strands of Palestinian and Diaspora tradition in a message to the brotherhood in Asia Minor in order to demonstrate and foster the unity and consolidation of the worldwide Christian movement.

3. In 1 Peter 2:18–25 such a fusion of traditions and themes serves to introduce and accentuate the social condition and divine vocation of household servants as paradigmatic for the entire household of God.

4. In order to explain and legitimate the instruction of servants to endure innocent suffering for doing what is right in obedience to God's will, appeal is made to the believers' divine vocation and the fact that Christ also suffered on their behalf and left them an example to follow. In explication of this fusion of kerygma (2:21a, b) and exhortation (2:21c, d), use is made of an early Christian hymn employing terminology and motifs from the fourth servant song of Isaiah in order to portray the Christ as the obedient and innocent, suffering servant of God. Christological tradition concerning the suffering servant thus serves to reinforce the resolve and praxis of suffering servants. Bound as servants subordinate to the will of God, believers and Lord are also united in their innocent suffering for doing what is right. The *passio iusti* is example and empowerment of the *passio iustorum*.

5. While solidarity in suffering is an accent which pervades 1 Peter, the concept of following in his steps is not. The combination of suffering with the notion of following Jesus in a symbolic rather than literal sense—a combination already made in the tradition upon which 1 Peter was dependent—explains its abrupt appearance in 2:21. In the Gospels this tradition was expanded through the use of the images of teacher and disciple. In Mark we see the beginning of a process in the Gospels in which discipleship and the διδάσκαλος—μαθηταί relationship assumes an ever-increasingly important role, statistically and thematically, for articulating the relation of Jesus and those who follow him in his ministry, mission, and destiny.[44] In 1 Peter, on the other hand, this image of solidarity is overshadowed by others and receives only momentary and muted expression. Despite this and other differences between 1 Peter and Mark, their many affinities point to a common ground which deserves further exploration. Not the least important among these points of contact is the similar manner

in which the household of God plays a major role in the identification and instruction of the Christian community. In both documents the community as οἶκος τοῦ θεοῦ and household instruction establish the socioreligious contours and help define the specific features of the Christian calling, of following Jesus and sharing his suffering, and of solidarity in experience and hope.

6. Finally, this Petrine text involves an issue which takes us beyond merely exegetical concerns to those of a broader theological and ethical scope. I am referring here to the implications of the Petrine term "example" or "pattern" and its relation to the long-standing debate regarding the role of *imitatio Christi* piety in the history of Christian theology, ethics, and spirituality.

## Implications for Theology and Piety

Ethicians and theologians as well as exegetes have been sensitive to certain problems posed by the model of discipleship in general and by certain biblical expressions regarding Christ as pattern in particular. One Danish Lutheran theologian, N. H. Søe, writing on the subject of discipleship in the compendium *Religion in Geschichte und Gegenwart*, candidly admits:

> The Lutheran Christian often does not know what to do with the doctrine of Christian discipleship. He opposes a Roman Catholic Imitatio piety and talk of a 'Christ-like life' in English and American circles as well as the interpretation of Jesus as an ethical-religious ideal popular in continental protestant circles at the turn of the century.[45]

But such opposition, Søe implies, is not balanced by a clear conception of what discipleship positively connotes.

A prominent American ethician, James Gustafson, underscores this same uncertainty in his splendid study, *Christ and the Moral Life*.[46] What, precisely, does conformity to Jesus Christ entail, he asks. In tracing the course of theological history, he observes various modes of response conditioned by various philosophical, social, and theological frames of references. He, as well as Søe, refers specifically to Sheldon's novel, and both note the popular attraction yet ethical inadequacy of Sheldon's enormously influential moral principle: namely, that in every situation of life you should ask yourself the question, What would Jesus do? The enormous popularity of this maxim and Sheldon's book is eloquent testimony to the fact that earnest Christians will find their own moral guidelines if the denominations and the theologians fail to come up with convincing proposals of their own. And yet this is no adequate solution to this urgent and vexed issue. For indeed, as Gustafson insists, "The answer to the personal moral question refers to objective criteria and norms."[47] The task of theology is precisely to clarify these norms, their scriptural warrant, and their ultimate legiti-

200

mation so as to control and critique personal projection and subjective fantasy.

To deny the need for models and the function of examples and models in everyday living would be to deny all that we have learned of the nature and process of human socialization and education. It would be equally ludicrous and pointless to assert that in the formative stages of the Christian movement it was otherwise. The issue is not and was not the need and use of moral models for ordering and guiding Christian life in society but precisely which assumptions regarding human nature, divine grace, salvation, and community inform the choice and use of these models.

Modern theology, particularly Protestant theology, is marked by a distinct animus against what is labelled "Imitation of Christ Piety" (*Imitatio-Christi Frömmigkeit*). This animus, moreover, appears in virtually every exegetical treatment of our Petrine text. On occasion, as with Hans Dieter Betz's brief treatment in his *Nachfolge und Nachahmung*,[48] it is claimed that traces of such an *Imitatio-Jesu-Frömmigkeit* are evident in 1 Peter. Far more often, however, scholars dissociate the letter from any "taint" of imitation theology. Seldom, if ever, however, do the exegetes define this opprobrious concept, apparently assuming that the course of theological history makes its definition as well as dangers self-evident.

It is interesting, nevertheless, to note that in the course of history, the concept of imitation of and conformity to the Christ regularly served the interests and programs of spiritual reform movements, from those of the Middle Ages down through seventeenth- and eighteenth-century Protestant and Roman Catholic Pietism to the popular "edifying literature" of works like Sheldon's. Ironically, even the Protestant father of modern existentialism, Søren Kierkegaard, it has been noted, did not fully escape its clutches,[49] nor presumably does any exegesis which is indebted to and informed by these existentialist perspectives. The issue of an *imitatio Christi* problematic, in other words, is not simply a matter of vulgar Protestant versus vulgar Catholic theology and morality. Once used as a polemical slogan in the Reformation and subsequent confessional wars to decry moralism, merit, monkery, mysticism, and other Roman Catholic instances of opposition to a biblically based doctine of justification (*Rechtfertigungslehre*), the notion of imitation and Christ conformity, historically viewed, is more like a fog or gas which persistently wafts over all the trenches. A contemporary reassessment of the entire matter, in any case, is long overdue, for the sake of exegesis as well as of ecumenical dialogue.

However this concept eventually is to be clarified, the heart of the issue it represents, I would suggest, concerns what we have come to call the relation of imperative and indicative, parenesis and proclamation, *ethos* and *salus*. An *imitatio Christi* theology, in its most negative form, is not the combination of one with the other but the *isolation* of one from the other, with the predominant or exclusive emphasis upon behavior divorced from belief, ethos separated from evangel, and ecclesiology divorced from christology and soteriology.

In both material and formal ways, the letter affirms this interrelation of indicative and imperative. Christians are given in Christ an example to follow, not an ideal to aspire to or an achievement to ape. The Christ of 1 Peter is an exemplar of obedience because he was first an instrument of empowerment. Jesus Christ the model is Jesus Christ the means. In his subordination to God's will without sinning, in his doing what was right, in his innocent suffering, just as in his rejection and righteousness, election and holiness, vicarious death, and glorious vindication, he expresses the unity which binds himself and those who believe with the merciful and gracious God of glory. At the same time Jesus as the Christ is singular, unique. He alone is the righteous one who makes others righteous; his suffering alone is vicarious; his suffering, death, and resurrection alone break the power of sin and inaugurate new life and righteousness; he alone is the chief shepherd. 1 Peter thus shows how the singularity of person and action affirmed in the kerygma becomes the enlivening power of salvation and the pattern for behavior. Christ the enabler is Christ the example. To illustrate this correlation, I recall an analogy from Eduard Schweizer's study, *Lordship and Discipleship.* The story with which his book opens is a fitting one for bringing this study to a close:

> When in a valley in the mountains there is a sudden heavy fall of snow, a child visiting his grandmother may not be able to reach home again. But when father comes home from his work he will fetch him, lead the way and with his strong shoulders make a way through the snowdrifts. The child follows, step by step, in the footsteps of the father, and yet in an entirely different manner. If the father wanted to be just an 'example' to the child, then the child would have to make his own way ten yards away from the father and merely imitate the manner in which the latter makes his way. If the father wanted to act 'vicariously' for the child, in the strict sense of the word, then the child would stay with grandmother and think: Father is going home in my stead.
>
> This example [Schweizer notes] *cannot* have the intention of emphasizing that the child "too must do something." He certainly does do something, and something very concrete at that. He follows a road on which there is sunshine and cold wind, soft snow and hard ice. But what he is doing is a matter of course. He is going home just as he went home yesterday, and he is pleased to go home. But this is certainly true: that he is involved in what Father is doing, involved 'after the event,' but yet involved step by step; so much so that he learns to see what Father is doing before his eyes and step by step practices what he sees.[50]

To follow in the steps of Christ is to have not only a model but a means. The steps in which the faithful are called are the prints of the Lord, who has first broken the way.

The specific terms of this Petrine correlation are unique. The unity of kerygma and exhortation which they express, however, locates the letter and its conception of *salus-Christus-communitas-ethos* not on the periphery but, rather, at the very center of New Testament proclamation and praxis.

## NOTES

1. C. M. Sheldon, *In His Steps* (Grand Rapids: Zondervan, 1967).

2. D. Bonhoeffer, *The Cost of Discipleship* (trans. R. H. Fuller; New York: Macmillan Co., 1948).

3. E. Schweizer, *Lordship and Discipleship* (SBT 28; London: SCM Press, 1960).

4. L. Goppelt, *Der erste Petrusbrief* (MeyerK 12.1; 1st new ed.; ed. F. Hahn; Göttingen: Vandenhoeck & Ruprecht, 1978) 200.

5. For a more extensive discussion, see J. H. Elliott, *A Home for the Homeless. A Sociological Exegesis of 1 Peter. Its Situation and Strategy* (Philadelphia: Fortress Press, 1981) esp. 205–8. N. Brox (*Der erste Petrusbrief* [EKKNT 21; Zürich: Benziger Verlag; Neukirchen-Vluyn: Neukirchener Verlag, 1979] 127–40) also notes the importance of this "Schlüsseltext" (129) within the larger context of 1 Peter.

6. On the significance and function of the household within 1 Peter, see Elliott, *Home for the Homeless*, 200–237.

7. A. "For one is approved [τοῦτο γὰρ χάρις] if, mindful of God"
   B. "If when you do wrong" (εἰ ἁμαρτάνοντες)
   B'. "If when you do right"(εἰ ἀγαθοποιοῦντες)
   A.' "You have God's approval" (τοῦτο χάρις παρὰ θεῷ)

8. E. Best, *1 Peter* (NCB; Grand Rapids: Wm. B. Eerdmans, 1971) 118; or J. N. D. Kelly, *A Commentary on the Epistles of Peter and Jude* (HNTC; New York: Harper & Row, 1969) 114, 116, 118: "For this is a fine thing (in God's sight)."

9. Goppelt, *Der erste Petrusbrief*, 189, 194, 197.

10. E. G. Selwyn, *The First Epistle of St. Peter* (2d ed.; London: Macmillan & Co., 1955) 176.

11. Besides the common terms χάρις and ἀγαθοποιέω (the latter, an infrequent New Testament term occurring only once [3 John 11] beyond 1 Peter [2:15, 20; 3:6] and Luke [6:9, 33, 35]), note: (a) the similar issue of how believers are to interact with outsiders; (b) the similar use of rhetorical questions; (c) the comparison-contrast between sinful and righteous behavior; and (d) the stress upon "doing what is right" as the conduct which receives God's approval or reward (χάρις and μισθός in Luke; χάρις in 1 Peter).

12. Only μισθός occurs in the Matthean version (5:46) of the Q saying.

13. BAGD, s.v., μισθός: "In these passages [Luke 6:32–34; see *Didache* 1:3; *2 Clement* 13:4. Cf. 1 Cor. 9:16 v. 1.] the meaning comes close to *reward*." There are at least four reasons for distinguishing the sense of χάρις here from its use in the rest of 1 Peter and hence for doubting the interpretations of Goppelt (*Der erste*

*Petrusbrief,* 192–98) and Brox (*Der erste Petrusbrief,* 127–40). (a) In other occurrences of χάρις in 1 Peter, it is clear explicitly (4:10; 5:5, 10, 12) or implicitly (1:2, 10, 13; 3:7) that God is the source or donor of χάρις. In 2:19–20, on the other hand, instead of a genitive construction is the phrase χάρις παρὰ θεῷ which has the sense of "in the sight of," "before, with" God (i.e., *coram Deo*) as the same phrase in 2:4. (See BDF par. 238 concerning παρά with the dative case and other New Testament examples.) (b) χάρις is synonymous here with κλέος, a New Testament *hapax legomenon* meaning "credit" and never used as a synonym for "grace" in the theological sense. (c) Goppelt and Brox fail to consider the sense of χάρις as determined by sources common to 1 Peter and Luke. (d) 1 Peter 2:21–25 relates to and describes not χάρις but suffering (πάσχω), which is the linkword joining vv. 18–20 and 21–25.

A further comparison of vv. 19–20 (χάρις, παρὰ θεῷ) and 2:24 (τῇ δικαιοσύνῃ ζήσωμεν) with the wider context of the Matthean version of the Q logion—namely, Matt. 6:1 (τὴν δικαιοσύνην ὑμῶν, μισθόν, παρὰ τῷ πατρὶ ὑμῶν)—while indicating no literary dependency or use of common sources, nevertheless clarifies the conceptual connection in 1 Peter 2:19–20 and 2:23 between "doing what is right," "righteousness" (in a Matthean, not Pauline sense), and "God's approval."

14. See especially Goppelt, *Der erste Petrusbrief,* and several of the studies in *Études sur la Première Lettre de Pierre* (ed. Charles Perrot; LD 102; Paris: Cerf, 1980).

15. This union of addressees and their Lord is expressed here in *form* as well as content. An *inclusio* which begins and ends with statements concerning the *readers* (second person plural passive verbs, second person plural possessive adjectives) frames traditional material pertaining to *Christ's* suffering (vv. 22–24). In vv. 21, 24, and 25 this interrelation of subjects and its salvific implications is most pronounced.

16. Compare 2:21a and 3:9; 2:21b and 3:18a (perhaps a fragment of the same hymn); 2:22 (ἁμαρτία) and 3:18, 4:1, 8; 2:22 (δόλος) and 2:1, 3:10; 2:23 (λοιδορέω) and 3:9 (an identical stress on nonretaliation); 2:23c (κρίνω, of God) and 1:17, 4:5–6, 17; 2:24 and 4:1; 2:24 (ζήσωμεν) and 1:3, 23, 2:4, 5, 3:18, 4:5, 6; 2:24 (δικαιοσύνη, cf. δίκαιος, 2:23) and 3:14 (cf. also δίκαιος in 3:12, 18, 4:18); 2:25 (comparative ὡς, a hallmark of 1 Peter) and 1:14, 19, 24, 2:2, 5, 11, 12, 13, 14, 16, 3:6, 7, 4:10, 11, 12, 15, 16, 5:3, 8, 12; 2:25 (πρόβατα) and 5:2–4 (ποίμνιον); 2:25b (νῦν as the "now" of salvation) and 1:12, 2:10, 3:21; and 2:25b (ψυχή in the sense of "yourselves, your lives") and 1:9, 22, 2:11, 3:20, 4:19.

17. On the structure and origin of the hymn, see Goppelt, *Der erste Petrusbrief,* 204–7. For the pertinent literature, see 204 n. 29 and, more recently, J. Schlosser, "Ancien Testament et Christologie dans la Prima Petri," in *Études sur la Première Lettre de Pierre,* 65–96, esp. 83–93; and M. Carrez, "L'Esclavage dans la première épître de Pierre," in *Études sur la Premiere Lettre de Pierre,* 207–17.

18. Especially 1 Peter 1:18–21 and 3:18, 22.

19. R. Deichgräber, *Gotteshymnus und Christushymnus in der frühen Christenheit* (SUNT 5; Göttingen: Vandenhoeck & Ruprecht, 1967) 142; see also 140–43.

20. Goppelt, *Der erste Petrusbrief,* 206–7.

21. Commentators are unanimous concerning the influence here of the Isaianic servant song; see n. 17 above for the literature. Over against H. M. Orlinsky ("The So-called 'Servant of the Lord' and 'Suffering Servant' in Second Isaiah," in *Studies on the Second Part of the Book of Isaiah* [VTSup 14; Leiden: E. J. Brill, 1967] 1–33),

I follow the conventionally accepted division of Isaiah 52 at vv. 12 and 13 (LXX) and do not find convincing Orlinsky's arguments against the association of 52:13– 15 with Isaiah 53. Thus, "servant" in 52:13 (ὁ παῖς μου) belongs to and identifies the verses which follow as a "servant song." 1 Peter 2:21–25 contains no explicit mention of a term for "servant," but it is implied by (a) the Isaianic text influencing these verses and (b) by the link of 2:21–25 with the preceding servant exhortation. οἰκέτης in the Septuagint (fifty-six times) regularly translates the Hebrew *ebed*. Here in 1 Peter, the *ebed* YHWH is the example for the *ebedim* YHWH. On the influence of the Isaianic servant song on early Christian tradition, see the literature cited by K. H. Schelkle, *Die Petrusbriefe, der Judasbrief* (3d ed.; HTKNT 13.2; Freiburg: Herder Verlag, 1976) 84 n. 1 and 82–84.

22. See 1 Peter 2:3 and the numerous parallels cited by W. Bornemann, "Der erste Petrusbrief—eine Taufrede des Silvanus?" *ZNW* 19 (1919–20) 143–65. Though Bornemann's proposal that 1 Peter constituted a baptismal homily based on Psalm 33(34) has found little scholarly support, the many traces of this Psalm in 1 Peter deserve more attention than thus far received. A somewhat longer quotation of the same Psalm text (33:12–18) occurs in a later Roman document which reveals a knowledge and use of 1 Peter—namely *1 Clement* (22:1–7).

23. The existence and common New Testament use of a "joy in suffering" tradition has been proposed by W. Nauck ("Freude im Leiden. Zum Problem einer urchristlichen Verfolgungstradition," *ZNW* 46 [1955] 68–80; see also Selwyn, *First Epistle of St. Peter,* 439–58). Goppelt (*Der erste Petrusbrief,* 299–304) notes the combination of material from Isaiah and the Psalms in the development of this theme but is skeptical of a fixed *Traditionszusammenhang* (304 n. 24).

24. R. Pesch, *Das Markusevangelium* (2 vols.; HTKNT 2: Freiburg: Herder Verlag 1976–77); see especially 1:63–68 on pre-Markan tradition and 2:1–27 on the pre-Markan passion history and the *passio iusti* motif. Pesch's proposal draws on the research of L. Ruppert (*Der leidende Gerechte. Eine motivgeschichtliche Untersuchung zum Alten Testament und zwischentestamentlichen Judentum* [FzB5; Würzburg: Echter-Seelsorge, 1972]; idem, *Der leidende Gerechte und seine Feinde. Eine Wortfelduntersuchung* [FzB6; Würzburg: Echter-Seelsorge, 1973]; and idem, *Jesus als der leidende Gerechte? Der Weg Jesu im Lichte eines alt- und zwischentestamentlichen Motivs* [SBS 59; Stuttgart: Katholisches Bibelwerk, 1972]). According to Ruppert, (*Jesus als der leidende Gerechte?,* 23) Wis. 2:12–20 and 5:1–5, an "Aktualisierung des leidenden Gottesknecht von Jes 52, 13–53, 12" play an important role in the development of this theological motif. Although there are no indications of direct literary dependency, it is noteworthy that here in Wisdom, as later in 1 Peter, a correlation is made between the *passio iustorum* (3:1–9; 5:15–23) and the *passio iusti* (2:12– 20; 5:1–5).

25. For a critical evaluation of Pesch's work, see F. Neirynck, "L'Évangile de Marc. À propos d'un nouveau commentaire," *ETL* 53 (1977) 153–81; and idem, "L'Évangile de Marc (II). À propos de R. Pesch, *Das Markusevangelium,* 2. Teil," *ETL* 55 (1979) 1–42.

26. On the atoning death of Jesus in 1 Peter and its ethical and ecclesiological implications, see Selwyn, *First Epistle of St. Peter,* 90–101; E. Lohse, *Märtyrer und Gottesknecht. Untersuchungen zur urchristlichen Verkündigung vom Sühntod Jesu Christi* (2d ed.; FRLANT 46; Göttingen: Vandenhoeck & Ruprecht, 1963) 182–87; idem, "Paränese und Kerygma im 1. Petrusbrief," *ZNW* 45 (1954) 68–89; Schelkle, *Die*

*Petrusbriefe, der Judasbrief,* 112–13; and H. Goldstein, "Die Kirche als Schar derer, die ihrem leidenden Herrn mit dem, Ziel der Gottesgemeinschaft nachfolgen: Zum Gemeindeverständnis von 1 Petr 2, 21–25 und 3, 18–22," *BibLeb* 15 (1974) 38–54. On Markan theology, see the literature cited in Pesch, *Das Markusevangelium,* 1:63.

27. This tradition, in other words, would embrace not merely the theme of "joy in suffering" but also "solidarity in suffering," as articulated, for instance, in 1 Peter 4:12–16.

28. J. H. Elliott, "The Roman Provenance of 1 Peter and the Gospel of Mark: A Response to David Dungan," in *Colloquy on New Testament Studies: A Time for Reappraisal and Fresh Approaches* (ed. B. Corley; Macon, Ga.: Mercer Univ. Press, 1983) 181–94.

29. That to which εἰς τοῦτο ("to this," v. 21a) refers is not the final χάρις of v. 20 (thus, Goppelt, *Der erste Petrusbrief,* 197, and Brox, *Der erste Petrusbrief,* 134) but "doing what is right under suffering," as Goppelt later observes (199 and n. 1). This is indicated by (a) the multiple occurrences of the verb πάσχω, which links these two sections (cf. vv. 20, 21, 23); (b) the fact that Jesus' actions illustrate "doing what is right" (nonretaliation, v. 23); and (c) the parallel between 2:21 and 3:9. As Jesus' nonretaliation when reviled (2:23) is the model for the nonretaliation of the reviled community (3:9; cf. 2:12; 3:16; 4:4, 14), so εἰς τοῦτο in 2:21 refers to the whole thought of 2:18–20, just as εἰς τοῦτο in 3:9, which with 2:21 frames the section, refers to the whole summarizing thought of 3:8–9.

30. The passive voice of ἐκλήθητε and ἐπεστράφητε (vv. 21 and 25) expresses God as the ultimate author of redemption. For further examples of this theocentric focus of 1 Peter, see also 1:2, 3, 12, 14–16, 17–21; 2:9–10, 12, 17; 3:18; 4:2, 6, 11, 14, 17–19; 5:2, 5–7, 10–11, 12.

31. The clause "Christ also suffered for you" here and in 3:18a most likely derives from the *Passionslied* echoed in 2:22–24 and 3:18 and 22, with the modification of ἡμῶν ("us") to ὑμῶν ("you") for hortatory purposes. The hymn, as Goppelt plausibly argues (*Der erste Petrusbrief,* 206–7) represents an expansion upon a primitive ὑπέρ formula ("Christ died for us" [χριστὸς ἀπέ θανεν ὑπέρ ἡμῶν], cf. 1 Cor. 15:3, Rom. 5:6; 8:34; 14:9, 15; 2 Cor. 5:14–15; 1 Thess. 5:10) with the aid of Isaiah 53. At this stage of pre-Petrine development, ἔπαθεν replaced ἀπέθανεν and with πάσχων in v. 23 marks the hymn as a *Passionslied.* Thus, ἔπαθεν, rather than ἀπέθανεν, is the most likely original Petrine reading in both 2:21 and 3:18. It is the verb πάσχω, not ἀποθνῄσκω, which links both of these verses to their immediate contexts (2:20, 3:17) and which expresses the solidarity of Christ and Christian throughout the letter (so also Brox, *Der erste Petrusbrief,* 135).

A further element of the ὑπέρ formula in 3:18, "the righteous for the unrighteous" (δίκαιος ὑπὲρ ἀδίκων), indicates the relation of the hymn to the *passio iusti-iustorum* theme mentioned above. The atoning death of the righteous is an important motif in Jewish martyr theology (see Lohse, *Märtyrer und Gottesknecht,* 29–32, 64–110; and Goldstein, "Die Kirche als Schar derer," 48–49). This Jewish martyr tradition may well have provided the conceptual basis for the merging of *passio iusti* and *passio iustorum* elements in early Christian thought. (See Ruppert, *Jesus als der leidende Gerechte?,* 27–28, 40, 57–71.) At the same time, both 2:21 and 3:18 (*hapax legomena*) express the characteristically Christian adaptation of this tradition. It is the singular, once for all, suffering and death of *the* righteous servant Jesus Christ on behalf of the unrighteous which makes endurable the suffering of the now righteous servants. It is hardly surprising to find the use of such tradition in a letter that must be read, as Brox aptly describes, against the background of a massive threat against the community from the outside and thus as a *praeparatio ad martyrium*, "a preparation for martyrdom" (*auf dem Hintergrund seiner pastoralen Intentionen in einer massiven Bedrängnis der Gemeinden von aussen [und insofern als* praeparatio ad martyrium] *zu lesen*" (*Der erste Petrusbrief*, 139).

32. The related ὑπολείπω ("to leave remaining") occurs only in Rom. 11:3.

33. For one of the most extensive discussions of these terms and their significance in 1 Pet. 2:21, see H. Millauer, *Leiden als Gnade. Eine traditionsgeschichtliche Untersuchung zur Leidenstheologie des ersten Petrusbriefes* (Europäische Hochschulschriften 23.56; Berne: Herbert Lang; Berne: Peter Lang, 1976) 65–84.

34. Compare also ἐταπεινοφρόνησεν (16:17; 16:1, 2) with 1 Peter 3:8 (ταπεινόφρονες), 5:5 (ταπεινοφροσύνη, ταπεινός), and 5:6 (ταπεινώθητε).

35. ὑπογραμμός occurs twice elsewhere in *1 Clement;* once in 5:7 (of Paul) and again in 33:8 (of God the creator).

36. Compare 8:1 with 1 Peter 2:24, 22, and Isa. 53:9.

37. A comparison of 1 Peter and the Pauline material would also be pertinent but must be omitted here in the interest of space. H. D. Betz (*Nachfolge und Nachahmung Jesu Christi im Neuen Testament* (BHT 37; Tübingen: Mohr/Siebeck, 1967) has analyzed the Pauline interpretation of the theme of *Nachfolge Jesu,* and much of what he says concerning a continuity of intention underlying different symbols and modes of expression in Paul and the Gospels applies to 1 Peter as well (cf. 186–89). My remarks in this paper, however, should make clear why I cannot concur with his brief assessment of a supposed "Imitatio-Jesu-Frömmigkeit" commencing with 1 Peter (see 181–82). For a study of Paul more useful for comparing Paul and 1 Peter on this point, see D. M. Stanley, "Paul and the Christian Concept of the Servant of God," in *The Apostolic Church in the New Testament* (Westminster, Md.: Newman Press, 1965) 312–51.

38. G. Schrenk, "ὑπογραμμός (ὑπογράφω)," *TDNT* 1 (1964) 772–73.

39. Ibid., 772, as illustrated in Clement of Alexandria, *Stromateis* 5.8.49, 1. See, similarly, Selwyn (*First Epistle of St. Peter,* 92): "The Greek word here translated 'example' admits of two meanings. It was used sometimes of an outline design or sketch of some work of art, as it might be a painting or an embroidery, which the master drew and left for his pupils to fill in. Or again the word might be used as a pattern, such as the handwriting of a copy-book, which was meant to be copied faithfully, detail by detail, by others."

40. Compare 1 Peter 2:21 and Mark 8:31–34, and προσκαλεσάμενος ("he called to him") in Mark 8:34 with the previous call narratives of 1:16–20, 3:13–19, and 6:6b–13. Millauer (*Leiden als Gnade,* 77, 83–84) correctly notes the Hellenistic character of the Petrine terminology and formulation and reaches a similar conclusion regarding the association of 1 Peter 2:21 with the synoptic "way of the cross" (*Kreuzesnachfolge*) tradition. However, his attempt to trace the Petrine phrase τοῖς ἴχνεσιν αὐτοῦ to "a conventional Old Testament-Jewish-New Testament *Wegvorstellung*" ("way of the cross") fails to convince. For this phrase there is no exact Old Testament or pre-Petrine source, and 1 Peter nowhere else explicitly develops a conception of "the way of God or the Lord" which Christians are exhorted to follow. For a formal but not material analogy to 1 Peter 2:21c, d, see Philo, *Virt.*

64. For τὸ ἴχνος in the sense of "example" to follow, see Rom. 4:12 (Abraham) and 2 Cor. 12:18 (Titus); and for Jesus as example (ὑπόδειγμα) for the conduct of his disciples, see John 13:15—all texts, however, which do not associate "example" and "following" with suffering or call.

41. For textual documentation and pertinent literature, see Elliott, "Roman Provenance of 1 Peter."

42. See Elliott, *Home for the Homeless*, esp. 132–50, 227–28.

43. A. Vanhoye, "1 Pierre au carrefour des théologies du Nouveau Testament," in *Études sur la Première Lettre de Pierre*, 97–128.

44. H. D. Betz (*Nachfolge und Nachahmung Jesu Christi*, 5–44) notes the growth of this discpleship theme, beginning with its limited origins in Q. Martin Hengel (*The Charismatic Leader and His Followers* [trans. J. Greig; New York: Crossroad; Edinburgh: T. & T. Clark, 1981]), moreover, stresses the importance of distinguishing the later concept of teacher and disciples from an earlier understanding of "following" as association with Jesus the charismatic leader. In the light of the history of this development, the proper question is not, What accounts for the *absence* of this teacher-disciple model in 1 Peter and the rest of the New Testament? but, rather, What accounts for its *appearance and growth* in the Gospels and Acts?

45. N. H. Søe, "Nachfolge Christi. III. Theologisch," *RGG* 4:1292–93.

46. J. M. Gustafson, *Christ and the Moral Life* (New York: Harper & Row, 1968); see esp. the chapter on "Jesus Christ, the Pattern," 150–87.

47. Ibid., 152.

48. H. D. Betz, *Nachfolge und Nachahmung Jesu Christi*, 181–82.

49. See E. Kähler, "Nachfolge Christi. II. Dogmengeschichtlich," *RGG* 4:1288–92.

50. Schweizer, *Lordship and Discipleship*, 11.

# APPENDIX

| | 1 Peter | Mark | 1 Clement | Polycarp to the Philippians |
|---|---|---|---|---|
| Servants | 2:18–20 | 9:33–37; 10:35–45; cf. 10:13–16 | (Humility) | 5:1–2 |
| Christological Tradition | 2:21–25 (Isaiah 53) | 8:31–34; 9:31; 10:32–34 (Isaiah 53) | 16:1–17 (Isaiah 53 quoted) | 5:2; 8:1–2; cf. 1:2; 10:1 (Isaiah 53) |
| Wives and Husbands | 3:1–7 | 10:1–12 | 21:6c–7 | 4:1–3 |
| Ps 33 [34] | 3:10–12; 3:15; 1:18 | (8:31–33); (10:45; 14:24) | 22:1–7; 21:6a | |
| Elders, Youngers | 5:2–5a | 10:35–45; cf. 9:33–37; 10:13–16 | 21:6b, 8 | 5:3—6:1 |

# Selected Bibliography

Barth, G. "Matthew's Understanding of the Law." In *Tradition and Interpretation in Matthew*, ed. G. Bornkamm, G. Barth, and H. J. Held. Philadelphia: Westminster Press, 1963.

Best, E. *Following Jesus: Discipleship in the Gospel of Mark*. JSNTSup 4. Sheffield: JSOT Press, 1981.

————. "The Role of the Disciples in Mark." *NTS* 23 (1976–77) 377–401.

Betz, H. D. *Nachfolge und Nachahmung Jesu Christi im Neuen Testament*. BHT 37. Tübingen: J. C. B. Mohr [Paul Siebeck], 1967.

Betz, O. "Die Geburt der Gemeinde durch den Lehrer." *NTS* 3 (1956–57) 314–26.

Brown, R. E. *The Community of the Beloved Disciple: The Life, Loves, and Hates of an Individual Church in New Testament Times*. New York: Paulist Press, 1979.

Cothenet, E. "Imitation du Christ." In *Dictionnaire de Spiritualité*, ed. M. Viller et al. Paris: Gabriel Beauchesne, 1937– . Vol. 7,2 (1971) 1536–1601.

Crouzel, H. "L'imitation et la 'suite' de Dieu et du Christ dans les premiers siècles chrétiens, ainsi que leurs sources gréco-romaines et hébraïques." *JAC* 21 (1978) 7–41.

De Boer, W. P. *The Imitation of Paul*. Kampen, Neth.: J. H. Kok, 1962.

de Jonge, M. "The Fourth Gospel: The Book of the Disciples." In *Jesus: Stranger from Heaven and Son of God. Jesus Christ and the Christians in Johannine Perspective*, ed. and trans. John Steely. SBLSBS 11. Missoula, Mont.: Scholars Press, 1977.

Delling, G. "ἀρχηγός." *TDNT* 1 (1964) 487–88.

Donahue, J. R. *The Theology and Setting of Discipleship in the Gospel of Mark*. The 1983 Pere Marquette Theology Lecture. Milwaukee: Marquette University Press, 1983.

Elliott, J. H. *A Home for the Homeless. A Sociological Exegesis of 1 Peter, Its Situation and Strategy*. Philadelphia: Fortress Press, 1981.

Fiore, B. "The Function of Personal Example in the Socratic and Pastoral Epistles." Ph.D. diss., Yale University, 1982.

Goldstein, H. "Die Kirche als Schar derer, die ihrem leidenden Herrn mit dem, Ziel der Gottesgemeinschaft nachfolgen: Zum Gemeindeverständnis von 1 Petr 2, 21–25 and 3, 18–22." *BibLeb* 15 (1974) 38–54.

Gutiérrez, P. *La Paternité spirituelle selon Saint Paul*. Paris: J. Gabalda, 1968.

SELECTED BIBLIOGRAPHY

Hengel, M. *The Charismatic Leader and His Followers.* Eng. trans. J. Greig. New York: Crossroad; Edinburgh: T. & T. Clark, 1981.

Kelber, W. H. *The Kingdom in Mark: A New Place and a New Time.* Philadelphia: Fortress Press, 1974.

————. *Mark's Story of Jesus.* Philadelphia: Fortress Press, 1979.

Lindars, B. "Imitation of God and Imitation of Christ." *Theology* 76 (1973) 394–402.

Lumpe, A. "Exemplum." RAC 6:1229–57.

Luz, U. "Die Jünger im Matthäusevangelium." *ZNW* 62 (1971) 141–71 (Eng. trans.: chap. 7 in *The Interpretation of Matthew,* ed. G. Stanton. IRT 3. Philadelphia: Fortress Press; London: SPCK, 1983).

Merki, H. ΟΜΟΙΩΣΙΣ ΘΕΩ *von der platonischen Angleichung an Gott zur Gottähnlichkeit bei Gregor von Nyssa.* Fribourg, Switz.: Paulusverlag, 1952.

Michaelis, W. "μιμέομαι, κτλ." *TDNT* 4 (1967) 659–74.

Moreno Jiménez, R. "El discípulo de Jesucristo, según el evangelio de S. Juan." *EstBib* 30 (1971) 269–311.

Schmahl, G. *Die Zwölf im Markusevangelium. Eine redaktionsgeschichtliche Untersuchung.* TTS 30. Trier: Paulinus Verlag, 1974.

Schrenk, G. "ὑπογραμμός (ὑπογράφω)." *TDNT* 1 (1964) 772–73.

Schulz, A. *Nachfolgen und Nachahmen: Studien über das Verhältnis der neutestamentlichen Jüngerschaft zur urchristlichen Vorbildethik.* SANT 6. Munich: Kösel-Verlag, 1962.

Schüssler Fiorenza, E. "Apocalyptic and Gnosis in the Book of Revelation and Paul." *JBL* 92 (1973) 565–81 (Rev. ed.: chap. 4 in her book *The Book of Revelation—Justice and Judgment.* Philadelphia: Fortress Press, 1985).

Schweizer, E. *Lordship and Discipleship.* SBT 28. London: SCM Press, 1960.

————. *Matthäus und seine Gemeinde.* SBS 71. Stuttgart: Katholisches Bibelwerk, 1974.

Segovia, F. F. *Love Relationships in the Johannine Tradition:* Ἀγάπη / Ἀγαπᾶν *in 1 John and in the Fourth Gospel.* SBLDS 58. Chico, Calif.: Scholars Press, 1982.

Seitz, O. J. F. "Afterthoughts on the Term 'Dypsychos.'" *NTS* 4 (1957) 327–34.

————. "Antecedents and Significance of the Term 'Dypsychos.'" *JBL* 66 (1947) 211–19.

Stanley, D. M. "'Become Imitators of Me': The Pauline Conception of Apostolic Tradition." *Bib* 40 (1959) 859–77.

Stock, K. *Boten aus dem Mit-Ihm-Sein.* Das Verhältnis zwischen *Jesus und den Zwölf nach Markus.* AnBib 70. Rome: Biblical Institute Press, 1975.

Talbert, C. H. *Literary Patterns, Theological Themes, and the Genre of Luke-Acts.* SBLMS 20. Missoula, Mont.: Scholars Press, 1974.

————. "The Way of the Lukan Jesus: Dimensions of Lukan Spirituality." *PRS* 9 (1982) 237–49.

Tannehill, R. C. "The Disciples in Mark: The Function of a Narrative Role." *JR* 57 (1977) 386–405 (= chap. 7 in *The Interpretation of Mark,* ed. W. Telford. IRT 7. Philadelphia: Fortress Press; London: SPCK, 1985).

Thysman, R. "L'Éthique de l'imitation du Christ dans le Nouveau Testament: Situation, notations et variations du thème." *ETL* 42 (1966) 138–75.

Tyson, J. B. "The Blindness of the Disciples in Mark." *JBL* 80 (1961) 261–68 (=

chap. 2 in *The Messianic Secret*, ed. C. Tuckett, IRT 1. Philadelphia: Fortress Press; London: SPCK, 1983).

Via, D. O. "The Right Strawy Epistle Reconsidered: A Study in Biblical Ethics and Hermeneutics." *JR* 49 (1969) 253–67.

Weeden, T. J. "The Heresy That Necessitated Mark's Gospel." *ZNW* 59 (1968) 145–58 (= chap. 2 in *The Interpretation of Mark*, ed. W. Telford. IRT 7. Philadelphia: Fortress Press; London: SPCK, 1985).

———. *Mark—Traditions in Conflict*. Philadelphia: Fortress Press, 1971.

Williams, D. M. "The Imitation of Christ in Paul with Special Reference to Paul as Teacher." Ph.D. diss., Columbia University, 1967.